MENTAL HEALTH CASEWORK

MENTAL HEALTH CASEWORK:
ILLUMINATIONS AND REFLECTIONS

edited and written by
J. P. J. Oliver, P. J. Huxley and A. Butler

Manchester University Press
Manchester and New York

distributed exclusively in the USA and Canada by St. Martin's Press

Copyright © Manchester University Press
1989

Whilst copyright in this volume as a whole is vested in Manchester University Press, copyright in the individual chapters belongs to their respective authors, and no chapter may be reproduced whole or in part without the express permission in writing of both author and publisher.

Published by Manchester University Press
    Oxford Road, Manchester M13 9PL, UK
    and Room 400, 175 Fifth Avenue, New
    York, NY 10010, USA

Distributed exclusively in the USA and Canada
    by St. Martin's Press, Inc.,
    175 Fifth Avenue, New York, NY 10010,
    USA

ISBN 0 7190 2230 4 hardback

British Library cataloguing in publication data
Mental health casework : illuminations and
    reflections.
    1. Great Britain. Welfare work with
    mentally ill persons
    I. Oliver, J.P.J. II. Huxley, Peter III.
    Butler, Alan, 1946–
    362.2'0425'0941

Library of Congress cataloging in publication data
Mental health casework : illuminations
    and reflections / edited by J.P.J. Oliver,
    P.J. Huxley, and A. Butler.
    p. cm.
    Bibliography: p. 166.
    Includes index.
    ISBN 0-7190-2230-4 : $40.00 (U.S. : est.)
    1. Psychiatric social work—Great
    Britain—Case studies.
    I. Oliver, J. P. J. (Joseph P. J.) II. Huxley,
    Peter. III. Butler, Alan, 1946–
    [DNLM: 1. Mental Disorders—case
    studies.   WN 40 M549]
    HV690.2'0425—dc19
    DNLM/DLC

Photoset in Joanna
by Northern Phototypesetting Co, Bolton
Printed and bound in Great Britain by
Anchor Press Ltd, Tiptree, Essex

Contents

LIST OF CONTRIBUTORS

Ms Jane Akister, BSc, MSc (Oxon), CQSW
Senior Social Worker
Department of Psychiatry
Gaskell House
Manchester

Mrs Judith Baron, MSc (Oxon), CQSW, ASW
Social Worker
Oxford Area Health Authority

Mrs Monica Baynes, BA, Dip. Mental Health, AAPSW
Team Leader
Psychiatric Social Work Department
Tameside Hospital
Ashton-under-Lyne, Cheshire

Mrs Reba Bhaduri, MA (Econ), AAPSW
Principal Teacher/Supervisor in Social Work
Medical Social Work Department
Withington Hospital
Manchester

Mr David Brandon, BA (Soc. Studies), Dip MH
Psychiatric Social Worker/Psychotherapist
TAO Clinic
Preston, Lancashire

Mr William Farrell, MSc, CQSW, ABPsS
Senior Psychiatric Social Worker
Social Work Department
Maelor General Hospital
Wrexham, Clwyd

Miss Jill D. Ford, MLitt, AAPSW
Acting Head of Department
Department of Social Administration and Social Work
University of Glasgow

Dr P. J. Huxley, BA, MSc, PhD, Cert. PSW, AAPSW
Senior Lecturer in Psychiatric Social Work/ Director of Research and Staff Development Unit
Department of Psychiatry
University of Manchester

Mr J. A. Ingram, BSc, Cert. PSW, AAPSW
Lecturer in Psychiatric Social Work
Department of Psychiatry
University of Manchester

Dr M. Kerfoot, Dip. Soc Adm, MSc (Leeds) PhD (Man.), Cert. PSW, AAPSW
Lecturer/Principal Social Worker
Department of Psychiatry
University of Manchester

Mr I. Leighton, MA (Oxon), Dip. Psycho-therapy, Dip. Soc. Studies, CQSW
Senior Social Worker (Forensic Psychiatry)
Whittingham Hospital
Goosnargh
Preston, Lancashire

Mrs J. Mawer, BA, Cert. PSW, AAPSW
Senior Social Worker
Manchester Royal Infirmary

Dr David Millard, MA, MB, CHB, FRCPsych.
University Lecturer in Applied Social Studies
Department of Social and Administrative Studies
University of Oxford

Mr B. Minty, MA (Oxon), MSc, AAPSW
Lecturer in Psychiatric Social Work/ Senior Social Worker
Department of Psychiatry
University of Manchester

Mr S. Newton, BA, CQSW,
Controller for Mental Health
Lancashire Social Services Department

Mr David Nichols, BA (Socio. and Social Work), MSW
National Training Co-ordinator, NSPCC

Mr J. P. J. Oliver, BA, MSc (Leeds), MSc (Oxon), CQSW
Lecturer in Psychiatric Social Work/ Senior Psychiatric Social Worker
Department of Psychiatry
University of Manchester

Ms Annabelle Page, BA, CQSW
Casework Consultant
St James's Hospital
Leeds

Ms Daphne Shepherd, MA, AAPSW
Senior Research Fellow
Department of Social Work Studies
University of Southampton

Mr David Southgate, MA, CQSW
Social Worker, Barnet General Hospital
London

Mr David Smith, MA, CQSW
Project Leader Crisis Intervention Team
Coventry

Mrs Ann Taylor, BA, MSoc.
Senior Psychiatric Social Worker
Park Side Hospital
Macclesfield, Cheshire

Mr C. Turner, MA, Dip. App. Soc. Studies,
  CQSW
Community Social Work Manager
Hammersmith and Fulham Social Services

Dr S. Wasserman, BA, MS, PhD
Lecturer/Casework Consultant (retired)
Reading, Berkshire

Ms J. Webster, BSoc. Sci.(Social Work),
  DPSW, CQSW
Lecturer in Psychiatric Social Work/
Senior Social Worker
Department of Psychiatry
University of Manchester

INTRODUCTION

THE NEED FOR A CASEBOOK

Practitioners are under daily pressure to account for the actions which they take in their work and social work education and training needs to take account of this fact. It would not be an exaggeration to say that competition from other occupational groups to undertake work which has traditionally been within the province of social work is currently very marked. Sadly, recent research reveals a tendency for social workers to be unclear about their potential contributions, especially in respect of therapeutically directed work. This corresponds with criticisms of the overall effectiveness of social work generally (Brewer and Lait, 1980), and casework in particular, which have been voiced both at home (Sheldon, 1979) and abroad (Fischer, 1973).

A good example of this is reported in *Mental Health Social Work Observed* by Mike Fisher and his colleagues (1984) from the University of Sheffield. Their survey, which was sponsored by the Department of Health and Social Security (DHSS), investigated social work services for the adult mentally ill in an English shire county. They revealed what can only be described as a dismal picture of professional social work activity which focused more or less exclusively on the 'amelioration' of client problems rather than the 'alleviation' of them. They portray a picture of social workers able to act in a wide variety of functions, such as liaison, co-ordinator, advocate or provider of material and financial help. While no one would wish to deny that such 'ameliorative' work is useful, alone it 'usually fails to contribute to the resolution of underlying problems or to prevent the recurrence of social difficulties. Thus it tends, in effect, to perpetuate needs, so that social work resources become absorbed in long-term ... aimless work to the exclusion of new referrals' (Fisher *et al.*, 1984, p. 193). Most alarmingly they showed that 'the fundamental causes of distress in clients' lives often remained unexplored during social work intervention; and even where such cases were obvious but largely unchangeable...., social work was rarely directed towards changing the client's responses to stress. When clients themselves raised questions as to the cause of their problems, social work help rarely built upon this questioning attitude....; where, more usually, clients were reluctant or unable to focus on the reasons for their circum-stances, social work help largely avoided the attempt to turn the attention to the issues' (Fisher *et al.*, 1984, p.194). If these findings are to be believed, contemporary mental health social work appears uncertain about its own ability to conduct 'direct', therapeutic work with clients, a most worrying scenario.

One of the basic tenets of contemporary British social work is that the worker who has recently completed a basic 'generic' professional training course, more often than not, will have been through a very general introduction to theory and practice and will have achieved a level of basic competence to prepare himself or herself for work in the field. Although there are plans currently afoot to lengthen social work training and to introduce an element of specialisation into it, many social work students complete their training without ever having had the opportunity to encounter some of the problems which they will have to face in day-to-day work. To account for this, most newly qualified social workers will still require close supervision for a period of time to ensure that they are able to deal effectively with the many new challenges they will meet when assuming the responsibility of a qualified member of staff. It is of particular importance that in the period immediately following training, the new worker is given a chance to consolidate the progress he or she has made during training (at best a period of rapid personal and professional development) which was meant to be a 'springboard' into practice and not a final endpoint in their career or educational growth. There is no doubt that the quality of work in practice is closely related the level of supervision available, and observing the contemporary scene, we can hardly help but notice the confused state of affairs which currently exists in respect of training.

As if this were not sufficient reason to promote concern, the field is currently plagued by uncertainty in respect of many other issues, including the relative place of statutory work (i.e. the role of the 'approved social worker', under the 1983 *Mental Health Act*) and how it might be objectively assessed, the proposed reorganisation of professional training and the relative merits and demerits of specialised practice. Thus, perhaps, it has never been of greater importance for social workers in the field of mental disorder to have a clear notion of the nature of competent social casework practice.

Informing social work practice has never been an easy task. As editors, we were interesed to find that while most of the material which we received was of a high standard, in only a few cases did the contributors seek explicitly to relate their practice to some coherent theoretical psychological approach such as learning theory or the more traditional psychodynamic theory. This gives many of the cases the appearance of being either atheoretical or eclectic in method. Alas, British casework remains a thoroughly eclectic activity, with few practitioners being willing to wholeheartedly commit themselves to any one style completely (we include some totally psychoanalytic and behavioural examples just to prove ourselves wrong). Having said this, while there are one or two things on which we would take a different view, we readily endorse the material as we have presented it.

Casework, as with other psychotherapeutic approaches, tends to be a 'hidden' endeavour not easily made available for public scrutiny. While no-one would wish to suggest that casework (the particular social work activity with which this book is concerned) is identical to psychotherapy, there are certain points at which the two overlap, the factor distinguishing the two residing more in the 'capacities' of the worker and client rather than their intentions. This point has been raised recently by Kraemer (1987, p. 209) who, in referring to other work in the field, concludes that such investigations of how the two are actually performed is rendered difficult by the fact that 'even widespread practices do not get written up as so many workers do not publish, the knowledge being passed on through training and supervision rather than in the literature' (Kraemer, 1987, p.211).

Textbooks exist because informed training and practice depend upon making our knowledge base both relevant and accessible. Acknowledging this, the purpose of this volume is not to serve as yet another text on mental health social work. Readers will be aware that two of the editors have already supplied such texts recently (Butler and Pritchard, 1984; Huxley, 1985). However, we are well aware of the lack of attention being given to casework as a method and neither of the works just cited nor others recently published in the field (e.g. Hudson, 1982; Olsen, 1984) contain even single chapters devoted to the topic. We also cannot help but observe the increasing tendency in the past few years for books on social work theory to be relatively free of case material. This is very damaging, as without making work public it cannot be properly scrutinised and criticised. Although this is sometimes discomforting, it is also a source of progress. In the end, without such discussion an endeavour will wilt and decay. There is no doubt that even in a social work profession preoccupied with its organisational forms of service delivery, continually testing yet another new approach to helping clients to solve their problems, that the major form of social worker-client interaction remains the individual face-to-face confrontation. The present book is an attempt to make some of this work more public. More often than not the cases are about the caseworker using his/her 'self' as the principal resource for helping the client (usually one person) to improve their condition; not really that much different from Mary Richmond speaking in 1915 who defined casework as 'the art of doing different things for and with different people by cooperating with them to achieve at one time their own and society's betterment' (Brown, 1977, p.79).

THE CONTENT OF THE BOOK

This is a collection of case studies. It is intended to help to rectify the lack of published material just discussed. The studies are not meant to be a 'representative' sample of casework as it is being practised. Social work has more than sufficient bad publicity at present, much of it relating to the publication of examples of hopelessly incompetent practice. We hope, at the worst, not to add to it. Moreover, we desire to do the opposite, to show the public some examples of at least 'competent' practice and at least a few examples of outstanding practice. Having said this, the cases are probably not 'perfect'. In a sense, no real case ever is. As we edited the cases we were posed with the dilemma of whether to try and make every submission 'perfect' in both detail and analysis. We decided against this. Instead, we feel that the actions taken in cases (those of the editors included) are 'right enough' to be defensible and that the analyses, while inclomplete, focus on important things. It is, perhaps, our way of saying that it is all right not to know exactly how things get done, sometimes. What the cases do have is that sense of *déja vu*, of common experience which will enable them to be debated.

The exercise of compiling the book also made us realise that while the state of casework could be better, and that while it is clearly unfashionable even to admit to practising it (though, after all of numerous points are debated, looking at the cases, we can hardly imagine why), the fact remains that social work within psychiatry often requires the worker to provide some continuity of care for the client and his/her family; to attempt to reduce stress on the client where possible; to promote their general welfare; and to try and foster primary prevention where possible. These things seem to be real among the cases which we continually encounter both as practitioners and as teachers overseeing the work of students.

This collection of cases is by no means complete; of course, it could not be. The area of work is far too broad, the issues raised far too contentious to be answered by twenty-four cases. We must frankly admit to being none the wiser for having written the book as to how many cases it might take to cover the contemporary casework scene adequately. Certainly the range of disorders and caseworker responses to individuals and the situations in which they find themselves are often unique and so variable as to seemingly make any catalogue virtually endless. Although we have managed to provide cases which address the major diagnostic categories in psychiatry notable by their omission are cases involving, for example, cogent examples of work with physically handicapped, blind and deaf people and the many interesting and challenging problems such work poses; any examples of work with the more than eighty mental handicapping conditions; some flavour of the many, many implications of the 1983 *Mental Health Act* for England and Wales; and interventions with solvent and alcohol abusers.

Instead of being a complete text or even a companion to a text, this volume is meant more as a 'sampler' highlighting areas of interest of the many experienced practitioners, managers and academics who have contributed. It is intended to be a practical guide designed to help practitioners, educators and students in their task of surveying the field by selectively drawing to their attention instances of competent practice, aided by an analysis of why a particular method or style might have been considered desirable in the circumstances. In this sense the book seeks, as the title states, to illustrate (i.e.

to make clear by means of decorative examples) and to reflect (i.e. to throw back an image) casework practice as it currently exists in the UK. Rather than to invent theory or practice, it has sought to establish what it actually is practised and to allow practitioners, managers and academics the opportunity to make some thoughtful comments which, to them, highlight a vital area of work which is currently poorly illuminated and present the entire thing in a form most likely to be read.

The aim of this book, then, is to present a collection of cases in which the central issue is one of mental health and in which the worker is actually employing casework as a method of intervention. The task of trying to define casework is a treacherous one and it would seem that practically everyone who writes on the subject uses a different definition. One is tempted by the cynical description that casework is what caseworkers do. However, it is certain that within the broader endeavour of social work, casework represents one method of helping people from among many (e.g. groupwork, community organisation and development). It takes as its starting point the concerns of the individual and sets them in the context of his/her own dynamic 'person-situation configuration' and recognises that the caseworker's involvement could include a 'large number of constituent activities' (Brown, 1977, p. 81). It centres on the task of adjustment, especially personal adjustment.

In respect of mentally ill people, the caseworker's activities have tended to take place in clinics or hospital settings where the mental health social worker shared the concerns of the other members of the clinical team: the study of the patient, the analysis of the information about the patient and the consequent diagnosis, and the formulation of a treatment plan (French, 1940). It used to be said that the psychiatric social worker had to answer three questions: what are the facts?, what do I make of the facts? and what do I intend to do about the facts? But time does not stand still and casework has changed. New techniques have been introduced and new approaches have developed as different (non-dynamic) theories have competed with the traditional for pre-eminence. Factors such as economics and technology have combined to place an ever increasing emphasis on effectiveness and consequently evaluation. Many new questions have now been added to the three above, for example 'does what I do work? if not, why not? if so, at what cost to the employer and benefit to the client?'

Drawing from contemporary accounts of practice, this book displays the manner in which mental illness, the individual's perspective and his or her current psychosocial situation intermingle to produce the 'predicaments' by which we are confronted. By acknowledging the difficulty in properly addressing the complexities of these issues except through a biographical presentation, cases show how the proper assessment of these factors can be used in a helpful manner, how casework practice fits into a general pattern of professional social work activity, and how therapeutic change occurs in a total context of events.

HOW THE BOOK WAS WRITTEN

As a means for addressing the problem of setting meaningful standards for practice, the idea of such a single reader presenting the work of recognised individuals seems sound, fitting in well with the established tradition in social casework of teaching by case material (e.g. Selby, 1965). Focusing on individual instances of disorder and subsequent casework intervention, the book seeks to capitalise on the recognised strengths of single case reporting by seeking (a) to strengthen links between theoretically informed observations and practice examples through case histories and worker commentaries; (b) to convey a feeling of intimate contact with the client and his/her disorder as well as with the worker and his/her style; (c) to provide case material which can be used for a critical comparison of interventions where there are several competing approaches; (d) to highlight areas of intervention which are novel and have not yet been explored by large scale research; and (e) to provide a forum for the presentation of actual work in situations and with problems which occur infrequently (Hersen and Barlow, 1976).

With each case study, we have endeavoured to present a clear example of some aspect of social work practice with a client who has a recognisable form of mental illness. Because of the limitations of size and our own orientation we were looking for instances where the practice depicted falls clearly into the category of casework. We have not given contributors strict guidance on other aspects of the case, unless specifically requested to do so. Such factors as the particular type of disorder, the setting in which the client was seen or worked with, whether the work was direct or indirect, what theoretical orientation was used, what aspects of the casework processes are highlighted (e.g. interviewing, assessment, planning, monitoring and evaluation, treating, etc.) were left entirely to the contributor's discretion. Thus, to begin with, we had no clear idea of the scope of material that might be submitted. This depended entirely on what became available to us and the ultimate shape of the book was determined chiefly by this factor. We were interested, as far as possible, in having each author recount the case in his/her own particular style of reportage, attending to the points which they considered most noteworthy and, if necessary, ignoring those they thought less so.

It is important to note here that we recognise the vast array of issues which are raised and dilemmas needing to be confronted in our practice. It is not our present desire to suggest that such things as simple solutions exist for a great many of them. We are well aware of the complexities of casework in reality. We do, however, feel strongly that if the book is to serve the purpose stated above it must be based on examples which can be justified, at least to some substantial degree, as reasonable and effective.

We have also sought, where possible, to include cases reflecting the current interests and thinking of the contributors and have encouraged them to submit material which is, for example, illustrative of recent academic work. Nevertheless, we were also aware of the fact that, over time, lecturers and fieldwork teachers have developed material which is both frequently used by and familiar to them. This book can be seen as an opportunity to see some of these cases finally put into print.

Each case study is composed of two parts. The first, called the *Case History* is a description of the work undertaken.It is meant to provide sufficient detail to enable the reader to focus on the process or issue under discussion. The second part, called the *Commentary*, attempts to draw out specific teaching points highlighted by the worker's intervention. Each commentary begins with a discussion of the *Mental Health Aspects* of the case. This generally entails a brief explanation of the diagnosis as it relates to the signs and symptoms presented along with any other pertinent facts about the disorder which relate specifically to the case. Following this, the commentary focuses on *Casework Aspects* of the case. The latter are linked to relevant theory or research, though the purpose is not to demonstrate the superiority of one approach over another by recourse to an analysis of the relative weight of empirical backing. More particularly, we were looking for examples of successful practice and for principles which could be extrapolated from them.

The submissions are presented in such a form as to protect the anonymity of the client. Contributors were expected to ensure that details which could easily identify the clients were suitably altered prior to submission. To ensure this further, cases have not be directly attributed to any one contributor. Rather a list of contributors is given in the prelude to the book without reference being made to which case each submitted. This is also important since the editors have altered many of the original submissions (particularly the commentaries) considerably in order to produce a book which, as far as possible, is unified, emphatic and coherent.

In using this book we would suggest that it may be beneficially employed in several ways. These cases may usefully provide the basis for discussions in tutorials and/or seminars prior to students beginning placements, or soon after entering an agency, by either tutors or fieldwork teachers as a means of preparation. As there is a reasonable range of material, there should be little difficulty in integrating at least some of the material to more didactic elements of a course curriculum. Not only can knowledge factors be identified and strengthened, but also emotional factors which may potentially inhibit learning progress can be identified and worked through.

Where fieldwork teachers are seeking to provide the student with useful standards against which to compare his/her own progress, these cases, if sensibly employed, should be of assistance. They certainly present some useful views expressed by very experienced fieldworkers and teachers about their own practice. In some respects, they are a good example of how to look at one's own work critically. In the same vein, where the full range of mental health cases are not forthcoming during a placement, these cases could act as a useful supplement to give the student at least a flavour of what unfamiliar cases might be about.

Also, they provide some opinion which might be of use to field or hospital-based social workers who perhaps came from generic training courses without the benefit of a mental health placement, and who wish to change direction in their career or make better sense of the mental health cases which they have. We have little doubt that they can form a useful basis for ongoing seminars and training for already qualified staff who would like to look at case material in training sessions but for whom producing one's own cases is troublesome (perhaps too time-consuming or, in some cases, even threatening). We have found that experienced practitioners undergoing training for the task of 'approved social work' under the 1983 *Mental Health Act* actually rate additional casework skills as a high priority for further training. As well, when given an opportunity for further training centred on case exploration, fieldworkers in practice (often those uninterested in other lecture-based forms of teaching) can be engaged in education by means of case discussions.

1 *Albert:*

public enemy number one?

CASE HISTORY

It is a lie. In fact Albert was not his real name. But perhaps I can be forgiven for altering some of the details, for this is a most unpleasant case where many untruths were told. It is an account of an assessment of sexual offences committed against a young child and Albert, the man who committed the offences.

Albert was referred to a forensic psychiatric unit (staffed by a multi-disciplinary team) by a specialist social worker in child care for out-patient assessment. Albert was then being prosecuted for indecent assault on Mandy, his four-year-old stepdaughter, and we were being asked for our opinion as to his psychiatric condition. An initial assessment revealed that Albert was not suffering from an acute mental illness. Nevertheless, it was felt that he might be mentally disordered within the meaning of the 1983 *Mental Health Act* as he had many of the characteristics of a psychopathic disorder. After an initial mental state examination by a psychiatrist, it was decided that a psychiatrist would not be involved in the assessment work, but that this would be undertaken by a team of four social workers (from both mental health and child care services). At the onset, the client signed a contract which provided for six interviews using video, a two-way screen and the quartet method of interviewing (cf. Dale, 1986). Albert agreed to co-operate after being advised by his solicitor that a favourable report could help to save him from prison.

When a sex offender is referred to me for assessment, I make two working assumptions. The first is that the protection of the child from further sexual assault overrides all other considerations. The second is that, until proven otherwise, the offender is a dangerous man and must be treated as such. At that time, Albert was admitting one offence of oral intercourse against Mandy, and I knew that he had two previous convictions for indecent assault against two other four-year-old girls six years earlier. My concern about the case was dramatically increased when I realised that the social work department had decided not to take either care or wardship proceedings in respect of the abused child. She was described as being happy normally and even-tempered, but was displaying behaviour problems including disturbed sleep, fear of strangers and nocturnal enuresis. Now aged six, at school Mandy was moody and attention-seeking; she lacked concentration and was continually 'picking her face'. Additionally, Albert was still living at home and neither he nor his wife had any appreciation of the seriousness of the situation, or of the disturbed behaviour the child was exhibiting. The assaults had not been reported to the mother by the child for twelve months though the child's memory of the incidents was very clear and she was able subsequently to demonstrate the events with dolls.

The purpose of the assessment was to construct a personality 'profile'. The team agreed to become involved in the assessment if three conditions were fulfilled: (1) that the Social Services department agreed to 'contract out' the family for the duration of the assessment and give us complete control; (2) that Albert remove himself from home forthwith and have no further contact with either of his children until the matter was resolved (he reluctantly agreed to do this, but it was eventually made a condition of bail by the court); and (3) that he would agree to our contract for assessment and that his wife agree to the child being assessed concurrently, but separately, from him. Albert attended all of his interviews, except for the last one which he cancelled because of pressure of work. A further interview was offered but Albert refused, stating that he was concerned that the content of the video, on which we were recording the interviews, could be used as evidence in court.

We proceeded to take a very detailed life history, tracing his development through childhood and adolescence from his earliest memories. It was his life story, and emphasis was placed on the quality of his relationships with significant other people as he saw them.

Albert was aged thirty-one. He was a quiet, passive man of very average build and looks with bright red hair and freckles. He came from a working-class family where he was the eldest of two children, both boys. We unearthed a dominating, controlling mother to whom he found it difficult to relate to and a weak father with whom he could not identify. He could share nothing with his parents and he eventually was displaced by a younger brother who he felt had taken all of his parents' affection. Paradoxically, he claimed to have been attached to his brother and used to enjoy taking him for walks. More predictably, his brother had married and eventually settled away from home. Albert had remained behind and did not keep up contact with him.

Although he was materially well provided for, Albert recalled his childhood as being a lonely time, 'an emotional desert'. He had been frequently and severely punished by his mother, who also limited his contacts with other children. She strongly admonished him never to bring a girl into the home. In later life his father died, but at this time his mother was still alive, living in the next street, and Albert visited her daily.

Albert was not academically inclined at school but liked to do practical things such as metalwork and woodwork. While at school he had no close friends. He tended to be bullied by the boys while always being rather uncomfortable in the company of girls. He was not strong and when he tried to defend himself against more aggressive adolescents, fighting being a frequent event, he was usually beaten. He strongly disliked all sports and games and, though he got on well with his teachers, to whom he was subservient, he was glad when he finally left school at sixteen to begin work as an apprentice electrician.

He first discovered the 'facts of life' from friends at school. He recalled having his first girlfriend when he was sixteen. The relationship lasted for only a week and was a source of 'no satisfaction' to him. He remembered his second girlfriend as 'a bit of a nymphomaniac. I didn't know it at the time. She wouldn't leave me alone. She frightened me off. I wouldn't tell friends that I was going out with her as it was a joke that she was a man eater. She put me off a bit. I nearly got raped and it frightened me. I can remember kissing and cuddling and then wandering hands and what would mum say.' When asked if he had had sex he replied 'No, but we'd have done it if she didn't behave the way she did. She frightened me ... it terrified me. I thought men were meant to be the dominant ones and didn't know about the other side.' He also had the fear of making her pregnant. Again he was left frustrated and masturbated to satisfy himself. Later, for a short period he took to drinking heavily, got blind drunk and couldn't remember what he had done.

Albert's later adolesence was uneventful. He was a reliable worker and tended to stick with the same employer. He worked hard to develop a trade, the necessity of which, he said, both parents had 'pounded into me'. He married at twenty-one a girl from a large family who had just turned sixteen. She was very inexperienced but wanted to leave home because she was fed up with being overcrowded. He and his wife managed to buy a house and at first the relationship seemed to be successful. They had one child but the marriage soon began to deteriorate. After the baby arrived, they began to have violent rows and and she once came after him with a knife. One day he returned home unexpectedly to find his wife in the house with someone else, kissing on the settee. Soon after, they were divorced, the marriage having lasted two years. His wife kept the house and he returned home to live with his parents.

In his mid-twenties Albert committed offences of indecent assault against two young children. At that time he was employed on a building site and the two, both around age four years, came to watch him at work. He offered them chewing gum and then sexually assaulted them. The police brought charges against Albert but these were eventually dropped because there was insufficient evidence to prosecute. During this period he committed several criminal offences, mostly to do with being drunk and fighting or being involved in petty theft. He never served a prison sentence but had completed a period of probation.

At the time of the offence, his second wife was aged twenty-five. She and Albert had been married for three years and they had two children, Mandy being the elder and the child of his wife's previous marriage.

The referral, due to the child's behaviour, was originally taken by a community psychiatric nurse (CPN) from the mother. She had complained that Albert was treating Mandy 'different than our own'. Soon the mother began to become overprotective of the child and before long this led to marital disagreements. For some time their sexual life had not been satisfactory and at the time of the offence, his wife had taken an evening job leaving Albert at home to care for the children.

As we interviewed him, his deep hatred of homosexuals dismayed us, but it was not until we began looking at his adult relationships that his deep hatred of females was revealed. Women were objects for his gratification and while he was capable of some affection and able to provide materially, this rapidly transformed itself into a frightening anger when he was deprived of a sexual outlet.

Throughout the assessment, he insisted that there had been only one incident of child abuse: that of inserting his erect penis into the mouth of his stepdaughter and that she had not objected. Independent investigation, however, revealed that he was lying on many accounts. First, several assaults had taken place on Mandy. Also, it was independently established in interview with Mandy that he had placed his penis between her legs and had tried to have intercourse but had failed. When confronted with this evidence, he admitted placing his penis but denied attempting intercourse. Finally, investigations by the police revealed that the child had, indeed, initially objected but had acquiesced finally, probably out of fear.

This version differed from interview to interview and this was a matter of great concern, giving us reason to doubt his veracity. It was a cornerstone of our approach that if we were to consider recommending an alternative to a custodial disposal to the court, then he would have to be completely honest about the extent of the abuse. This is only to say that truthfulness is a prerequisite to treatment and rehabilitation. It seemed important to recognise that therapy would be no guarantee that he would not offend again and that the likelihood of failure would be increased by Albert's reluctance to explore emotional issues openly and honestly.

As we formulated the assessment, various themes began to emerge. In the first place, Albert showed no real remorse for the offence and displayed no concern or appreciation for the effect that his assault would have on his daughter. He often said that he told her that he was sorry but that it was 'not as if I have hit her. You would think that one small thing was enough to make me "Public Enemy Number One".' Instead, his main concern was for himself and his own future. One object of the assessment was to get to his emotions and on more than one occasion the topic which made him break down into tears was the fear of being imprisoned. He always tended to minimise his offences, to display reluctance to discuss them or to forget or block details when pressed for information. Faced with this level of secrecy, it is essential to have the child's own account and this must be gained under circumstances where the child is free from intimidation. Also, Albert was unable to confront his own hostile or negative feelings about females and sexual matters in general. This was not an issue to which we addressed ourselves in any great detail in assessment, but would have been an important component of any effective treatment, if he were to be prevented from re-offending. He had considerable anger, though this was usually well concealed. We hypothesised that the abuse may have been precipitated by anger and frustration towards his wife because she was not able to perform well sexually at the time, ostensibly due to gynaecological problems. Albert also displayed a strong need to exert power and control in his relationships in general. That is why it was essential for the team to take control of the family for the period of assessment. He was perfectly able to manipulate situations to his own ends and it was essential to prevent professionals being played off against one another. Finally, his attitude towards his previous offences was that he had been punished (fined) for them and that they could now be 'forgotten'. He added that he saw his previous period on probation as punishment.

We concluded that Albert was not fully honest about the extent of the assaults, but the nature of his admissions indicated that there was more than one incident. Secrecy is one index of dangerousness and Albert's lack of openness in general meant that we were unable to come to any conclusion as to whether he had revealed the full extent of the abuse of the child. Albert had a strong need to define his personal relationships in terms of control and this was another measure of his dangerousness. Where power and control are set within the family dynamic, his wife would be unable to resist this and any child in the family could be at risk. Finally, his desire to abuse children was probably related to his inability to confront his hostile or negative feelings about females and this may have been rooted in a pre-verbal anger which could be explored in psychotherapy. Unfortunately, we felt that the longstanding nature of his difficulties in combination with his personality would strongly militate against success, and that untreated he would offend again should the situation arise.

Albert came to trial where he was found guilty and sentenced to a term of imprisonment by the court.

COMMENT

Mental Health Aspects

The case of Albert and those like him presents a dilemma for those working in the mental health field, challenging our abilities at every stage of an intervention from referral and problem definition to follow-up. The many diagnostic terms used to describe such people range from being a psychopath or sociopath to having a psychopathic personality, a personality disorder, moral insanity or character disorder. While intellectually such people can be dismissed as a 'rag bag' of residual characteristics, not properly the province of psychiatry, they cannot in reality when they have presented as actual clinical entities demanding attention. The 1983 *Mental Health Act* (Part 1, Section 1.2) refers to 'psychopathic disorder' as 'a persistent disorder or disability of mind (whether or not including significant impairment of intelligence) which results in abnormally aggressive or seriously irresponsible conduct on the part of the person concerned' and provides grounds for compulsory detention for those likely to benefit from treatment. Although the area is very controversial and riddled with uncertainty, it is convenient to think of persons with disorders of personality, with psychopathy being an extremely severe form (see Prins, 1986 for a most useful discussion).

Although he clearly had many abnormalities of mind, there was no trace of any disease entity at work to create his condition. Instead, his behaviour is better explained as being a reflection of his personality (i.e. those relatively enduring aspects of himself which are manifest in his social relations such as his character or moral sense, intellect, attitudes and opinions, motivation, judgement, etc.), as influenced by temperament and personal history. Here, he had many deficits, some of which are illuminated in this incident from his life. He was prone to lie; in the past, he had been found out to be a thief; he was an exploiter of other people who were unable to protect themselves. What was 'wrong' with Albert himself was not insanity in the usually encountered sense (i.e. being out of touch with reality) but more what personal characteristics were lacking. His form of 'insanity', if one could call it that, was of the moral kind. He seemed to have no true moral sense, no real desire to obey commonly accepted rules when no one was watching, or a desire to do something, simply because it was the right thing to do. He did not seem to be able to benefit from previous experience but broke the same rules again and again.

Many such people have all of these characteristics but are much more anti-social in their behaviour, more dangerous and violent than Albert, and misbehave in more areas of life. These people could be said to be 'essential psychopaths'. Likewise, there are many people with disorders of personality whose abnormalities are much less marked. These would include people who are too suspicious, too orderly, too extravagant, too melancholy as a regular or persistent, characteristic of their personality. Such people are often treated as neurotic or personality disordered. Albert, like many, remains in the no man's land between the extremes; his behaviour a matter of concern, his degree of menace to society, a matter of debate.

Casework Aspects

Psychiatry, social work and the law

Section 12 of the 1983 *Mental Health Act* imposes an obligation on courts to ask for a psychiatric report. It is, however, rare for sex offenders to be mentally ill. They may be suffering from a personality disorder which may, or may not, be susceptible of treatment, but they are generally responsible for their actions and fit to plead. As mentioned above, psychopathic disorder is defined in the Act as a form of mental disorder, but few psychiatrists outside the special hospitals are willing to offer treatment to this type of offender. Inter-familial sex offending tends to have its roots in the individual family dynamic and social workers by their training are often ideally placed to offer a service to the offender and the court. Not every sex offender is a psychopath, but a sympathetic assessment will evaluate the extent of the disorder and be of help in formulating plans for the future. We need to have the confidence and expertise as a profession to offer such a service.

The Assessment Team

In the case of Albert there were apparently both psychiatric and child care aspects requiring attention. This method of interviewing, as well as having both mental health and child care social workers involved, addresses this issue as well as providing control, protection and support. Now that the real extent of child sex abuse is becoming more apparent, social workers will have to address themselves to the issue. But to do so they will need to have clear understanding of what is involved, not just in terms of the family, but also of their own mental health and sexuality. This raises a number of considerations for such a team of workers.

Firstly is what I call the male 'conspiracy' of sexuality. Male attitudes towards women as 'sex objects' are deeply ingrained in our society and a male worker can easily be drawn into the offender's world, where women and children are objects to be dominated and abused. This can be obviated by having a strong female as a co-worker who is not afraid to confront the man on this issue.

Secondly, clear roles in the assessment are important. Sex abuse can give rise to strong feelings of anger, loathing and pity in all of us because it strikes at the core of our being. The offender and the victim should have separate workers unless the victim is old enough for a family assessment to be indicated.

Thirdly, while careful planning and feedback from each session is important, the team needs to be flexible and resilient enough to allow for resistance and for the unexpected. Each case is different and will throw up its own set of problems. Each team is different and team members come to the assessment with their own experiences and expectations, so an exercise in team building will help the workers to get to know each other, sort out their roles and plan the assessment. While I have attempted to explain a working model, in practice, each team will have its own contract with the family and with each other.

2 Ann:

a problem in mothering

CASE HISTORY

Ann was twenty-two when she was referred to the Eating Disorders Clinic with symptoms of binging, vomiting, some weight loss and amenorr-hoea. At the lengthy initial interview Ann gave the following history: she had grown up, together with her sisters, in a village-styled children's home. She knew that she and her sisters had come into care because her mother had had a drink problem and 'could not cope'. There had been no further contact from their mother, although there was with their father. He would visit, and later they went home for weekends. He worked in a brewery and he, too, had a drink problem.

Most of Ann's memories of the children's home were pleasant ones. They included manipulating new staff and students, particularly when she began to truant in secondary school. The latter came about because for six years the children had lived with the knowledge that their children's home was too close. In preparation for this, Ann left the children's village school and went to a large comprehensive school near to where her father lived. This was some considerable distance from the children's home and she had felt different and out of place there. She did not tell anyone where she lived and, despite good intellectual ability, Ann began to truant.

During a routine medical examination, Ann was found to be five months pregnant. She and the father, a West Indian boy, were both aged fourteen at the time. Ann left school but continued her education by having a home tutor, which she enjoyed, until she went to a mother and baby home. After this, she lost contact with the child's father, who had also been from the children's home. Despite pressure to give up the baby for adoption, Ann decided to keep the child and was placed, together with her daughter, in a foster home right away from the area—a prospect which initially terrified her.

While Ann was adjusting to her new role of being a mother, the children's home closed and Ann's sisters returned to live with their father. She and her daughter, Tracy, joined them there soon after Ann had turned sixteen and they were all still together six years later.

Ann said that she had been miserable for some years prior to the interview. She had not wanted her family to know of her eating problem. At home, as the only unemployed adult, she had taken responsibility for all of the domestic arrangements, including the cooking. She had found no reward in this and in identifying how she might begin to change her eating pattern, it was obvious that there were many unresolved problems around the family budgeting arrangements, for which Ann felt responsible. She did not feel that she could afford to eat differently and she was the person who bought all the food. Because she wanted to keep her problem a secret, she could not see how she could change this arrangement. She was already sensitised to any comment about her eating and felt particularly upset by her father's criticisms and lack of support.

Despite initial resistance to the idea of having contact with a social worker, she agreed to see me again. She also agreed to keep a diary of all the food that she ate and to record any thoughts that she was having when she wished to either binge or vomit. She also agreed to attempt to eat three meals per day.

At the next meeting a week later Ann came with her diary. She had kept it carefully, recording her food intake, but had found the task terrifying. She had not been able to describe any feelings, but had binged for three days after the interview and then eaten very little for the rest of the week. She was, however, able to talk in this session, about her difficulty in accepting advice and, again, about her childhood.

Ann spoke of her current problem as that of housing. She wished to live on her own with Tracy (who had problems with poorly controlled asthma), but she thought her desires wicked. Various people had told her, 'it would kill your father if you left home'. She had secretly put her name on the council list, but she worried about who would care for him, even though he grumbled at her constantly.

We continued to meet fortnightly. Ann often used the time to speak of the staff of the the children's home, whom she recalled with mixed feelings. For instance, she felt they had been unhelpful over her preparation for starting her periods, while she remembered herself as having been anxious. Ann used the diary regularly, and a pattern emerged where she would binge following her appointments with me and visits to her foster parents. By this time, she had stopped vomiting. As she began to record her feelings, it became clear how desperate and despairing she felt at times and she used the diary as a means of communicating with me between sessions.

Also, at about this time, a number of changes began to take place in the case. For the first time, Ann began to express anger and resentment towards her family about the organisation of the work. An example of this was that she finally gave over the responsibility for paying the rent to her eldest sister because the council was beginning to think of taking action against them for their rent arrears. The family had been reluctant to give Ann rent money, the father having spent most of his own money on drink.

At one meeting, following a holiday, Ann sat seemingly paralysed with fear, having discovered that her weight had increased. We discussed this increase, and though she hardly spoke, in the end she did relax somewhat. She eventually began to understand that the rest of the family ate excessively and were irresponsible. While she still felt responsible for curtailing these excesses in them, she began to feel less desperate and her eating gradually stabilised. As we examined Ann's way of undervaluing herself, it became clear that despite her perception of herself as being intellectually inept, she was gaining useful insights from reading books by leading academics on the topic of eating disorders.

While beginning to make progress, an indicator of how much remained to be done with Ann was the degree to which she was still severely debilitated by her continuing anxiety. For instance, she began to consider the possibility of further training for herself, but she was too anxious to consider allowing anyone else to look after Tracy, now seven, for any part of the day. Also, during this period she was offered a twelfth floor flat by the council but had to refuse it because of the great degree of apprehension that the thought of using the lifts roused within her.

When Ann and Tracy were able to move into a new flat six months after her first contact with the clinic, it marked an important turning point. For one thing, Ann found it less lonely than she expected. I visited her there soon after she moved in and found it well furnished, tidy and rather homely. Tracy's asthma had finally disappeared.

Suddenly, there was a series of several consecutive missed clinic appointments and following these I took the initiative and visited Ann at home. When I arrived she hid under the bedclothes. When she finally spoke, it was about a variety of anxieties. She seemed to need support and reassurance in her new venture of living in her own home. She had been dwelling upon her childhood experiences and had recently become interested in the experiences of people who had been 'in care'. She was anxious about her ability to 'mother' Tracy and remembered the arguments which she had encountered at the time of Tracy's birth. She said, 'Social workers warned me that I would become a 'battering parent''. She recalled how badly she had behaved with the foster mother and social workers but had invested her love in her daughter. I told her how I saw things: that she had given birth to Tracy when the children's home was closing down and that she wanted to care for someone and to be cared for. I said that the two of them were together, she was ill and was wondering if Tracy was capable of caring for her.

When her father died suddenly, about six months after Ann and Tracy had moved into their flat, Ann was devastated. She seemed to get over it, however, until she was allowed access to her case notes and learned some factual information about her parents. Her distress at that stage was such that, once again, she was rendered quite unable to speak. She was particularly upset by her father's life, although what these details were, she was never able to say. She also learned from the notes about her difficulty in speaking which emerged in the social work reports as her refusal to speak. She said that the 'first five social workers' had described her as a happy-go-lucky child and then, in later years the records show how she would not speak, although invited to do so.

In the last few sessions Ann spoke of her ambivalence towards her daughter, who was well-liked by everyone who met her and was doing very well in school. At home, however, it seemed that she treated Ann badly.

COMMENT

Mental Health Aspects

Anorexia nervosa, or the 'slimmers' disease', is, of course, a psychiatric condition which varies greatly in severity where substantial loss of weight occurs in the absence of either any organic condition, or where the symptom is not secondary to some other form of mental disorder (such as depression or schizophrenia). Ann's condition displayed many of the characteristics most commonly identified in people suffering from *anorexia nervosa*. To begin with she was a young, unmarried woman with at least average intelligence and suffering from amenorrhoea, a very common picture.

Her history shows that she was anxious about reaching a normal weight and felt uncomfortable about her sexuality (despite her premature sexual experience) as described by Crisp, 1980. She had an anomalous family background typified by a dominant father and absent mother (both of whom had disordered behaviour in respect of alcohol consumption) and having been raised in care.

Psychologically, she was very conscientious; she had a distorted self-image (her own idea of her physical appearance did not closely correspond to that held by others); her personality was markedly oral (food refusal, binging, vomiting and mutism). As can be seen below, her condition was not so serious as to require hospitalisation and responded to psychologically based help-giving. Nevertheless, her disorder was very much in evidence throughout, as where the use of the diary to monitor and to control the binging and vomiting (Lacey, 1983) needed to be modified because of her anxiety and guilt about her food intake. This was indicative of her anorexic thinking, although she was not severely low in weight.

Casework Aspects

The choice of casework as a method of treatment was made because of the multidimensional nature of Ann's condition, which corresponded to Perlman's (1970) view. Her eating disorder indicated the many intra-psychic problems she had: poor self-esteem, despair, and conflicts arising from any assertion of her own views or needs. The reality of being a woman and a mother filled her with anxiety. In addition, she was experiencing difficulties in her social functioning, partly related to these internal conflicts, but also because there were external problems within her family and her home (e.g. economic, interpersonal) that sometimes intruded into her relationship with her daughter.

The only tasks set for Ann were around her eating, with the aim of controlling the symptoms and getting her to eat three meals per day. Alternative approaches to some of her problems were often explored. Ann asked for help in direct negotiations with the Department of Health and Social Security (DHSS) once. Dependency was both fostered and contained by regular meetings at two or three-weekly intervals. Ann contacted me outside these times only rarely, for example to change an appointment or to inform me of her father's death.

The content of the interviews moved from food-related issues to those relating to the problems at home. She had taken it upon herself to be a 'mother figure' in the family and this proved to be both unsatisfactory and unsatisfying. The problems in her relationship with Tracy emerged as they became a separate unit although Tracy's asthma disappeared.

Whilst use was made of understanding transference, this was never interpreted to Ann. It was acknowledged that she probably had some unsatisfactory social workers in her childhood. Having access to her case notes (from another authority) proved to be a most painful experience, but one that she needed in order to find out about her family and about her time in care. She did not acknowledge this to the local authority in case they stopped her from reading her files. It was helpful for Ann to see how her difficulties in speaking – a feature of the casework – had previously contributed to her problems with social workers. It had been easier for Ann to go through the process of getting access to her notes than to ask her father directly about herself, her mother, and how they had first come into care.

On occasions Ann brought Tracy to the interview. It was in this way that Tracy's mixed racial origins became known. In seeing Ann alone at the clinic, it was possible to support the part of Ann that wanted to be in better control of her life, and the occasional joint interview and the two home visits were made to support Ann and to reassure her. She knew a great deal about bad mothering and judged herself harshly. Gradually Ann had been able to free herself from the unsatisfying mother roles that she had with her sisters and her father until she was able to take on the more appropriate, but sometimes lonely, role of being mother to Tracy.

3 Tony Brown:
the case of Prometheus Unchained

CASE HISTORY

It was Sunday evening and Pam Brown had just rung me at home. She was seeking advice about her twenty-two-year-old son, Tony, who has been severely depressed for nearly a year, with five weeks of in-patient psychiatric care in the local psychiatric unit early last summer. He was very withdrawn. Also, he was neglecting himself—not eating or washing—and he hardly spoke. He had been having an affair with an older married woman, Rose, which was ending.

On the next day Pam was to see the consultant psychiatrist. She feared that he would suggest ECT (electro-convulsive therapy) for Tony and wished my opinion. I asked what other treatment Tony was receiving. He was on amitryptiline prescribed by the general practitioner. I advised against ECT, saying that other treatments needed to be tried. She asked if she and Tony could come to see me and I agreed.

On Tuesday both Mrs Brown and her husband arrived with Tony. He was a very tall, thin, slow-moving young man. The two parents discussed him but he responded only occasionally with eye movements and a brief chuckle at one point. The parents were clearly frustrated as he ate rarely and never went out of the house. When he was in hospital, he was not properly fed so 'starved'. The relationship between Mr and Mrs Brown was poor and she looked very sad.

I saw Tony on his own. I massaged his back on the couch whilst explaining about therapy. I said that I would tell his parents nothing without his permission but would simply report to them as to whether things were progressing well or not. I could see that he understood and gave him a booklet on meditation and asked him to read it. He nodded his head.

On the following Saturday Tony arrived accompanied by his father who waited in our office whilst I worked with his son. I was nervous about this encounter and had searched for medical references on depression and 'elective mutism' and found little which was not about Sioux Indians! I prepared some coloured felt tip pens and a notepad for him to write on.

Tony laid down on the couch and I slowly massaged his back from top to bottom with long firm strokes. The right side was very stiff and he reacted with pleasure. The circulation seemed cut off from his hands and feet which were very cold and I helped him to sit up but it took great effort for him to do so. 'Nod or shake your head in reply. Have you been well since I last saw you?' 'Not very well', came the answer. I was relieved as I could put the felt tip pens away. I talked slowly and there were long delays. Sometimes he tried to speak to me and nothing came; sometimes he got stuck in mid-sentence. Another time a slow, brief and complete answer emerged.

All day he did nothing but think a great deal which is very tiring. I asked if it was all right to ask his mother to do notes on his background. He was not keen and said slowly that he would give me any necessary information.

'How long have you been depressed? Your Mum said since about last Christmas.' He smiled briefly. 'That's as good a time as any ....I can't link it with any specific event.....It had been coming on for some time....'

He had read my booklet on meditation. I gave him a wooden meditation stool and sat him on it. I straightened his back and showed him how to sit properly and breathe slowly. 'Try to sit for ten minutes a day and to say under your breath the words "I am worthwhile..." over and over again' I said. He nodded his head in agreement and I felt tearful because he tried so hard. Every answer seemed to be a tremendous effort. We finished the session early and I simply told Dad that Tony was talking. Dad looked dumbfounded.

Tony arrived with his mum for his next appointment on Thursday. There had been some difficulty in getting him from the car and I went to help. He walked along with me but at a very slow pace. That session began with me massaging him again. The right side of his back was still stiff and sore, and again I sat him up forwards with a great struggle. I held his face and looked closely into his eyes. It was very difficult for him to keep eye contact; he kept looking away and I pointed this out.

After some time we began to talk. I put one hand on his shoulder and said, 'Tell me about your family.' 'My twin brother Sam is in the Army.....My Dad was in the Fleet Air Arm......is now an engineer........My sister Bess lives away from home......works in a nearby pub......She is expecting a baby.' Every time the young man answered, his heart went into palpitations and his whole body tensed. 'I get on much better with Dad....than with mum.' 'Mum seems very sad,' I said. He agreed but went on to tell me about meditation. It was very difficult for him but I asked him to persist and promised to help him as much as possible. I could see how quickly he tired and massaged his back again and gave him a hug.

On Tuesday Tony was again accompanied by Mum who, however, looked much better than before. I massaged Tony's back again and his right side was still very stiff. I sensed a lot of anger this time and we began to talk with considerable difficulty. His father had gone on business to Saudi Arabia for two weeks. He seemed to be eating better, though his mother had complained of him picking at his food.

'I am frightened of losing control,' he said. 'Are you talking about anger?' He smiled and struggled soundlessly. 'Tell me how you get on with mum?' 'She dominates me.' 'How?' The smile came again but no words.

'When we talk about feelings, you have great difficulty in talking.' He smiled again but again was speechless. 'Will you think about that before our next meeting?' He silently nodded consent. I touched him as he was tearful. He looked very sad and I hugged him. He muttered, 'I'm frightened of losing control.' 'Tell me what that means?' I responded. But still, no words came.

Before they left, I had a brief discussion with his mother. She had just arranged for a second consultant psychiatrist's opinion. She was trying to organise a holiday in order to 'get some sun'. Mrs Brown said that there had been some quarrel between herself and Tony's girlfriend Rose. According to her, the girlfriend thought that Tony should have gone back into hospital and had ECT. Mrs Brown said that now that Tony was discussing his difficulties with me he shared less with Rose and seemed pleased of this. She recounted that Rose was older than Tony, a married woman still living with her husband and three children. She added significantly 'still sharing the same bed'. The green-eyed monster strikes again!

They came again early the following week and Mrs Brown sat in the kitchen alone while I spoke to Tony. I massaged his back and noticed that his hands and lower back seemed less cold than usual. I helped him to sit up and his face looked more lively. Laboriously, he focused his eyes on my face and grinned.

'How are you?' I enquired. It was with considerable difficulty we began to talk. 'O.K.' he replied in a whisper. I asked about Rose and that stopped conversation altogether. Knowledge of Rose had come from his mother and not from him. His mouth moved several times but no sound came. Big emotions seemed to block his speech, so I changed direction: 'You seem frightened.' He nodded his head vigorously. 'What about?' No sound came even after two or three minutes of agonising atempts. 'When was the last time you cried?' His eyes reddened and he whispered 'Last week.' In a relative flow of words, he told me that Rose and three friends had taken him to a prayer meeting. While there he had been overwhelmed by the sympathy and cried. 'They held me,' he said and I hugged him. He resisted the tears which welled up and muttered something about religious experiences. 'Do you know I am a priest?' He looked incredulous. I showed him a photograph taken at ordination. He examined the photo carefully and I said he could keep it. He was tiring quickly so we ended the session.

On the following Tuesday Tony arrived, accompanied by his mother as usual. I was told that she had a heart complaint—angina—and has suffered one heart attack already. I speculated to myself as to whether it was a product of stress. I massage Tony and can hear his reaction—grunts and groans. 'Tell me how you have been feeling?' 'I am not very good at feelings.' I asked about crying and about fear. He finds it very difficult to express anything. I ask if he is frightened and he nods his head. He mutters, almost inaudibly, '...about losing control.' 'What would happen if you lost control?' Neither sound nor gesture came in reply. 'How loudly can you shout? Repeat after me the sentence "I am worthwhile!" ' After some hesitation he said it louder and then very loud. His face reddened and filled with an infectious grin. I handed him a mirror to see himself and he was embarrassed. 'What do you do during the day?' 'Just watch TV?', he replied. He had a way of turning every statement into a question. I told him that he seemed very frightened of something or somebody and that related to his family. He looked blank and puzzled. I tried to explain it a different way, but he still looked blank. It was an ill-timed remark; too much, too soon. I am better at intuition than thinking.

'Is there anything that you want to know?' I asked, changing tack. 'Tell me how I am doing?' 'You are doing very well. But we both need to work hard to get you better.' He nodded approval.

I had a brief word with Mrs Brown who was worried about going into hospital and thought it necessary for Tony to go in as well. He had come off amitryptiline completely now.

On Monday I received a telephone call from Mrs Brown who later came to see me. According to her Tony had been very difficult over the last few days refusing to wash and simply watching the television all day. 'I thought he was going to hit his father last evening,' she said. 'He shouted at him.' I explained how Tony was beginning to 'thaw' emotionally and that he was part of a difficult and complex triangle (dad, mum and Tony). Dad is stiff and disciplined. Mum is bitter and broken-hearted. Tony is angry and sullen. 'I know all this anger coming out is good. But if I couldn't turn to you, I would have rung the doctor and had him admitted to hospital again.' 'What about Tony coming to spend some time with me? That will take some of the strain off you.' She looked delighted at this suggestion. Also, she had started to attend yoga classes at the golf club.

The following day Rose rang. She said that she loved Tony very much and wanted to be with him always. However, she had three young children and a husband to look after and that made life difficult. I was sure that it did! Rose felt strongly that Tony had been crippled by his mother. 'She doesn't like me coming around. Between his Dad's insistence on being a real man and avoiding this arty farty stuff and his Mum's constant messages that men are no good, always letting you down, he has been crippled. He left college after doing art and design with the half promise of a job which never materialised. He went to London to look for work and came back after three days very depressed. He went all moody and just got worse. We went on holiday to Yugoslavia last May and he was fine. On return, he got deeper into the depression and went into the psychiatric unit not long after.' The chat with Rose was very helpful. The triangle had become a square!

Later the same day Tony came with his father. After the massage we talked more fully than before. 'How do I get my father off my back?' It appeared that if I waited long enough and encouraged him to comment sufficiently, he would. 'I totally lack confidence.....I just wallow in despair....I cannot cope with my parents.....They are destroying me altogether.'

Everyone in this square was destroying everyone else! He commented enthusiastically about his Auntie Sandra, who was staying with them. They walked on the seafront earlier in the day amid the wind and the rain. He enjoyed it and liked her pleasant discipline.

'Do you prefer bossy older women?' He smiled. 'Would you like to spend the day with me tomorrow?' His eyes lit up. I asked him to bring along his paints and he agreed.

The next day was Wednesday. Tony arrived with oil paints and we spent most of a pleasant day together. We played pool in the basement. He took several minutes to get into position for each shot but, to his delight, played well. He obviously benefited from working in a pub.

We had a slow lunch. He could not face the pie and baked beans which looked enormous to him. Instead, he ate a toasted cheese sandwich with much prompting. After, we played chess and I taught him Fox and Hounds. Nevertheless, he was a young man plagued by self-doubt and extremely concerned about being a failure. 'I'm no good at anything. I have lost confidence.' 'It will return, gradually.'

I taught him some yoga-style exercises. He enjoyed these and gained considerable energy. I should have introduced him to them days earlier. At 5 p.m. his mother came to collect him, and I took her into the kitchen to stress the importance of his relationship with Rose. I asked her to encourage Rose's visits. She responded 'I needed to be told that.'

On Sunday Tony greeted me with a smile. There was no massage but instead we practiced the yoga exercises. He stood up and I got him stretching and breathing out explosively. His body was full of energy when we finished, both huffing and blowing together.

We started to play a game of free association. He started off and I replied. Then, I called out the subjects. His response was quite speedy until we got into feelings. I shouted out 'anger' and the response was 'mad'. Suddenly, the words came quite quickly. 'It has been a difficult few days since I saw you last. Dad has been trying to wind me up. He plays lots of games. He made me feel very angry over something—I can't even recall what it was now—but I wanted to throw the TV out of the window. I resisted that. Turned my mind away to other things. What can I do to get better? I know I have to concentrate more effectively but what else?'

I suggested a few more daily exercises to get his body moving and better co-ordinated. I asked him to close his eyes and see a white candle slowly flickering in a slight breeze. He closed his eyes for a few moments. 'I can see it. I can see it,' he said excitedly. I should have tried visual imagery before. It works much better with someone of artistic ability.

The next session was two days later, Tony being brought by his father. When I entered the room, Tony, who was seated stiffly in the chair, greeted me with a smile. 'How have you been feeling?' 'O.K.,' came the reply. 'How have things been going with your family?' 'O.K.' 'Have you seen Rose?', I asked. 'Only a fleeting visit. Half an hour. It went quite well though. I got angry with my mum yesterday. She doesn't understand and harasses me. I managed to control myself. I kept it all inside.' 'What happens if you don't...control it?' This question seemed too near the fear because his concentration went and his chin tensed up and his eyebrows went up and down. I imitated the tension on his face and he laughed.

We played the free association game where I said a word and he responded. His responses came very slowly and contained invisible question marks. 'You seem to be afraid of not saying the right thing....of failing? Where did you get this sense of failure?' 'It came from not being able to cope. I cannot succeed at anything.' We searched around for the source of this but his mind was fogging over and his concentration going. I asked whether he wanted to come for part of the following day and he was delighted. I suggested that we could play some more pool and that we should record a tape to help his meditation practice.

The next morning his mother dropped him off saying 'He doesn't like me. He wouldn't get washed or anything this morning.' We spent most of the day together. He was very withdrawn. He played pool with my son Stewart and then beat me in two frames. He seemed to be better co-ordinated than the week before, although his movements were still very slow, sometimes freezing into positions, almost as though forgetting to move. He spoke a little when prompted, but gradually began to show more initiative.

'I am lost. I am still struggling through all this. Quite lost.' I made some lunch and he showed a much improved appetite from the last time we had eaten together. Lentil soup followed by toasted cheese sandwiches, a Danish raspberry slice and washed down with mugs of sugary coffee. Also, it felt good to be a 'mum' preparing the meals and enjoying someone eating them.

We finally got around to making the relaxation tape. It was a simple self-hypnosis programme about meditation and his personal value and he enjoyed making it. 'You are worthwhile...You are worthwhile...' Later, I suggested some drawing with paint and pencils. He drew a pleasing abstract patern for about half an hour.

On Sunday, when I next saw Tony, he looked tired and battered. His mother had phoned me during the week. As she had planned, she had taken him to a second consultant psychiatrist for another, independent medical opinion. Tony, however, had refused to co-operate and did not speak to the doctor. The consultant had informed her that I was Tony's lifeline.

'It is hard... to keep up.... the resistance... all the time. I have... to be.. on my guard ...against.. their interference...I am having ....these nightmares. I wake up... during the night... several times.... feeling... frightened... but can't recall what.. the dream.. was about.' Words come very slowly for him again. I used a stop-watch to time his delayed responses and they speeded up. We played the free association game and he laughed a lot.

'How do you feel?'

'O.K.'

'That tells me nothing. Tell me what feeling words are?'

'I don't really know.'

'Is anger a feeling word?'

'Yes.'

'What about sadness?'

'Yes.'

'Come up with one of your own.'

'Resentment.'

'That's absolutely right.'

'I feel such a failure.'

I shook my head in disagreement. 'No, we are both succeeding. Both working together.' He smiled. 'I understand the resistance to your parents but you still need to eat. Is it possible to bend rather than continually to tire yourself out with this rearguard commando action?' He seemed to understand. We did some yoga exercises together and I massaged his back. When his father collected him, he told me that his son had gone back to his art.

When he arrived for his next appointment on the following Tuesday, Tony looked like something rescued too late from the river—large, lifeless and scruffy. At first, he spoke with great difficulty. I encouraged him to do energetic yoga exercises and really concentrate. Concentration came slowly.

'It is such a struggle keeping them away. I get so angry with dad and mum. They don't really understand anything. I have to imprison myself in the bedroom; shut myself off from everything. All these thoughts coming from my unconscious. These thoughts could destroy both of them. I have to keep control, to sit on top of the thoughts. Keeping control...it's difficult because I don't have any discipline...at all. Just sitting and thinking all day...I get very sad... and I am wasting my life. I'm no good at anything any more.' A small tear came from the right eye. He looked very sad indeed.

I suggested that he did exercises daily but we both seemed to be struggling against the power of this family and its capacity to cripple its members. By the time he left, he had life again but for how long....? His father greeted me in an accusatory tone saying, 'He is much worse you know. He won't wash or shave. Sometimes he looks at me with such hate...I simply don't understand it.' No doubt, therein lies a large part of the trouble.

We spent the next day together. We played some pool, which he won two frames to one, so I surmised that I must be improving! He ate lunch with some prompting; celery soup, steak pie and chips, followed by a Viennese whirl. We had shopped together earlier and when we returned home he had looked at some French Impressionist books of mine. We talked about my hobby of sailing and I promised we could go sailing together when the weather improved.

I showed him these notes and he was very excited. 'I will be famous. I would like to see them when they are finished.' 'The finish depends more on you than on me.'

He talked haltingly about his parents. He found them increasingly difficult. We discussed other ways of coping which don't necessarily involve refusing to eat, wash, bathe or shave; for instance, doing daily exercises followed by a short period of meditation, to establish a discipline. 'I am poorly motivated,' he said. 'It is easy here but very hard at home.'

His mother arrived to collect him and told me that she had had a good day. 'My husband and I are trying to get on better, for Tony's sake. It is working.' With Tony's permission, we discussed the family situation. I explained to Mrs. Brown that it was not so much what she did which was the problem but rather who she was. Tony felt that he had to defend himself against both her and her husband. She understood a little and gave me a big hug on leaving.

On Sunday, Tony looked washed out. We did some yoga exercises together and the life returned to his body. I explained that I was going to pretend to be his father and he must just talk to me as if it were really so. He found this amusing. 'Dad,' he said, 'you are intimidating me.' 'I can't intimidate you. You are bigger than I am.' Tony laughed at this. 'You see he doesn't understand anything.' Emotions began to flood in and he froze up.

We acted out the relationships between him and his mother. 'Mom— you intimidate me. You are always bullying me.' 'I try hard to get you to take care of yourself but you won't co-operate.' Again, I could see the emotions flooding in and again, he froze.'I cannot see anything clearly. So much is coming in.'

We talked about feelings that his parents might have about him. I tried to help him by assigning them colours: green for envy and jealousy; red for anger; yellow for fear. Tony saw that his parents might feel envious about his youth and potential freedom; might be angry about his lack of progress as they saw it and particularly his unco-operative attitude; they might also be afraid of his physical size and power. He began to see and feel how it was for them and the flooding of emotion began to take place once more.

His father came to take him home and was pleased to say that Tony had been painting again; an oil sketch of the view over the road. This painting was one important measure of how they saw him progressing. Mischievously, I commented that I hoped it had lots of yellow, green and red colours. Tony added quickly 'and brown'.

When Tony arrived on Tuesday I had never seen him looking as well. He was washed and shaved which made an important visual difference, but more than that, he was animated and actually initiated conversations. He seldom had to be prompted. 'I am feeling much better, almost serene and relaxed. It has been nice having Dad home for a short holiday. We've got on really well together. Even relations with mom have improved. Sam will come home for Christmas. I admire him. He knows where he is going. I have been enjoying my painting of the house over the road.'

This session was botched up because I was so pleased. My enthusiasm got the bettter of me and I tried to push him to discuss his feelings in a deeper way than before but was rewarded, instead, by all the old hesitation coming back. I made a serious mental note about remembering casework basics: work at the customer's pace not your own. He left with a tense and puzzled expression and we decided to spend the following day together to go into that.

When we spoke then, deeper currents began to come up from within Tony. His mind was troubled and more accessible. 'I am really lost. I feel invaded by ...People are penetrating me...My defences are not strong enough to protect me...from myself.' He looked both puzzled and bemused.

We played snooker together at the club and he enjoyed it. We had ham sandwiches for lunch and bought a cake from the shop. Over several hours he began to come alive. When his mother came, he looked lost again and very unhappy. The time he spent with us was still a rest from the battle which resumed on going home.

On Sunday Tony arrived with his twin brother, Sam. He looked well. Comments came much more quickly than usual, but he still required prompting. 'It is good to have my brother home again. I miss him. A lot is happening in my unconscious mind. Whirlpools. I had a disagreement with dad this afternoon. I can't remember what it was about. I think that it was quite silly, but before that I had felt much freer than for a long time. Freedom is very important.' I got him to close his eyes and focus on the dispute with his father, but nothing seemed to come except a lot of tension. It seemed as if his father was threatening his very existence.

'I feel this panic which wells up inside. I can't control it.' His breathing started to get shallower and shallower. I put my hand on the diaphragm and told him to close his eyes and concentrate on my hand. His breathing got deeper and he became less agitated quite quickly.

Now, seven months on, Tony is talking much more fluently and generally feeling much better. In addition to seeing me, his psychiatrist has started him on a major tranquilliser and Tony feels that this is helping him as well. I have shown him this case study and we have discussed it thoroughly. Presently, he wants to have more of a social life. He has enrolled in a pottery class and is using the ordinary bus for the first time in over a year. Next week he begins to help out in a day centre for old people. He and I go sailing regularly.

COMMENT

This complex case study shows, in detail, a great many aspects of direct work with someone who is currently going through a schizophrenic breakdown such as this. It features many of the psychological, social and psychiatric characteristics which frequently emerge as striking in our contacts with such people, and gives valuable insights as to how to work with them and their families.

Mental Health Aspects

Tony is a young person and this is a problem of the young with cases usually occurring before the age of forty-five. The commonest period of onset for men is in adolescence and early adulthood and its appearance is sometimes preceded by an 'affective' disorder. Tony's mental problems were severe and widespread and grossly interfered with his ability to live a 'normal life'. Typically, he showed signs of change, particularly disintegration, in his personality; eccentricities of thought and behaviour; emotional blunting; social withdrawal; deterioration in his personal and work habits; all of these things occurring without any firm evidence of organically based illness. Also, physically Tony is tall and thin (asthenic), a body type often associated with schizophrenic disorder. There are family factors present (discussed below) which have been shown to be associated with this problem. Although neither parents nor twin have developed the condition, such an event would not have been unusual as there is a high rate of concordance for this condition among first degree blood relatives.

Casework Aspects

Family and social factors and schizophrenia
In the light of the parent's behaviour one is immediately tempted to attempt to associate the cause of Tony's disorder with family processes in line with one of the many social causation hypotheses in existence. At this point, however, the ultimate cause of this condition remains unknown, and the place of family factors, as with biological and genetic ones, is still speculative. Tony's parents' relationship was indeed strained but, in making an assessment, one must also recall the stress that having a person with such a condition creates within even the most stable and nurturing family. Unravelling such tangled webs and working to improve the situation is one of the principal tasks of the mental health social worker.

Nevertheless, whatever part such pressures may play in the development of the condition, it is certain that family pressures can influence considerably the course and outcome of a given case. Certainly, some of Tony's behavioural deficits amount to what is called 'the clinical poverty syndrome' (i.e. apathy, mutism, social withdrawal) which has, itself, been found to be a product of untreated schizophrenia in a disabling social environment (Wing and Brown, 1970), not unlike what he was experiencing at home.

Likewise there is evidence that specific 'life events' (Birley and Brown, 1970) such as Tony's unsuccessful trip to London and his break-up with Rose could also have acted as precipitants to the particular episode described. Finally, there is little doubt that the high level of explicit criticism of Tony, the degree of overprotection and intrusiveness which his parents exercised on his life, and the high level of hostile face-to-face contact present in his home relationships were important in this case. There is solid observational and experimental evidence that such high levels of expressed emotion (EE) play major parts in schizophrenic relapse (Vaughn and Leff, 1976) and that lessening the amount of contact, such as was done here, can substantially reduce the risk of further acute episodes (Leff et al., 1985).

Practice issues

The question of whether or not to employ psychotherapy or psychotherapeutic techniques with people with schizophrenic disorder remains controversial. Such direct work is often seen as hazardous for the patient, difficult for the therapist and of lesser therapeutic impact than drug treatment for a condition which many consider to be a true illness. Nevertheless, psychotherapists of very considerable stature, like Sullivan and later Laing and Jackson, have reported successes, and it is probable that it is best to consider each case on its merits when trying to determine the appropriate style of work.

One point raised by the case of Tony is the unqualified value of having sound interviewing skills. The essentials still involve a balance between gathering useful subjective and objective information upon which to make an assessment, and using the interview as a basis for forming a therapeutic relationship. For the information-gathering task, active techniques for eliciting feelings such as expressions of sympathy, direct requests for feelings, picking up on emotional cues, asking open-ended questions and giving interpretations of responses, as a group, were frequently employed. Also, but less frequently, techniques for eliciting factual information, such as raising specific topics, probing and requesting detailed descriptions, were used. All these have been investigated and found to be useful and their presence and absence an essential characteristic of psychotherapeutic style from directive to non-directive types (Rutter et al., 1981).

The psychological state of Tony presented special problems to the initiation of the casework process. When an individual is withdrawn, as was the case here, it is especially difficult to make contact and begin the process of relationship-building, because vital areas of the personality are inaccessible to external influence. Here, the somewhat unconventional methods of massage, yoga exercises and later recreational activities were employed successfully to overcome this blockage. Making contact then allowed the worker to help Tony to concentrate his attention on the external world and develop a basic sense of trust from which point treatment was able to take off.

This case shows particularly the need to be patient and to be able to work at the client's pace, as well as be flexible in one's choice of methods. Two methods which are infrequently used and which require careful assessment and 'timing' are the use of behavioural reinforcement (i.e. stop-watch) which helped to eliminate pauses in conversation and the use of what might be classified as 'projective' techniques (e.g. the use of colours). These techniques might be applied usefully in a wide variety of cases.

4 Colin:
a quality of life

CASE HISTORY

In June 1983 I was called to the window of the psychiatric clinic attached to the district general hospital, and was asked to observe a man of thirty-seven years as he walked to his car. He had been referred by his general practitioner for assessment and for advice on the management of his behaviour. A paranoid psychiatric illness had just been diagnosed at interview, but it was observed that he walked with a broad-based, unsteady gait and that his hand movements, seen as he fumbled to unlock his car door, were poorly co-ordinated. This view of Colin marked the beginning of lengthy contact between him, his family and the multi-disciplinary psychiatric team. The team consisted of nursing staff, three medical staff, a clinical psychologist, two occupational therapists and a social worker (me). The unit served a rural population, with specialist psychiatric facilities based over twenty miles away.

I was asked to support Colin's family whilst the diagnosis was clarified and a management plan instituted. I use a particular format to report and review social work contact, in order that assessment, goal-setting and monitoring work can take place. The description that follows demonstrates this review system.

First Review
Client: Colin—37   years—electrician   Family: Jean—39   years

(wife)—school cleaner Dawn—17 years (daughter)—waitress   Simon—15 years (son)—attends school Russell—12 years (son)—attends school.

1. Outside Agencies Involved
a. General practitioner.
b. Employer's personnel department.

2. Situation At Time Of Review
Over the preceding twelve months, Colin has become increasingly suspicious, irritable and violent in the home. The problems began four years ago coincidental with his brother's conviction for murder and Colin's conviction for sexual assault. Colin now hears voices telling him that he is mad. A paranoid illness has been diagnosed, but neurological problems are suspected. His wife appears supportive, but hints at longstanding marital difficulties and problems with the children's behaviour.

3. Problem Assessment
a. A severe disruption of family dynamics.
b. Child behaviour problems.
c. Difficulty in maintaining a consistent management plan with Colin whilst the diagnosis is unclear.
d. Financial problems due to long-term sickness.

4. Practical Services
a. National Insurance benefits.
b. Day hospital attendance to provide relief for Jean.

5. Social Worker's Goals
a. To support the family unit so that decisions about its future can be taken in the knowledge of Colin's diagnosis and prognosis, the family members' wishes and the support available.
b. To provide the team with information to help management and diagnosis. These goals are shared with Colin and his family.

6. Social Worker Activities
a. Family counselling services, in conjunction with the consultant psychiatrist.
b. Home visiting, to document the precipitants of violent outbursts in the home and the family relation to them.
c. To give advice and information on state benefits.

7. Client Contact
Fortnightly family sessions, either at home or in the clinic and open access for the whole family to the team in times of acute stress.

Second Review
1. Outside Agencies Involved
a. General practitioner.
b. Community occupational therapist.
c. Consultant neurologist.

d. General hospital ward.
e. Department of Health and Social Security (DHSS).
f. Housing authority.
g. Solicitor.
h. Approved social worker (area team).
i. Genetic counsellor.

2. Situation At Time Of Review

A diagnosis of Huntington's chorea has been made, and investigations in Colin's wider family reveal this previously undiagnosed disorder. The paranoid features of his illness continue. His cognitive ability is being periodically assessed and shows a marked decline. He is becoming depressed on occasions. His compliance with medication is poor. His violence towards his wife, and now his children, is increasing. The younger children's behaviour is leading to problems in the school and the community. Colin and his family, nuclear and extended, now know of the diagnosis and have received genetic counselling. Colin's self-care and physical abilities are decreasing. At times of admission for relief care, he has to sleep on a ward of the general hospital because he is unsafe on the stairs of our Victorian building. He is choking on food and prone to bed sores.

During the intervening period, there has been one formal emergency hospital admission under the Mental Health Act, 1983 (Sec. 4). Jean is considering divorce and has also considered an injunction to prevent Colin's return home, as well as appointing a solicitor to represent his interests.

3. Problem Assessment

a. The family's distress at the implications of the diagnosis—particularly for the children's future health.
b. The difficulty in distinguishing between behaviour resulting from the illness and that resulting from Colin's dependency and distress. Differing interpretations among family and staff are leading to management problems in the home and clinic.
c. The difficulties all involved face in tolerating the violence towards Jean, leading to confusion amongst staff over who is the patient/client.
d. Behavioural techniques to control or modify behaviour are now difficult to institute because Colin can no longer agree or maintain contracts or remember contingencies.
e. Colin's future placement has emerged as an issue as he is becoming increasingly difficult to nurse either at home or at local hospital facilities. Consideration needs to be given to the family's wish to keep in constant contact with him and to be involved in his care.

4. Practical Services

a. Day hospital attendance.
b. Holiday relief hospital admissions.
c. Adaptations to the home and aids for daily living.

d. Disability and housing benefits.

5. Social Worker's Goals

At this point the main goal of social work is to enable staff and Colin's family to work together in an alliance which will achieve the maximum quality of life for Colin, support for his family and maintain the positive aspects of family life. This goal is shared by everyone who is involved in Colin's care.

6. Social Worker Activities

a. To perform a 'key worker' role co-ordinating services.
b. Family counselling, in conjunction with the consultant psychiatrist, around genetic implications.
c. Exploring long-term placements and sources of funding.
d. Assessing the ongoing need for domiciliary services.
e. Linking home and hospital, to clarify and explain management and treatment.

7. Client Contact

As before.

Latest Review

1. Outside Agencies Involved

a. General practitioner.
b. DHSS.
c. Private nursing home.

2. Situation At Time Of Review

Colin now presents a considerable nursing problem, for both his mental and his physical state. District nursing services and the social services home care team have been involved in the home, to help Jean with his physical care. He still has paranoid delusions and is violent. His memory has deteriorated significantly. His daughter has married and left home. She is pregnant. This was an elective pregnancy, but she is showing signs of uncertainty about the decision. Simon is about to leave home to join the army. These two moves will leave Jean little practical support in the home.

A new local private nursing home specialising in the care of the chronic and terminally ill, and run by an registered mental nurse (RMN), has opened recently and has offered Colin a bed which Jean and the family have accepted. The decision was taken after careful consideration of alternative National Health Service provision. This placement has meant a large reduction in the family income as Colin has forgone many disability benefits and is funded in the nursing home by the DHSS. Jean's income in the family home cannot rise above Supplementary Benefit level without her having to make a contribution to Colin's fees.

3. Problem Assessment

a. Adjustment to low income.

b. Continuing need for support for Colin's family.

c. The ability of the nursing home to contain Colin's aggressive behaviour.

   4. Practical Services

a. DHSS.

b. Housing benefit.

   5. Social Worker's Goals

No change.

   6. Social Worker Activities

a. Support for the family during the adjustment to life without Colin in the home.

b. Linking the nursing home with the psychiatric team to help in Colin's management.

   7. Client Contact

Indirectly, through others when they perceive problems in relating to him.

COMMENT

Mental Health Aspects

Huntington's chorea is a progressive degenerative condition of the central nervous system which is traditionally considered one of the 'pre-senile' dementias. The most outstanding features are the involuntary, jerky (choreiform) movements which the individual develops, seen initially in Colin's uneven gait and loss of manual dexterity. These normally precede the onset of the second outstanding feature, dementia, including loss of memory and irritable behaviour, as seen here. 'Because the condition is due to a non-sex-linked dominant gene, approximately 50 per cent of the children of an affected parent are themselves liable to be affected' (Trethowan, 1979). Its onset tends to be in mid-life and since there is, at present, no way of detecting the gene's presence before its actual emergence, it can be transmitted to future generations before the carrier (i.e. parent) is aware of its presence. This raises the serious question of genetic counselling in relatives as shown in this case. The course of the illness is relatively slow, so that there is a gradual deterioration and planning for and managing the medical, social and psychiatric consequences of such cases can take this factor into account.

Casework Aspects

As the reader progresses from one review to the next, a picture develops of the role taken in the multi-disciplinary team by the social worker in response to the needs of the client and his family. The review system described in this case study is also useful when teaching and supervising students, drawing attention to key aspects of their work. It also keeps team members informed of social work input and its role in the team effort. The Problem

Assessment and social work activities are discussed with the team and, on occasions, activities are shared with other team members. For example, the nursing staff also supported the family and monitored reactions and precipitants of violent behaviour; this work was then used by the clinical psychologist to set behavioural programmes for all to follow.

The review system thus acts as a description of task and role in a team and as a teaching tool, but not as a description of the process of interaction between social worker and client. The latter, of course, can be done separately. It is based on work by Goldberg and Warburton (1979). It can include a section at the end of each review stating which problems the social worker intends to address and which problems are seen as of major importance, and reviewing the success of previous social work activities. In this team, an integrated file is kept, so notes from all disciplines keep team members informed of progress.

The review system can highlight important issues relating to social work practice. In this case there were issues relating to consent and risk, to identifying the client, and to the innovative use of state and private resources to provide appropriate care for the client's needs.

Every effort was made, at the early stage of treatment, to include Colin in planning, and to ascertain his views on his future. There was full discussion with his nearest relative who, despite ambivalent feelings towards him, was concerned to act responsibly and in accordance with his best interests. In the efforts to keep him in the home, in the community, the family were able to tolerate significant risk, and were supported in this by the primary health care team and social services. The problem of how to involve a person who is progressively becoming incapable of informed consent was a difficult one, and I was grateful for the comments on the matter of 'consent of informal incapable patients' made by the Mental Health Act Commission (1985).

There were occasions when the family was more able to tolerate the violence and risk than were the team. It was tempting to treat the wider family as the client and to forget the needs of the referred patient. Involving the family in management, to work alongside the team and develop effective strategies to deal with these outbursts, helped resolve this problem (Reading, 1985) and on only one occasion was it necessary to use a section of the Mental Health Act. The possibility of a Guardianship Order to provide a framework in which to work was constantly under review, and may be required in the future.

Colin's case demonstrates the work needed at the interface of physical, neurological and mental illness. Social workers in the psychiatric sector are frequently faced with chronic and deteriorating clients in a setting where hospital-based services for the chronically and terminally ill are decreasing, and a partnership is being pursued with community-based services—private or state funded—often before such resources are uniformly available. It requires co-operation and imagination on the part of many agencies (who might previously have had little experience of the particular disorders) to achieve good patient/client care.

As can be seen, when the diagnosis of Huntington's chorea was made, the possibility of genetic risk to other members of both the immediate family and other relatives rightfully became a therapeutic consideration. As a result, the content of the caseworker's sessions was adjusted appropriately. This is very important as research shows the many ways in which professional staff, faced with this situation, often shy away or even collude with family members to avoid discussing the implications of the diagnosis. Defence mechanisms commonly used by the client such as denial, rationalisation, projection and even reaction formation, are shared by the professional worker. By doing so, professionals can actually perpetuate the spread of the disease through generations by undermining the possibility of preventative medicine (Martindale, 1987).

Lastly, this review system leaves the worker free to use the most appropriate social work method to attain goals. In this case a combination of behavioural, problem-solving, task-centred and counselling methods were used. Changes in social work method were explained to the team members, the client, the family and the outside agencies, and this flexibility in method and organised review has helped this difficult case to its current stable position.

5   Denise:

avoiding the game of pass the parcel

CASE HISTORY

Denise first became known to the Probation Service at the age of twenty-two, following an offence of criminal damage. Her pattern of life had already marked her as a 'problem'. She was received into care at the age of six months. Three years in a local authority nursery were followed by a foster home placement until the age of fourteen. This and a series of short-term placements in residential homes all ended because of her behaviour. She was aggressive and unpredictable, with manifestations of stealing, wandering and sexual acting-out.

Denise's first psychiatric assessment, at the age of fifteen, gave a tentative diagnosis of manic-depressive psychosis and recommended out-patient treatment. She was described as 'depressed, lost, childlike and attention-seeking'. She was admitted to an adolescent psychiatric unit at fifteen and a half years and, formally, to an adult ward at sixteen. An informal admission foll- owed at twenty-one, with intervening periods of out-patient treatment. Diag- nosis fluctuated between manic depressive psychosis, hypomania and perso- nality disorder with manic episodes. Treatment was mainly with lithium therapy. Denise was a difficult patient, noisy, demanding, abusive, threatening and violent. The violence was not serious, but the possibility must always have been there since Denise is a big girl and her sudden and unexpected loss of control must have been alarming. At one period, her behaviour led her to be banned by the hospital.

Denise had been a Social Services client all her life. As well as displaying anti-social behaviour and having an inability to make relationships, her presenting problems were accommodation and finance. Denise had neither family nor friends; private landlords turned her out; hostel placements always failed, either because Denise walked out or because she was asked to leave on account of her behaviour.

Fragile self-control and inchoate aggressive feelings inevitably brought Denise into conflict with the law. Her offences included 'actual bodily harm', assault on the police, criminal damage and using obscene language. She had already served a six-month prison sentence before a further offence of criminal damage resulted in a twelve-month probation order with a condition to reside where directed. The Social Services department had by now banned her as a client after she punched a social worker.

There was no time to plan probation intervention with Denise or to work out a contract. She had nowhere to go. The lodgings found for her lasted one night before she was thrown out. A hostel run by nuns asked her to leave when she threatened one sister with a knife. Another hostel tolerated her for four weeks before evicting her. Two weeks later she was back in prison, for two months, following a further offence of criminal damage.

Prison offered a breathing space. Denise was surprised and please to be visited by her probation officer, Naomi, and by Sister Ursula, a hostel nun. Sister Ursula agreed to try and persuade her colleagues to take Denise back, and arrangements were made for Denise to attend the probation day centre and the local psychiatric out-patient department. Denise accepted the day centre well. She attended several times a week without persuasion, always finding someone to give her the attention she craved, either a fellow client, a volunteer, a probation officer or Naomi herself. Naomi's plan, shared with her colleagues, was to offer Denise an accepting relationship while, at the same time, giving her firm boundaries and regular feedback about what was and what was not acceptable behaviour. Naomi also kept in close touch with Sister Ursula. Accommodation was, as usual, the major problem. Denise was a difficult resident. She pilfered and was noisy and disruptive, coming in at all hours. She also claimed to be pregnant.

Tolerance was inevitably strained. Denise was dirty, inconsiderate in her use of toilet facilities, she wandered about half-naked and screamed and shouted and banged on doors during the night. She was finally admitted briefly to a psychiatric hospital where she was confirmed as being four months pregnant.

The next five months were particularly difficult. Because of her pregnancy, litihum therapy was discontinued. The hospital was reluctant to readmit her because she was so difficult. Naomi spent many hours on the telephone trying to arrange accommodation (Denise was now of 'no fixed abode') and eventually, with the help of Sister Ursula, Denise was admitted early to a mother and baby home run by nuns of Sister Ursula's order. Denise continued to attend the probation day centre where she tried everybody with her unreasonable and demanding behaviour. Naomi stuck doggedly to her plan of offering both positive and negative feedback, while maintaining a friendly interest with firm boundaries. This included calling the police to remove her, screaming, when she refused to leave at closing time, after a particularly difficult day in which she behaved provocatively, lying down and lifting her legs, shouting, swearing and insulting people.

Following this episode she was banned from the day centre for a week. Despite the problems, however, there were positive aspects. Denise could be charming and friendly. She attended ante-natal appointments regularly and behaved appropriately, and financial crises became gradually less frequent. And, once her outbursts were over, she showed no resentment towards Naomi and her colleagues.

Part of Naomi's work lay in liaison with other agencies. By now these included the psychiatric hospital, the maternity hospital, the mother and baby home, housing aid and the Social Services department, who were concerned for the baby. A case conference was arranged two months before the expected delivery. As the mother and baby home refused to continue with Denise, the psychiatrist agreed to admit her informally as the only way of providing care for the remainder of the pregnancy. Psychiatric nurses would liaise with the maternity unit in case psychiatric care was needed at the time of delivery. Denise was to be offered help in caring for the baby but if she proved incapable, the Social Services department would take out a care order; the Housing department would provide accommodation when Denise was ready for independence. Naomi would continue as key worker and co-ordinator of the complex plan.

Denise continued her usual course. She was discharged from psychiatric hospital for threatening other patients, but readmitted after persuasion from Naomi when it was discovered that Denise was sleeping rough. When Naomi visited her in the maternity unit just before the birth, Denise was at her best, quiet and rational, reflecting intelligently on the pros and cons of keeping the baby. She found more reasons for giving the baby up, but those for keeping it were stronger, namely that she would have, for the first time, someone to whom she would belong.

Denise had a normal delivery of a healthy baby, but soon showed signs of hyperactivity, resulting in her grabbing the baby and trying to run out of the hospital in her night clothes. The maternity hospital felt unable to manage her and she was transferred back to the psychiatric hospital. Denise agreed with Naomi to the baby going into temporary care. She acknowledged anxiety about her ability to look after him.

By now the end of Denise's probation order was approaching, and the transfer of responsibility had to be planned. Because Naomi was one of the few people Denise trusted, she agreed to maintain voluntary contact, and Denise would continue at the probation day centre. The psychiatric hospital was persuaded to take primary responsibility for Denise, now given the diagnosis of 'intermittent mania', and an attached social worker would accept the baby as 'client-in-chief' and work with Denise towards accepting long-term fostering.

Over the next six months Denise made real progress. She visited the baby regularly and came to realise that she could not manage him. She discussed this with Naomi, distinguishing between 'caring for' as loving, and 'caring for' as looking after, and grieved for him appropriately. She had many changes of heart about letting him go and talked of applying to the court to have him back, but accepted, without anger, Naomi's refusal to support her application. She saw the ending of her probation as an achievement and was proud of herself for having, for the first time, completed something successfully. Rows and scenes at the day centre continued, though less frequently, and she was, once again, temporarily banned after a fight. Later she managed to restrain herself when another client attacked her, and Naomi reinforced this with praise and encouragement. Perhaps her biggest achievement lay with her accommodation. Though she moved more than once, she eventually settled in a hostel where she behaved well and remained until allocated a flat by the Housing Department.

Eighteen months after Denise's first encounter with probation, the day centre closed when the lease on the premises expired. Naomi transferred to other work and Denise's case was not reallocated. She remained out of trouble, living in her own flat, for a further twelve months, until two further offences brought her back to the notice of the Probation Service. She was convicted of shoplifting, and shortly afterwards of attacking a stranger she believed was 'getting at' her. She was placed on probation for two years with a condition of attendance at the probation service's new-style day centre. A psychiatric report prepared for the court stated that at examination Denise showed no signs of illness. The new day centre offered a more structured regime. Attendance was on a regular basis, unlike the old 'drop-in' system, and offered social skills training within a formal groupwork context. Clients were younger than the now twenty-five-year-old Denise and all male. Denise was not accepted by them and her surpervising officer decided reluctantly to apply for removal of the condition of attendance. He noticed, in addition, that Denise was becoming 'high'. Denise is presently awaiting trial on a further charge, having attacked another probation oficer who was interviewing her. Psychiatric re-referral is contemplated.

COMMENT

Mental Health Aspects

Denise has a chronic mental disorder which has affected her life, at least since adolescence. In her 'career' as a patient, she has been frequently diagnosed as having some version of mania. This accounts for her hyperactive, 'high', noisy and sometimes aggressive manner. The problem is that this illness is being superimposed on a disordered personality. This means that even when her manic symptoms are under control she is likely to behave in an impulsive, childish and anti-social way. Also, because of the sort of personality which she does have, the management problems associated with her chronic illness are compounded because success doubtless requires a degree of compliance. This latter she resists and, as a result, probably suffers more frequent relapses than she might otherwise need to do.

Casework Aspects

The case of Denise is characteristic of many mentally disordered persons who wind up as active probation clients. Typical features include fluctuating diagnosis and 'difficult to manage' behaviour. Neither her offending nor her disorder is of sufficient proportion to warrant disposal via the Special Hospital or Regional Secure Unit Systems, yet each serves to make her difficult to contain within the ordinary National Health Service (NHS) or penal services. Denise's personality and behaviour make her unsuitable for community service or group work. She needs a sustaining relationship with firm boundaries, yet her insatiable demands and unpredictable aggression make her an impossible one-to-one client. The relative success of Naomi's approach (Denise completed her probation and stayed out of trouble for a further twelve months) lay in offering a casework relationship within the informal day centre environment. Both Denise and Naomi benefited from this. Denise had regular interviews with Naomi, but could attend the day centre as frequently and for as long as she chose. There was always someone to listen to her, and to share with Naomi the casework strategies of control, feedback and reinforcement of positive efforts at independence, as well as participate in the sisyphean struggle with her accommodation problems. This strengthened rather than weakened the relationship between Denise and Naomi. Denise never doubted that Naomi was 'her' probation officer. She trusted Naomi and came to regard her as a friend. Though Naomi and her colleagues were frequently exasperated and exhausted by the strain of coping with Denise, sharing the task enabled Naomi to pace herself, to have time for other clients and to tackle other aspects of the work with Denise (e.g. working with other services).

Listening to Sister Ursula and talking persuasively to Housing Aid and the psychiatric services were integral to the work. Naomi was not content to be a passive recipient of medical/nursing decisions, but was instrumental in helping the NHS staff to acknowledge the totality of Denise's needs, rather than viewing the situation from an exclusively medical perspective. In systems theory language, Naomi, as a change agent, with Denise as her client, had a range of target systems. These included Denise herself, but also Sister Ursula, Housing Aid and the psychiatric services. The case illustrates well the interlocking nature of the systems, since of the targets identified by Naomi, Sister Ursula and the consultant psychiatrist were change agents in themselves, and Housing Aid, the psychiatric services and voluntary hostels were all part of the action system.

The probation action system depended heavily on the availability of the day centre. The centre made few demands on Denise, but those few were inflexible: no drink, no drugs, no violence, leave when requested. Within those limits Denise was free to do as she pleased. The ratio of staff to clients was high. Skilled though she is, Naomi would have achieved little success without the collaboration and close support of a group of like-minded colleagues; witness the unhappy outcome of Denise's other social work contacts. Examination of Denise's case suggests that objectives can only be realised with a high input of resources in terms of manpower, time and accommodation, and with collaborative strategies both within and between agencies. Naomi could call on colleagues, not just in an emergency, but on a day-to-day basis, and the Probation Service worked closely with health, housing and voluntary services. Clients like Denise are often seen as unrewarding, and agencies tend to give up in despair. A genuine sharing of intervention, rather than games of 'pass the parcel' may be the only way of offering such clients the help they need.

6 Eddie's Story:
a fragment

CASE HISTORY

I do not currently work in a psychiatric setting. I was contacted, however, by an erstwhile colleague, a social worker in a large psychiatric hospital in a nearby town, to ask if I would see an ex-patient on an informal basis. She told me that Eddie lived in the town where I work and, being unemployed, found it difficult to travel to the hospital, although he had continued to attend a group there for a while after his discharge when he still lived nearer. When first in hospital, a few years previously, he had been through a very difficult time indeed; he had not been able to respond much to other people, or hold on to a sense of himself as a person. The later break-up of his marriage added to his sense of abandonment and unreality. He had lived abroad, with friends, for some months, but had returned home in considerable distress and had spent another few months in hospital, a different hospital, one near his present home. He was back at home now, where he lived with his widowed mother. He was managing—just—but felt he might have a better chance to continue to manage if he could see and talk to someone who could understand. I agreed to see him to discuss whether it would be worthwhile our working together and, if not, whether I could suggest someone else. Due to the nature of my present job, I could only begin such an enterprise with someone who could come to see me on an appointment basis, probably no more often than fortnightly, and my ex-colleague thought this should be possible.

Eddie did come to see me and we did agree to work together. He was a big man, physically, with a bearded, friendly face which could break into an engaging smile but which was mostly troubled by a slight frown, a look of strain. He seemed ready, indeed wanting, to talk. He talked of the past, his years at university where he met his wife and obtained his degrees. Good times, although looking back perhaps even then... He told me about his breakdown, how he had to give up teaching, withdrew into himself and, for months after admission to hospital, had crouched into himself, unable to speak, to relate, to make sense of anything, in terror and turmoil. His wife had stood by him for a long time, but had said eventually that she must have a divorce and was now remarried and out of touch. He spoke of the fairly immediate past, of a close relationship he had formed abroad and its break-up. He did not tell me a clear story and, indeed, I was often unclear about the timing and sequence of events, but concentrated rather on his feelings about what had happened. Indeed, it felt to me more as if he were telling me about his feelings, the enormous rage that was inside him (so great that he did not know how to contain it, how he could manage if it continued) and using what he was telling me of his life as a vehicle for expressing them. He was angry with his wife, his mother, friends who had not visited and particularly with the woman abroad who had caused him such heartbreak. He was obsessed by thinking of her, he said, unable to get her out of his head, unable to sleep and spending too much energy trying to stop himself contacting her, knowing that if he did so it would only make things worse. He suspected his desire for contact was, in part, a desire to hurt and disliked himself for that but was going round in circles with his need and loss and his rage. Eddie himself wrote about that time, recalling it some eighteen months later. He said:

at that time I was pretty low and emotionally confused, going through the trauma of divorce and with the 'normal' support systems afforded by family and friends virtually disintegrated. There are probably several factors in the aetiology of this situation but the most fundamental seems to be loss of love and affection from others and a lack of trust in other people. It may not be an exaggeration to say that I was quite desperate, having often felt in a panic and not knowing who to turn to for support. Relationships with others were fragmented and torn apart and I probably felt in a destructive frame of mind.

To me, the confusion was apparent as was the sense of family and friendly support having fallen away to blankness. I am not sure, however, that the panic and the feeling quite desperate were fully appreciated by me. Nor, I think, was I fully aware of the need, within such a blankness, to find someone who could fill, what is in in ordinary circumstances, a very ordinary human need. Eddie continues:

I think I saw our initial meetings as something of a risk, a make-or-break attempt to understand—with compassion—what I was going through and to consider my plight with some respect for me as an individual. I feel it is important that any threat of punishment or judgement was absent from our discussions.

For me, this last was not difficult. Eddie's judgement of himself, although it did contain, I thought, a measure of tolerance, was likely to be harsher than mine. Had I thought of punishment, I would have thought that nothing that I could do would compare with his present suffering. This may be only half true, though, if this were the 'make-or-break' he describes. Had he felt a negative judgement or a wish to punish from me, perhaps it would have been the final straw. The 'make' side of the either/or, however, takes time. Eddie again:

Gradually learning to trust implicitly again, I began to feel more confident and I looked forward to the meetings to get some emotional relief. The structure—however fragile—of once fortnightly sessions was also important particularly since enforced unemployment made the days long, fruitless, lonely and uncreative.

As so often, the pressure of the everyday present added to the difficulties. If only, I felt (the everlasting cry), I knew how he could get a job or somewhere to live that was not so close to his family. The emotional relief he refers to was, I think, the opporunity to talk about his consuming rage.

He talked of his rage with his father (in the past but still present) a very violent man in the home; with his mother for deserting him (though probably she had not from her point of view) and not giving him the unconditional loving he needed; with his grandfather for not being an adequate substitute father when his own father was left behind. His feelings at the time, particularly at his violent father, were probably stronger, we agreed, than he could remember—probably stronger than he had experienced them at the time. They would likely have included wishes to kill, for certainly now such thoughts could come. It was hard to sort out which anger was of the past and should, if possible, be worked through and left behind and which was of the present, to be integrated with other real feelings of the present (which, for much of the time, needed to be taken on trust) and not denied. It is worth noting, I find, that this process gave him some emotional relief in spite of the taxing work it involved.

In the present, Eddie got himself a job, not full-time and not forever, but a regular job. He continues:

Eventually work—however boring—added to this structure and I was able to be with people who were not confused and unhappy, having spent many months in the company of other patients in psychiatric hospital. Being able to contribute to something increased my feelings of self-confidence and self-esteem. I also believe that your support added to my recovery from what were termed psychotic symptoms and obviously reduced my isolation and fear. I now feel that I can rely on you to give me support in any crisis, while remaining apprehensive that you have other duties and commitments. Seeing you has taken the burden off my family and in the long run family relationships have improved and I don't feel the rejection I used to. I think the respect and tolerance of a human being's predicament are vital if the analysand is to regain some independence and self- esteem. The prospect of someone caring about me over a long period of time is also of importance I feel.

While seeing me, over a period of eighteen months or so, Eddie continued, much less frequently, to see the psychiatrist at his local hospital. At one time Eddie expressed some concern that seeing two people might be confusing. I said I could see the possible problem and if he felt he should see only one, I thought it should be the psychiatrist, as he could offer two avenues of help which I could not, namely medication and in-patient care when Eddie could no longer contain the build-up of inner rage and his what are termed 'psychotic symptoms'. He accepted that, thought about it and continued to see us both. Importantly, his psychiatrist continued to offer both and to be experienced by Eddie as genuine and 'straight'. At one point Eddie told me how relieved he was to have been given a diagnosis at last; borderline schizophrenia. I said that this made sense to me and used an example of his feeling (which came out of the blue) that his head was turning into a train. This feeling was very real (and hence, very frightening) and yet there was still a part of him which knew it couldn't be true. This added to the confusion and the fear of madness, but kept him on the 'borderline'. I did not attempt to interpret the possible meaning of this or any other 'symptom' but, instead, discussed the possible implications.

Eddie (which, as he wishes, is his real name) wrote the notes which are quoted here after his job had finished. Shortly afterwards he had one short spell of feeling disoriented and out of touch , but since then has continued, in spite of the continuing frustration of not finding work, much as his writing would suggest. We no longer meet but from time to time he telephones me to say how things are going and to talk things over.

COMMENT

Mental Health Aspects

Eddie's condition was described as 'borderline schizophrenia'. By this was meant that, though not obviously psychotic, he had the capability of deteriorating into a florid, acutely psychotic state. His condition was characterised by a core disturbance in his 'ego identity' wherein he experienced a sense of 'ontological insecurity', internal rage and confusion. His capacity for interpersonal relationships was consequently affected. This difficulty in establishing an atmosphere of basic trust with another person and maintaining an integrated sense of 'self' in the face of the stresses of human relationships is a particularly important factor in respect of psychotherapeutically directed treatment with such cases.

Casework Aspects

My work with Eddie concentrated on his feelings about himself, his sense of identity and well-being, his relationship to the world in general and some individuals in particular, and his strong and present feelings about past events, how they all intermingled and might possibly be sorted out, clarified and integrated. My understanding of how the personality functions in relation to its self and others is firmly rooted in 'object relations theory' and particularly the work of D. W. Winnicott (1958). Working with Eddie, I held on to the notion that all personalities have the potential for love and compassion as well as for anger and rage. My conviction, therefore, that although Eddie was flooded with his rage his capacity for loving and concern was also a real part of him was based not only on my impression of him as a person (initially bound to be impressionistic) but my 'knowledge' of his personality make-up— because he is a human being, a person. His need, in childhood, to 'split off' the rage had not dissipated it but meant that when eventually it overwhelmed him he could no longer hold on to his awareness of his capacity for concern. I could hold on to it because I could 'know' it.

In my view, this is one reason why the relationship element in helping is so important. It helps to shift the internal dynamic by introducing a new perspective. How to introduce it in a way that has meaning is perhaps the crucial issue and, I find, more difficult to pinpoint theoretically. It has echoes of Carl Rogers and his emphasis on a 'real' and 'congruent' relationship (1967). I hope I could emulate the work of Dr Fried (in reality Dr Frieda Fromm-Reichman) in the novel *I Never Promised You a Rose Garden* (1964) by Hanna Green (pseudonym for Joanne Greenberg, see Rubin, 1972).

For me, the theoretical underpinning of understanding the complex inner world of the individual in constant interplay with real relationships is vital. Nevertheless, those real relationships, to be therapeutic, must be ordinary (however extraordinary the circumstances), everyday and naturally person-to-person. I leave the last word with Eddie, who ends by saying:

> To sum up, I feel that the sessions have given me a new base from which to become operational again. I feel more whole and less alone and look forward to the future. I feel that I have done nothing else than ask for help from my fellow man and to avoid the emotional wasteland of aloneness and isolation.

7 Fred:

coping with long-term mental illness

CASE HISTORY

Fred, aged fifty-five, has been married for eight years to Mary who is aged fifty-two. He has been an in-patient of the local psychiatric unit for six months. Although he goes home most days, his psychiatric condition prevents him from staying there overnight. Mary is upset by this.

The consultant in charge of Fred's treatment operates a policy of involving relatives as closely as possible in the assessment and treatment of a patient. This is done by arranging for a member of the clinical team to act as the 'family worker' for a particular patient. The work of the family worker is to identify the key relative, to see them regularly and to create a link between the relative and the clinical team. The task of this role is to communicate clearly to the relative the team's understanding of the nature of the problem and/or illness, the treatment suggested, the length of treatment and the expected outcome. It provides an opportunity for the relatives to talk about the difficulties they have encountered and for advice to be given on possible ways of overcoming them. This close involvement is seen as crucial in reducing the length of hospitalisation and the successful resettlement back home. The team social worker had been asked to undertake this role for Fred.

Fred was admitted to the psychiatric unit six months ago because he was so terrified of being attacked by a group of people who were friends of a woman who had been his girlfriend fifteen years ago. He had been staying up all night, prowling about the house to make sure that the group could not make entry. This conspiracy to attack him had, he claims, started just after he had finished with his girlfriend. He did so because she had been unfaithful to him. She had retaliated by saying that he would live to regret his actions. A few weeks later in the street, a man, who was friendly with this woman, had said to him that 'they would get him'. The conspiracy has continued ever since. At times he did not feel too bothered by it, but at the time of the admission, the only place where he felt safe was in the psychiatric unit and during the first weeks of his stay in hospital he would not even leave the ward to attend occupational therapy.

His evidence for believing that the conspiracy continued was that when was out of the house there were groups of men, usually in cars, tailing him. On two occasions, a group of young men had got on to the bus on which he was travelling and, because of the way that they had looked at him, he was convinced that they would have attacked him had he been the only passenger. At home he was convinced that cars passing the house contained members of the group keeping watch on him. Also, he was sure that the fact that one set of neighbours often left their lights on during the day and that another kept her curtains drawn were all evidence that they were involved in the conspiracy as well. He admits that nobody has actually attacked him, but is sure that this is part of the plan to increase his anxiety.

A diagnosis of paranoid schizophrenia was made, but Fred resisted any suggestion that he was mentally ill, maintaining all the time that he was only in hospital because of extreme terror caused by the conspiracy.

Fred has had three previous psychiatric hospital admissions and on each occasion the clinical picture has been the same. The first admission occurred about two years after the relationship with the key woman had ended. For a year before he had been unemployed, because he had been convinced that the group would do something in the shop where he worked to embarrass him. With his first two admissions, the intensity of his symptoms had been controlled by neuroleptic medication, and he had been discharged after six and eight weeks respectively. On the second occasion he was offered (and he accepted) a place in the day unit as a means of helping him to prepare for full-time work again. Although various jobs were found for him by the Disablement Resettlement Officer, he could not be persuaded to accept any of them as he felt all of them would open up, in some way, opportunities for the conspiracy to act against him. At that time his mother, who was disabled by a chronic chest condition, needed a good deal of help. He spent most of his time helping her and continued to do so until her death.

Between admissions, he has been seen regularly for depot injections and psychiatric review. The relapse that led to his third admission two years ago he attributed to being left in the house on his own for the first time in his life while Mary was away on holiday with her sister. He was an in-patient for six months and it required considerable effort from the clinical team before he would consider making a plan for his discharge. He insisted that he could not return home. With the help of the psychiatric social worker, alternative accommodation was arranged with one of Mary's sisters, but Fred went back to live with Mary as soon as he was discharged. The last relapse appears to have coincided with a rather sharp reduction in the anti-depressant medication that he has been taking.

Fred's father died twenty years ago, aged fifty-five, from a heart attack. His mother also died eight years ago, aged sixty-seven, as mentioned above, from the effects of a chronic chest condition. He has one sister, Ann, aged sixty-one, who is married and childless. She and her husband live nearby on a council estate and Fred visits her regularly. Unfortunately Mary does not get on well with Ann, whom she feels is too argumentative and is always trying to persuade Fred not to take his medication. At times when Fred has been too scared to stay at home overnight, Ann has put him up, but as she has only a small home, he has to sleep on the settee. About thirty years ago Ann was admitted to a mental hospital for six months, but there is no further information about this.

Fred describes his early life as happy. He left school aged fifteen, trained to be a butcher and worked in a small shop. For fourteen years he has been unemployed. As a young man, Fred had many girlfriends. When he was twenty years old, he married but the marriage lasted for only three years. There were no children and his wife left him for another man. Following this, he had several relationships. The last one finished acrimoniously and is the focus of his delusional system. Before his first admission, he was described as cheerful, sociable and interested in sport. Mary says that when he is well, her family like him a lot and that he is a pleasant, cheerful and helpful person.

Fred and Mary met at a club, courted for three years and married five months before his mother died. Mary had been married before but had been very unhappy as her husband had been a heavy drinker and had physically abused her. Eventually, he left her to live with another woman. Following this, Mary suffered with depression and was an in-patient for two months where her treatment included a course of electro-convulsive therapy (ECT). She believes that her recovery was due to the fact that one day she realised that it depended on her own efforts and from then onwards she has not looked back. This influences how she views Fred's illness and makes it difficult for her to express any sympathy for him.

Until three years ago, Mary had worked in the canteen of a local factory but had to leave because of increasing pain due to her arthritic condition. She has two children, John, aged thirty, and Susan, aged twenty-eight. Both are married and there are five grandchildren. Whilst Mary was at work, Fred did most of the housework and at times looked after his step-grandchild, Steven. At present, Mary helps to look after Susan's daughter Ella during the day while Susan is at work. Ella also stays several nights a week with Mary to give Susan a good rest, but Mary also says that she provides the company that Fred should be giving her.

Mary is the youngest of six in a close family. They all keep in regular contact with each other. When Fred and Mary have stayed with them for weekends, he has found that he has been free of his fears.

At the initial visit by the psychiatric social worker, Mary continually emphasised that Fred needed to try harder and that only when he realised that he could help himself would he begin to improve. It seemed that Mary was being very critical of Fred and that this might be alleviated if Mary could appreciate that Fred was suffering from a different illness from her own. Mary was very upset over Fred's unwillingness to sleep in their house and his insistence that he was not ill. She always argued with him when he said something strange in the hope that she could shake him out of his beliefs, particularly those about the neighbours whom she found to be friendly and helpful. On the other hand, she found his arguments and constant insistence that he was right so very persuasive that she had almost come to share some of his beliefs. He was also trying to persuade her to move house as a means of escaping the conspiracy. She told the social worker that having someone from the hospital to explain the situation to her had been useful and said, 'it helped me to keep my sanity'.

The psychiatric social worker (PSW) discussed with Mary ways in which the couple's contact could be reduced and advised her that it would be better for her not to try and argue with Fred about his beliefs. If he insisted on talking to her about them, she should leave the room and that it might be necessary for her to leave the house as a means of reducing the arguments. From talking to both Fred and Mary, it was clear that each wanted the marrriage to continue, although on occasions, when Mary had been very upset she had told Fred that she would be initiating divorce proceedings.

At the following ward round, Fred asked his consultant whether it would be a good idea for them to move as a means of escaping the persecution for at least a few years. He was advised against such a move unless there were other compelling reasons. It was suggested to him that having a dog might be a way of making sure that no one could attack him whilst he was asleep. He had previously had a dog, but it had died soon after his third admission.

When the psychiatric social worker next visited Mary, he reported this to her and also told her about the changes in medication that had been recommended. He spoke with her again about the need to learn how to prevent an argument with Fred over his beliefs. Mary very much appreciated the opportunity to talk freely and brought out her distress over Fred's continual refusal to try a night at home.

During the following week Fred asked to see the PSW at hospital. On the previous weekend Mary had become so upset by his continual need to talk about his symptoms and his insistence that they must move house that she again mentioned divorce. He was very upset about this and asked the social worker to visit her again as she had found the social worker's previous visits so helpful.

A further home visit was arranged at a time when Fred would be there. The aim of seeing the couple together was to discuss with them both the strategies which had been suggested to them individually for the sake of improving their relationship. It was hoped that by talking with them together about the need for each of them to change their behaviour, there would be a greater chance that they would accept these suggestions. Mary used the visit to rehearse most of her complaints about Fred in a very critical manner and he listed all the evidence for his beliefs. It was apparent that he was so wrapped up in his beliefs that he could not recognise or respond to Mary's distress about being left on her own. Her barrage of criticism did not encourage Fred to show much sympathy. The caseworker again suggested to Fred that he should stop talking to Mary about the conspiracy. Instead, he should talk with members of the clinical team about this and that Mary should not argue with him if he did say something strange.

The next visit was arranged to see them both two weeks later. Between these visits, their relationship was easier for a few days, but then rapidly deteriorated.

When the PSW saw them again, the couple more or less repeated what they had said the time before. Fred and Mary were each trying to get support for their own views of the situation without listening to the other, or to the suggestions made by the worker. Joint work was abandoned and it was mutually agreed that Fred and Mary would be seen on their own in future.

During the next two months, three home visits were made to see Mary and there was further contact through phone conversations. This gave Mary an opportunity to voice her distress and for the PSW to try and help her to see that it was the illness that was pressing Fred to behave in such an apparently uncaring manner. Although seemingly agreeing with the worker's explanation in one discussion, Mary tended to start the next discussion with a further barrage of criticism about Fred's behaviour which seemed to show that she could not modify her ideas about the situation. Her ideas about mental illness were as fixed as Fred's delusional system. However, during this period she arranged that she would undertake voluntary work for her church as a means of developing further interests for herself and reducing the occasions when Fred could talk to her about his symptoms. Fred, rather unwillingly, got used to coming home from the hospital and finding Mary out.

This reduction in face-to-face contact between Fred and Mary was not sufficient to prevent one or two bad arguments between them, and after one of these Mary insisted on Fred leaving home and adamantly told him that she did not want him back. At the subsequent visit, the PSW listened to Mary's list of criticisms about Fred but also again tried to help her to see how his illness was affecting his behaviour. Mary told the PSW that at church the previous evening the preacher had urged the congregation to always be willing to forgive. Consequently, she would not go ahead with her plan to obtain a divorce and she concluded that, in honesty, she could not contemplate a life without Fred. To manage the future she would need to reduce the intensity of their relationship, but found this a difficult concept with which to come to terms. It seemed to her as if it was like 'losing your man to another woman'. Mary asked the PSW to tell Fred of her change of mind but before he could get back to the hospital Mary had phoned the hospital and had spoken to Fred.

At the PSW's next home visit Mary was still very critical of Fred. She felt that he had been in hospital for too long. She made the suggestion that he should spend more time at home so that he could redecorate some of their rooms. This was despite reporting that she felt that there had been no improvement in Fred's condition following a further alteration in his medication. On the ward it was observed that he was much more thoughtful towards other people and not hostile to the nursing staff. The following weekend Fred had his first weekend leave out of the unit with both of them staying with one of Mary's sisters. This was a modification on Mary's part and was in line with a suggestion made by the worker. Previously Mary had been insisting that his first weekend leave must be spent in their home.

The slow process of helping Fred to leave hospital has begun. The PSW plans to continue to be in contact with Mary in the expectation that she and Fred will live together once he is discharged, and that, with further assistance, Mary could modify some of her criticisms of Fred. This, no doubt, will lead to a more stable resettlement. It is very likely that the intensity of Fred's symptoms will flare up again and that Mary will need further assistance to help her to maintain their relationship which appears to mean so much to her.

COMMENT

Mental Health Aspects

This case presents a rather good example of several aspects of chronic paranoid schizophrenia. The key feature of the condition is, of course, the person's delusional ideas. These delusions are mistaken, irrational beliefs which are held, nevertheless, with an unshakeable conviction (e.g. the feeling that his ex-girlfriend was pursuing him). As part of a picture of paranoid schizophrenia, they most frequently appear in mid-life, in individuals who have functioned adequately previously. The ideas may be very specific and systematically focused on one area of life (he did not feel that his wife was out to harm him) with much of the individual's personality remaining very much intact. Their effects, however, can be far-reaching and, as in this case, affect home, social life and career. Chronic mental illness is a very disabling condition. Delusions may be of many forms (e.g. erotic, guilt, hypochondriacal, nihilistic, grandeur, unworthiness), but most commonly associated with conditions such as Fred's are delusions of persecution.

Also, this case demonstrates that with chronic mental illness, the symptoms never completely disappear, even with constant medication. However, the patient's willingness to comply with treatment is generally seen as a positive sign of his/her ability to live outside hospital, if for no other reason than it suggests that the patient's distrust of people is not universal and does not necessarily include those who wish to help him/her.

CASEWORK ASPECTS

Fred's case throws up several points of interest for the caseworker called upon to deal with such chronic disorders.

Social adaptations are often made that are not conducive to full rehabilitation. In this case, Fred's mother had been very happy to have him at home although this meant that he did not go to the day hospital or look for work when he was well enough to do so. Similarly, Mary was happy to have him at home while she was at work (see Stevens, 1972).

Patients living with relatives who are over-involved and highly critical of them have a fifty per cent chance of a further psychiatric relapse even if they are taking their medication (Leff *et al.*, 1982). This can be considerably improved if their face-to-face contact with each other is reduced to less than thirty-five hours per week (Falloon *et al.*, 1985; Leff *et al.*, 1985). It should be noted that Fred remained well during his marriage while Mary was at work. Following her retirement he has had two relapses.

The allocation of a 'family worker' to a patient can reduce the distress and difficulties experienced by relatives as well (Anderson, 1977). Mary's statements about the relief given by having the opportunity to discuss the situation with the PSW supports this practice. They also reiterate the need for professionals working directly with relatives to have established psychotherapeutic skills.

Though it should hardly need stating, it is still worthwhile pointing out that casework help to relatives can be useful in preventing the breakdown of relationships which have been strained by the effect of chronic mental illness. Also, the notion, now quite popular, that as such marital conflicts involve both partners interacting with each other, the treatment must do so as well, is clearly erroneous. In this instance, family-oriented treatment failed and the worker was forced to revert to dealing with each partner individually. This is a situation which may well occur frequently in practice and one with which we will be well prepared to deal providing that we have sound casework skills.

Relatives' understanding of the patient's illness is greatly influenced by their own personal experiences and beliefs. Simple explanations about the patient's medical condition will not be very effective if the relative's belief system has different basic assumptions (Tarrier and Barrowclough, 1978). Mary's belief that her own recovery was due to her own efforts led her to believe that all recovery flowed from trying hard. This, wrongly, led her to maintain that there a strong wilful element to Fred's inability to stay with her at night.

8 John:

mania

CASE HISTORY

John is fifty, divorced and lives alone. He is unemployed, owns his house and has a small income from his mother's legacy. He has a history of several admissions to hospital, mostly for manic episodes of illness, but also for depression, and on one occasion he was diagnosed as suffering from schizophrenia.

What follows is a description of one of his latest episodes of illness. John has been referred to the local Social Services by the consultant psychiatrist and has been allocated to me. I have been visiting John for nearly two years, during which time he has had two admissions to hospital. I am a senior practitioner based in a specialist team. Our department has undergone reorganisation which has involved the creation of neighbourhood offices, where a mixture of services is offered, including an initial referral system. One of the social workers in this system has been seeing John, who has started to drop in to the office uninvited (as have several of John's neighbours, who have come in to complain that John is up at all hours of the night making an amazing din.) At first this worker thought that John was perfectly well; and John explained that he had a business going at home which required the use of machinery at night on the off-peak electricity. He seemed quite rational, spoke quickly but made good sense, and the worker was quite impressed by his initiative. The neighbours protested that he was becoming ill and that this had happened before, but the worker, having interviewed John, could not find any sign of mental illness and decided he could to do nothing further.

John became a more frequent visitor to the office. He told the worker that his business was going very well but that he needed to have more money. He said that he was going to sell his house and asked if the worker wanted to buy it. More neighbours came in to protest to the housing manager about the noise in the middle of the night. He told the worker that he was nearly ready to launch his new product on the world and that when he did it was going to change everybody's lives. The worker contacted our team and made us aware that this was happening.

When I visited the house it was clear that pandemonium had been happening. The police had been called because John had caused an incident with a young woman in the next road. The girl's father had seen his unwelcome approach and turned a garden hose on him. He was in the front room, surrounded by police and neighbours, and wearing only a bath towel which kept falling to the floor and which was put back by one of the policemen. He was telling us that he was about to save the world with his new invention and referred us to the diagrams on the wall (on the wall, not pinned to the wall) which appeared to be an incomprehensible jumble of figures, quotations, and random scribbling. Several large boxes were scattered on the floor, some unopened, and there was obviously a large amount of computer equipment on the tables, chairs and in the hallway.

John had been buying computer equipment to help him with his grand plan, but he had not yet been able to use any of it. He had put his house up for sale and had ordered a yacht. John refused to get dressed at first and began berating the assembled company for stopping him from getting on with his work. He was walking around the room waving at the diagrams on the walls. He agreed to get dressed and went upstairs with one of the policemen. We heard a thump and then saw John running out of the back of the house and quickly out of sight.

He had not eaten and there was no food in the house at all. He did not usually drink and we did not know when he last had food or water. The woman and her father did not want him charged with an offence and so we decided for his own health and safety we would try to admit him to hospital.

First we had to find him. When we did eventually find him we pieced together his movements—he had been into the medical wards of the district hospital and had begun to preach to the patients; he evaded the nursing staff and made off to a fast food restaurant, where he ordered three meals, played in the children's play area and then indecently assaulted a waitress. He eventually turned up at his brother's home and his brother and sister-in-law were able to put him into the car and bring him to the psychiatric unit.

His brother took charge of his affairs and was able to send back the unused computer equipment, take his house off the market, redecorate the front room and cancel the yacht.

After a month in hospital, where he was treated with a neuroleptic drug, his excitement abated somewhat, but then he absconded. After another episode of treatment in hospital, he was re-referred to me and I began to visit him regularly, and he came to visit me in the office. He became more withdrawn but was stabilised on his medication. Some months later he told me that he thought he should get out more and that he was going to enrol for evening classes. My anxieties were aroused and we discussed the wisdom of taking on too much. He agreed not to enrol for all of the classes and decided to begin with Fine Art first. I was able to visit him often enough to be able to tell whether he was eating and whether he was looking after the house adequately. He talked a lot about his illness and about being lonely. The neighbours said how pleasant he was when he was well, and how sorry they were that he sometimes 'went off'. We shared a lot of what might be called ordinary conversation, not directed at his problems and his illness, but at his preferences and his 'wants'. This visiting reminded me very much of the sorts of visits I made to parents of mentally handicapped children. They did not 'want' a lot, but they did want to know that when they next had a problem they would know where to go for help. The difference between them and John was, I suppose, that John wasn't always sure when he needed help.

I continued to visit John; he no longer called in to the neighbourhood office. He attended the Art class for several months but became disenchanted and began to withdraw from social contact. I visited once every three to four weeks; if I arranged to see him in the office he failed to turn up. I discussed the possibility of John attending a day centre. I thought that if someone could get to know him that they could monitor his mental health and make arrangements for him to receive appropriate help. John was reluctant to attend—he did not want the bother of a regular routine, nor did he want to mix with people who had severe mental illnesses. He agreed to visit the day centre with me and decided that it was not as bad as he thought and that he would give it a try.

The day centre was two bus rides from his home. I took him at first and then he went alone. The day centre organiser was an experienced woman worker who was well liked by the centre staff and clients, and John got on with her very well. This arrangement had been working well for three months or so when she left to go on a training course. Soon after this John stopped going to the centre and the staff did not get in touch with me until three weeks later. I visited at once. John appeared at the door in his dressing gown. He ushered me in and almost in same breath asked after my health, told me he was very well, said he was sorry he hadn't seen me for a few days, offered me some tea, asked me to sit down and thrust a large pile of A4 sheets of paper onto my lap. He said he had never felt better and that all his problems were over, he never wanted any more treatment and he would never be ill again. (He could obviously see what I was thinking.) I told him I thought he was beginning to become unwell again and that he should perhaps go to see his doctor; I offered to ring the hospital and arrange an out-patient appointment. To my surprise he accepted this offer and I was able to take him to see the duty psychiatrist the same afternoon.

He reluctantly accepted some tablets and said he would go back to the day centre. The staff there agreed to monitor his medication. This arrangement broke down after a few weeks when John had another major episode of mania. This time he was compulsorily admitted to hospital and lithium treatment was started. This has stabilised his episodes of illness; he receives lithium tablets and attends a local clinic for monitoring of his blood lithium levels, and he has started to attend the day centre again.

COMMENT

Mental Health Aspects

John exhibits the main features of mania; the central features are elevation of mood, increased activity and grandiose ideas. He also displays irritability and disinhibition. His speech is rapid and he reports his thoughts are speeded up. When this is at its worst, his thoughts come faster than they can be spoken. He is convinced that his scheme for solving the world's problems is a divine mission, and this belief is held with conviction in the same way that a delusion is held. He has a decreased need for sleep and is very easily distracted.

There is an increased risk of depression during mania. Mania occurs in cycles and in some people these cycles are fairly regular. The natural history of bipolar illness (which has both manic and depressive episodes) is for the patient to have episodes of increasing frequency and duration over the course of his lifetime.

Casework Aspects

One of the main problems for the social worker approach is that in the early stages mania is very difficult to detect. What appears to be an elevated mood may not seem abnormal. It is understandable in such circumstances that social workers want to give the client the benefit of the doubt, but, as in this case, the dangers of doing so may be fatal. There is no substitute for a sound assessment of the case and for an intimate knowledge of the client and family. Some clients develop an understanding of the subtle signs of the first stages of a manic episode and can be the first ones to alert the worker to the forthcoming problems. These clients have a degree of insight and want to avoid a full-blown episode. In a minority of cases the client actually rather 'enjoys' the elation, especially if it replaces a depressed mood. This might have something to do with John's refusal to accept treatment.

Protecting the client and their rights and interests is of central importance in working with manic clients. The use of the authority of the Court of Protection arises in such cases. Here the worker is once again treading the narrow path between being over-protective and under-protective. There is little doubt that in the most serious cases it may be the only alternative. In the present case this was not necessary because John's brother was able to take care of his affairs. In some cases, however, there is doubt about the relatives' ability or trustworthiness, and it is necessary to consider alternative solutions. The Court of Protection may appoint a receiver to administer the patient's affairs and this authority lasts until revoked by the court. Manic clients are quite likely to enter into business arrangements beyond their means while they have grandiose ideas, and when the client is plausible and convincing and does not yet display any of the more profound disturbance of the height of the episode they are hard to restrain or resist. They have boundless energy to expend on their affairs and it is hard to keep up with them. One has to exercise great care not to be caught up in the more plausible aspects of their schemes and one certainly should take seriously the concerns of relatives. It is often helpful to work with another worker or a team in order to retain one's sense of perspective, and to share the burden of the work; this is more easily achieved in a structured environment rather than in the community.

The case also demonstrates the value of knowing the client and family well. Staying involved in some way with people with long-term problems is almost always justified by the ability it gives one to be able to know the signs of illness, to be trusted enough to provide help at an early stage, and to be involved in maintaining the client in the community, rather than trying to produce 'improvement' or closing the case because nothing much seems to be happening. Martin Davies (1981) has written of the role of social work that 'maintenance is the truth. And maintenance the goal.' The knowledge that someone is there when needed is profoundly important for most people. Weiss (1974) has called this relationship provision a sense of 'reliable alliance'. In John's case it was provided by the social worker and then by the day centre.

9 Karen:

the treatment of a case of phobic anxiety

CASE HISTORY

Karen (twenty-eight) was referred to the author, a mental health social worker, by her general practitioner due to neurotic symptoms such as a morbid preoccupation with being involved in a car accident, closely associated with fears of travel (particularly to work) and with losing her temper both at work and with her family at home. Both of these symptoms, as well as other morbid fears, had begun to display themselves recently and to a disabling degree. A previously healthy mother of boys aged six and three, she worked full-time in an electronics factory. Her husband Don (twenty-nine) was a skilled worker on permanent night shift.

She was seen throughout by the author at the community hospital near her home. Both Don and the boys came with her to the first interview, largely because of the difficulties in getting a baby sitter, but also due to Karen's need to be escorted out of the house. When Don was seen towards the end of the first session, he was obviously enthusiastic to be involved. This fitted in well with the author's preference for maintaining close links and working with the client's natural living group, particularly spouses. This is particularly true of such cases where the client's symptomatology so markedly affects, and is affected by, other members of the family. Karen was seen for eight sessions at two- or three-weekly intervals and Don, a relaxed and open man, was present for several of these. Sessions were audiotaped, a practice the author employs to enable supervision or self-supervision of his work and occasionally in order to let clients hear a session again. Karen and Don readily agreed to the taping after the purpose was explained to them.

Karen, an alert and attractive woman, began treatment by describing (at times with considerable feeling and difficulty) the emotional turmoil which she had experienced during the recent treatment of her child for non-compliance by a clinical psychologist. She had found herself becoming exasperated with the child's behaviour and had threatened him and his brother that she would harm herself if they did not behave. In doing this she was suddenly and painfully reminded of her own childhood and her own mother similarly threatening her, her brother and seven sisters. Furthermore, when she had threatened to leave home, her husband told her that he would be compelled to put the children into care if she did. At this, she was overwhelmed by anger, only later recalling that she herself had been in a home for a brief period as a child.

She then described how her father and, later, her eldest sister's husband had sexually abused several of her sisters, though not herself, and how her mother had been unreasonably strict with them, not allowing them to play out with other children. It transpired that she had previously dealt with the traumas of her childhood by denial, humour and frantic sporting activity (including playing squash and hockey at county level), but these mechanisms had temporarily broken down.

At the same time, she and her family had strengths; she was not keen either to take tablets or further time off work but wanted to work through the problems without being overcome by them. Nevertheless, she was fearful that she would not succeed since most of her siblings had received already, or were receiving currently, psychological help, in a few instances quite long-term.

Bearing the above factors in mind, the author made a number of decisions about the course of treatment at this point. The first was to offer a series of treatment sessions, since the client was a likely 'customer', seeking change, as was her husband, rather than having been 'sent' by an overwhelmed referrer.

The second was that it was safe to include the husband in the sessions, because Karen claimed not to have been one of those female children abused. Had this not been so, or if it had begun to emerge later that she had not told the truth initially, then the husband might well need to have been excluded in order to give Karen the confidential atmosphere where she could safely disclose her secrets and discuss them without fear of further consequences within her marriage. It was also true that her fears were more easily contained by her with her husband's physical presence, and at this point she was too fearful to make her way to the office unaided.

The third was to restrict initial participation to Karen and Don. Although the children were likely to be affected by the problems which brought Karen to treatment, she and her husband seemed to be able to draw a boundary between themselves and the children and to avoid triangulating the children either into their own individual problems or into conflicts between themselves.

The fourth was that, although Karen's symptoms were very much current, it seemed clear that issues from the past were influencing events in the present and it seemed important to bring some of these issues out into the open early on. This latter point seemed further justified in that the material as well as the association of present to past events was already emerging into the client's consciousness and she was attempting to explore it.

The fifth was to attempt to work 'briefly', which in the author's case, usually means over less than ten sessions. As well as according with the client's hopes (as it did here), this can serve to create an expectation of fairly rapid change as well a placing the major responsibility for change on the couple or other client system.

Karen and Don were seen again a week later, by which time she had returned to work for which she was congratulated. The bulk of this session was spent constructing a genogram of Karen's side of the family, stopping at points which seemed to be affectively important for her. Obviously, personal and distressing information regarding her past came to light and was examined. Hardly surprisingly, one point of interest in her relationship with Don was her concern about her own desire for him to be like a father to her, inasmuch as she was always yearning for non-sexual physical contact and demonstrations of affection. Another point of interest was the fact that she was made particularly angry when he was untidy, since she was fighting a family tendency to obsessionality which had been displayed already by several of her sisters. A major intervention in this session was to attempt to 'normalise' the feelings she had been having, suggesting that they were understandable given what she had been through and encouraging Don to help in this process. As a task between that session and the following one, they were asked to continue to fill in and talk about details on the genogram.

At the third session three weeks later, Karen was still at work but coping only with difficulty. She had lost her temper with a colleague who had said she had known the family as children and thought they were 'stuck up' because they wouldn't play with other children. She also reported feeling very anxious and fighting compulsions to clean the the house, etc. In addition, she had not brought the genogram drawn in the last session, but had left it behind her mending basket. Fortunately, the author had drawn a second copy whilst listening to the tape of the second session and that was used.

Although it would have been interesting to have had the time to explore the meaning of this oversight on Karen's part, at this point it seemed more important to focus on Don's family and his experiences, since a key question for the author was why it had become hard for him to help and support his wife as he had otherwise done throughout their marriage. Also, the author wished Don to take an active part in the definition and resolution of the problem rather than regard him as a spectator to Karen's treatment and, therefore, needed to address briefly the source of his resistance. The key points which emerged were that he too had, in a way, 'lost' his family (as Karen had tried to do), inasmuch as he had a large extended family in another part of the country, not seen since a move many years earlier. More importantly, he had been devastated recently upon receipt of the news of the death of his maternal grandfather, one of these abandoned relatives. Don broke down and wept at the memory of this, which not only helped him to resolve his feelings of grief but also seemed to bring the couple close and give Karen permission to display her own strong feelings. Also, it was possible to frame their behaviour positively as 'coping by concealment' rather than seeing this as resistance or avoidance, but simultaneously to suggest that they needed to understand better what they were concealing.

The subsequent session, a fortnight later, was an important point in the process of therapy. Karen reported experiencing a great deal of hurt and anger, as well as anxious situations at work, but she had been dealing with these emotions competently. Additionally, she was able to talk more openly about the abuse of her sisters, prompted by the fact that her father, divorced from their mother, had now reappeared and some of the children he had abused were proposing to look after him. This re-emergence of the father into the here and now had been distressing her for some time and it was therapeutic that it came to the surface and was able to be discussed openly.

This, in turn, brought to light a problematic relationship cycle between this couple: it transpired that before each session one of Karen's older sisters (herself a victim of sexual abuse) had called round, revealing more distressing information about the past. Don wanted his wife to stand back from her extended family rather than, as it were, recoiling from every new revelation like a blow struck by them due to her over-involvement. This had been her previous strategy for coping or not coping, as the case may be. However, much of what was taking place was a sworn secret between Karen and her sisters and this made it difficult for Don to comprehend the exact significance of events for her. The author wondered if his encouragement of her denial was in fact based on his own fear of not knowing how to cope with the strength of her surpressed emotion. Certainly rows would develop around these matters, Karen would 'explode', Don would refuse to continue and would withdraw, leaving Karen still fuming. The couple would then not speak for days on end. This represented a severe limitation on the client's ability to utilise her husband emotionally and was addressed.

Several indirect techniques were used to bring about change. The metaphor that it was 'as if you are carrying things around from the past' was used to point out to Karen that Don was really urging her to let go of a burden, but that she was unable to do so whilst she had yet to acknowledge or disclose what it contained. Following on from this, a concerted attempt was made to split the past from the present, and to point out that one could learn one behaviour in one context and a new behaviour, to replace it, in another. Here, a presupposition of a future without the problem was used to encourage Karen to move her focus to changes that were happening as well as paying attention to more distant goals. Of course, it served the more immediate purpose of helping Karen to distinguish her husband from her father and to enable her to act accordingly. In addition, a direct technique of 'pattern intervention' was offered to the couple: when Karen reached the point where she was about to lose her temper, she was told to go and get a mouthful of water and to hold it for five minutes before she carried on. Also, she was asked to let Don know (with her sisters' permission) some of the secrets.

At the fifth session, three weeks later, the feedback was mixed. It appeared that the couple had got on well and had shared some secrets about the past. The family taboo still worked to prevent this but Karen had made a deliberate effort in this direction. She had confronted her sisters as to how all of these disclosures to her was affecting both her and her marriage, demanded and gained some co-operation. Karen had not needed to use the 'water-in-mouth' technique with her husband, but had tried it once when she became angry with the children. At this time, a number of issues about her difficulties at work arose, including her 'over-sensitivity' when work mates were talking casually, or her feeling of being crowded by circumstances. These seemed to the worker to be inviting a more confidential atmosphere and the following session was scheduled for Karen alone.

During the sixth session, Karen again raised the problem of her tension, and following an exploration of these feelings several suggestions were offered to help her to deal with with these feelings. She was taught how to recognise when her emotions were mounting up and she was in danger of losing control, and how to respond by relaxing. Also, she incorporated some of Don's suggestions about 'standing back' from her thoughts as tactics for avoiding being drawn into a long, obsessional, internal dialogue, full of self-doubt. Karen had a strong capacity to visualise and a fine sense of humour, and these were employed to help her to divert mounting anger by a comic visualisation of her 'angry self'.

The author suggested that the situation at work would probably be more under Karen's control, but that she might be less successful at home. It is wise, in such situations, to prepare such clients for the possibility of a relapse. Again, this was framed as being 'understandable in the circumstances', giving Karen permission for her feelings and preventing an inevitable setback being seen as a complete failure and 'return to square one'. Progress is never 'onward and upward' but rather is more likely to be 'two steps forward and one backward', and clients can be helped to adjust their expectations to this.

Karen next attended alone what should have been a joint session. It transpired that there had been an argument three days before in which she and Don had exchanged some 'home truths'. Apparently it was still too recent for him and he had chosen not to come. We discussed her successes and failures over the intervening three weeks. As predicted, it seemed that she had managed well at work. At home, when she and Don had argued, she had managed to stay calmer than usual and Don had withdrawn before she actually lost control.

In the eighth and final session, both Karen and her husband attended. We reviewed the progress that she had made on the presenting problems. Both she and Don agreed that they had continued to have confrontations but were beginning to resolve these by talking, as they never had before. When asked to grade the improvement on a scale of 0-10, Don replied it was only 2 in terms of noise but 9 in terms of trauma. The impact of the disclosure of 'family secrets' was beginning to dissipate and with it some of the symptomatology which was apparently associated with them. Karen reported continuing changes at work, being more able to tolerate workmates. She was no longer threatened when people came to sit next to her in the work canteen and was beginning to be able to take the initiative to sit next to some of them. She was upset by contact with her extended family but was learning to behave calmly with them, managing the things which they told her. She had attended some of the sessions on her own and was overcoming her fear of travel generally. This was shown in an increasing readiness to assume some of the responsibility for her own transport to work, though she still did not travel there alone.

After some discussion, it was mutually agreed to terminate treatment at this point, since the presenting problems had shown considerable improvement and the couple were ready to continue working on their own. The author did point out that as their younger child went to school in the next few months, they were at a stage of transition as a family. They had many developments to face and Karen still had many problems which were, as yet, incompletely resolved. While there was every chance that they would now be able to manage without help, it would be strong and purposeful action to ask for more if it was needed.

The case was reviewed three months later. Karen had returned to playing hockey and had progressed to regional level. A month later, the family had requested a single session when Karen's mother had died suddenly and tragically in an accident. In addition, at their request, they returned for a further session at a period of nine months following the termination of treatment for continued work on their relationship.

COMMENT

Mental Health Aspects

Phobic anxiety can be defined as 'a form of anxiety, i.e. fear or apprehension, where the phobia acts as a defence, often an inadequate one, to protect the patient from situations or circumstances which may predispose to or initiate anxiety attacks. The patient recognises his fear is an irrational one, but is unable to overcome it and is usually unaware of its unconscious origin, though it is doubtful whether even if he were aware of it, the fear would necessarily be removed' (Sim, 1981, p. 285). This seems a particularly apt description of Karen's condition. In her case, the phobia was more diffuse than monophobic (i.e. related to any one specific class of stressor such as a cat, dog or spider), because she exhibited several, somewhat generalised fears. Such conditions appear relatively commonly in clinical work and, as here, are frequently associated with other neurotic symptoms, such as obsessional thoughts, themselves psychological defences being used to ward off unpleasant anxiety. While it is tempting to make psychoanalytic interpretations as to the symbolic association of the aetiology of Karen's fears with her psychosexual constitution, this case focuses more on the realities of casework treatment, in this instance, a short-term, eclectic approach being employed.

Casework Aspects

Overall, the treatment of this case can be seen as brief-focused problem resolution. The author feels such an approach has a compelling and coherent rationale applicable to the reality of late 1980s statutory agency practice. Thus, the goals are the client's and are, if possible, finite and identifiable, if not measurable. Goal attainment by any ethical and therapeutically defensible means, no matter how apparently absurd, is seen as being of far greater importance than the client's understanding of why the problem is what it is. The therapist is responsible for bringing about improvement, although he/she should attempt to utilise everything that the client and his/her environment have to offer to that end. A part of the implications of the latter point can be summed up in the maxim 'if it works, don't fix it'. De Shazer (1985) offers an elegant elaboration of the theory and experimental evidence generally underlying this approach.

With Karen, a particularly flexible and eclectic variety of this approach was used. The problem was assessed and formulated as being a transgenerational consequence of being part of a family where there had been child abuse. This understanding had been clearly shared with the client: the careful and patient use of the genogram in sessions two and three for this purpose also served to get the couple working together. It widened the context of the symptoms of anxiety, giving them a meaning which may have been more helpful than 'mental illness'. Also, the author values the understanding in Skynner et al. (1983) of how couples are attracted by what they are mutually unable to deal with, and generally looks for these features in the non-symptomatic (or rather non-diagnosed) spouse when working with referred patients. One could argue that ventilation of feelings was an important technique in this therapy. While this is probably so, the author feels it is as, or more, important how this effect is directively managed. By enabling individuals who have been traumatised to hand back the responsibility for their distress to caretakers and other adults, they are able to decrease the effects of strong feelings which have arisen, even where they have been surpressed for a substantial number of years. Specific techniques can be seen as having either intra- or inter-personal focus. Thus, the use of visualisation or humour with Karen to deal with her obsessional internal conversation was different from the pattern of intervention to disrupt the repetitive sequence of behaviour around fighting between Don and Karen. It would have been equally possible to get Don to do something different.

A further point of note in this case is the importance of the relationship with these clients, particularly rapport. More apparent in the audiotapes than in this summary is the extent to which the author matched and paced the client's verbal and paralinguistic behaviour. In reality a similar matching went on in respect of non-verbal behaviour which went unrecorded. Several of the techniques used, such as visualisation, humour and reframing are 'hypnotic-like' (Calof, 1985) and involve the creation of an atmosphere within a therapeutic relationship where influence towards, and suggestion and expectation of, positive behaviour change are effective.

Finally, the author believes it may often be important to get in and out of situations with clients as quickly as possible without getting in the client's way. It is seen as an advance that the couple have sought help with their relationship subsequently though the decision was theirs. This readiness to let clients go involves risk and can, at first, be unsatisfying. What it does do, however, is to serve to emphasise their contribution to, and responsibility for, effective casework.

10 Lydia:
crisis work with a client with long-term problems

CASE HISTORY

Lydia was a tall, fair, twenty-seven-year-old woman who was unmarried. She was referred to a Social Services Crisis Intervention Team (CIT) by a duty doctor at the local psychiatric out-patients unit at around midday on a Friday. He requested an immediate response in order to avoid a psychiatric admission, because he felt the risk of suicide by her to be great. In his request, the doctor explained that Lydia had been referred to him only that day by a clinical psychologist who had been treating her obsessional ritual cleaning behaviour. The psychologist had been using relaxation exercises and behavioural techniques to tackle her compulsion to clean the house constantly. This she did whenever she was at home alone.

Lydia had been sent to the psychiatric unit because upon arrival for her session with the psychologist, she was experiencing severe anxiety, and felt that she could not cope. She said she did not know why she should be feeling like this, but also subsequently had told the duty doctor that she was going to transfer jobs from where she was currently working to a town seventy miles away in order to live near or with her mother.

Whilst the CIT initially felt that the ritual behaviour was unlikely to be compatible with a crisis approach, it was agreed to look into the situation further since it sounded as though there were other aspects which had come to the fore.

The same afternoon, I and another social worker from the CIT went to the psychiatric unit in order to make a formal assessment of the case. We had a variety of resources as options to consider. The team operates on a seven day a week basis with up to four staff on duty during the day, two in the early evening and one at night. Clients can be seen at home or, if appropriate, admitted into residence for a maximum of seven nights.

Lydia was very agitated and at first it seemed to us that a psychiatric admission would be the probable outcome. However, after talking to her for about an hour, it became apparent that her feelings did correspond to the problems she was facing and that the danger of suicide was not extreme. The situation therefore, seemed a feasible one for offering crisis intervention.

In the course of the interview it transpired that she was still living in a house which belonged to her ex-boyfriend, even though their relationship had broken up three years earlier. Her mother had felt that Lydia would not manage on her own and had encouraged her to come home and live with her. This was made possible by the fact that the company by which Lydia was employed as a work study officer was aware of the fact that she was receiving professional help for her psychological problems and was able to offer her a position near where her mother lived. She said that work was normally a stable part of her life, but that recently she had felt that there had been a considerable amount of strain between herself and her general manager. In fact, Lydia had agreed to change work-places in an interview with her own supervisor, only that morning.

Apparently, the previous week Lydia had visited her mother and had stayed there for several nights. She described to us how her mother had treated her as a child. When at home, she hated being there and hated her mother, but when she was not visiting her mother she felt as though she should be and felt very guilty. She said that when driving back home from the visit she had been nearly overcome by feelings which 'seemed to get out of control'. Then she had nearly killed herself by crashing the car. When asked her if she often felt angry about things, she said that she felt she had bottled up her feelings for years!

Lydia then told us that her father had died eight years before and that he had been terminally ill for some time prior to his death, but that she had not been told of his illness. Thus the death had come as a sudden, horrible surprise to her, shocking her severely.

It seemed very clear that there were a large number of crises occurring in this young woman's life. We felt very uncertain about whether Lydia would, in practice, accept crisis counselling, because of the way in which she had ordinarily defended herself by channelling emotions into ritual behaviour. The situation seemed a living example of the old debate about whether behavioural techniques were the best way of tackling obsessions, or whether there were underlying personal issues which should be addressed. We decided to try and help, particularly as Lydia had not had treatment as an in-patient previously.

As it is frequently the practice of the CIT to work alongside other professionals, we offered her a contract with the following stipulations which would help to clarify our role for the client:
1. Lydia was to live in residence at the Crisis Centre for up to a week.
2. She was to receive intensive counselling and support.
3. She was to have help with the decision about whether or not to move home and live with her mother.
4. She was to be given the chance to explore the boundaries of her relationship with her mother and feelings about her father's death.

It was felt to be important to have an agreement with the psychologist that he would continue to treat the client's obsessions as such treatment seemed likely to outlast the CIT's normal maximum of twelve weeks' involvement. It was also agreed that if our approach did not work and Lydia was at risk, then a bed was to be made available at the psychiatric unit.

Late in the afternoon of the day of the referral, Lydia was admitted to the Crisis Centre. It was explained to her that the centre was staffed by a rota of experienced qualified social workers and that whilst she would have two keyworkers, the main aspects of the case would be passed on to whoever was on duty, so that she would not continually have to explain her situation to different workers. After showing her round and allowing her time to relax in the company of a volunteer, Lydia was given a further opportunity to talk about what she was feeling; at this stage great emphasis being put on acceptance of her feelings, answering any of her questions and addressing any concerns. In our experience it seems particularly important that a new resident can off-load their worries before going to bed on their first night away from home.

Despite advice to the contrary, Lydia was determined to continue working while a resident of the centre. She did not want time off sick for fear of what her colleagues would think and we were prepared to accept her feelings and comply with her wishes. Fortunately, there was at least the weekend during which she could give more time to attacking her problems rather than simply evenings, following a full day's work. Initially, counselling concentrated on her feelings about moving house; this was a useful focus around which it was necessary to talk about what had been happening in her adult life as well as to explore her feelings about her mother and father. The emphasis of crisis work is customarily on present decisions (Waldron, 1984).

It very quickly emerged that Lydia had an unresolved grief reaction over her father's death eight years previously. Her fondest memories were of spending time with him as a teenager. It was in the nature of such grief that this issue required numerous opportunities for lengthy ventilation of her feelings which, in practice, spread over the whole length of her stay in the Crisis Centre. She needed to be encouraged to cry a lot as well as talk about him. Lydia gradually came to be able to think about her father, accepting him as dead, whereas she had previously talked to him at night as if he were still alive.

Talking about her father enabled her to understand how angry she was with the way that her mother tried to control her. Not only had her mother hidden her father's terminal illness, but she had also been unable to discuss his death. This had led to difficulties in winding up her father's financial affairs. There was also a mystery about why her mother had a monthly injection; in fact there seemed to be a whole bagful of family secrets. As the sessions progressed, attention was turned to an examination of the way her mother engulfed her, made her feel guilty and generally inept. This required a number of sessions and we had several rehearsals of how to talk to her mother over the phone and spend time with her. During the ten weeks that Lydia was in counselling, she felt obliged to visit her mother twice, but did succeed in preventing her mother from interfering in her decisions about what to do. Dealing with her mother was the hardest issue to handle and on one occasion, later in the treatment, Lydia stayed overnight at the centre again because she was so overcome by her feelings following visits to her mother.

After five days in residence, Lydia decided not to move back home but to buy her own house locally instead. She came to this conclusion as a result of talking over what life with her mother would be like and realising that in moving home she, in fact, would be surrendering what independence she had achieved, leaving her with no life of her own. She was quite able to look for a house herself, but needed considerable support in handling the decisions that had to be made at each stage of the process. While, in itself, this was no different from the difficulties faced by anyone else, it was complicated because it involved exploring feelings about her mother. She also had to cope with the usual frustrations of house buying—her first house was lost due to 'gazumping'.

Throughout this period it was obvious that she was very socially isolated and this was an aspect of her life to which considerable attention was given during her period of contact with us. The CIT had two Community Service Volunteers who co-ordinated a programme of social activities to try and bridge the gap between coming to the centre and social life in the 'outside world'. Lydia attended some of the Social Committee meetings, which planned activities, and seemed to enjoy sporting activities which were arranged. Nevertheless, she continued to find it very difficult to make any trusting relationship with other people. This area was not resolved when she finished counselling sessions at CIT and was an important feature of the case which was eventually referred on to the psychologist for further help.

After ten weeks the major aspects of crisis counselling were completed. Lydia said that she felt much more in control, but was pleased she still had appointments with her psychologist, as she was still spending considerable periods of time compulsively cleaning. She insisted she could manage to find another house to buy on her own. She appeared to have overcome the most powerful feelings of grief in relation to her father, and to have created more of a boundary between herself and her mother. The immediate threat of self-destructive behaviour subsided without any attempts and the acute anxiety which she had felt on referral passed. It was emphasised, both to her and in a letter to her general practitioner, that she was welcome to return to the Crisis Centre should new problems occur in future.

COMMENT

Mental Health Aspects

When Lydia was referred to the Crisis Team, she was suffering from a number of psychiatric complaints of a neurotic type. Prior to her referral she had been treated for obsessive-compulsive disorder. An obsession, of course, is an unwanted thought or feeling upon which the individual continually ruminates. These were accompanied by compulsive behaviours which were ritualistic in nature and associated with cleaning. Her condition was, quite properly, being treated by behaviour therapy. However, she showed marked mood variation characterised by anxiety and depression to a degree serious enough to make suicide a possibility. Further investigations revealed that her anxiety and depression were reactive to various family stresses, personality traits and life events. As obsessions can also be symptoms of depression, an interesting point of differential diagnosis arises as the implications for management are considerable in cases such as these.

Sim (1981, pp.310-11) says that 'the distinction between a severe obsessional neurosis with depressive features and a depression with obsessional features can be a very fine one, yet it is not entirely academic. In the former, even though the depression may yield to anti-depressant measures, the obsessional symptoms may not be affected, while in the latter anti-depressant treatment may be enough to clear the whole symptomatology, the obsessional features being a secondary problem, linked to the major one and perhaps aggravated by it.'

In this case, Lydia was clearly an obsessional neurotic who became depressed. Her depression was treated by casework and she returned to her normal treatment for her still existing obsessional neurosis which had not cleared.

Casework Aspects

Crisis work carried out by social workers in mental health situations is most commonly practised with situational crises, and in cases with anxiety and depression. Often it is not thought to be appropriate for people with more long-standing problems. The case presented illustrates how crises methods can be of particular relevance in helping persons to overcome severe problems, even in the presence of long-term problems present, such as obsessions and compulsions.

Lydia's case is, of course, unique in its detail, as are any of our lives. Yet, in deciding how to help her and what resources were required, many important points arise which are illustrative of similar cases, and reflect findings about the nature of crisis intervention work, now familiar throughout the literature.

Facilities in the community

The 1983 *Mental Health Act* places on those social workers empowered to enact its provisions a duty to seek suitable alternatives to hospital. To be able to do this, there must be appropriate resources, available at times which meet people's needs. In Lydia's case, she would have been admitted to hospital if there was no overnight crisis accommodation available. Secondary facilities, such as a Crisis Centre, providing these alternatives are indispensable parts of a comprehenshive and effective system of community care.

One must never forget that in providing suitable alternatives to psychiatric hospitals, one still must take into account the client's need for such services as would otherwise be provided by them. A good example of this is the supervision given to persons at risk of self-harm. One of the reasons why community-based care could be considered at all here was the ability of the crisis service to monitor the client's behaviour in this respect with a properly devised and articulated plan as to what action to take should her condition deteriorate.

As important as the centre, however, were the skills and time of the professional staff. The availability of experienced community-based counsellors for Lydia when she was experiencing severe anxiety meant that she did not have to wait long periods of time for, or enter hospital to find such help. Additionally, the community-based professionals had a sound working relationship with other hospital-based professionals so that longer-term needs could be looked at from the onset. It was also useful to have social activities organised and facilitated from the Crisis Centre, to begin to counteract her isolation and intense loneliness.

Treatment for obsessional behaviour

The case history has a particular significance for discussions about whether to provide behavioural treatment for obsessional problems or whether to look at the 'underlying problems'. In Lydia's case it was decided to do both: crisis counselling was needed for tackling issues of unresolved grief and making clear, unconflicting decisions about her future. Obsessional thoughts and compulsive behaviour are often part of depressive pictures but, as can be seen here, the symptoms may not clear up with the underlying disorder. Here behavioural work needed to be continued because the problems persisted. It could well have been less help to Lydia to stick rigidly to one approach than to develop an integrated treatment plan.

The effectiveness of crisis intervention

All too often, people with entrenched symptoms, such as obsessions, find that this problem dominates the thinking of all those who offer treatment. It was clear, in Lydia's case, that there were several crises coming to a head in her life and it was worth seeing whether she could respond to the crises being tackled. The 'grief work' was very time-consuming but, nonetheless, proved a very rewarding area to tackle.

The intervention appears to have been successful. This in itself is useful, if modest, evidence in support of the contention that a crisis team consisting of social workers is particularly appropriate for dealing with cases of anxiety, grief and/or depression, when it is possible to make a contract with the client about treatment. As can be seen, the style of work used above incorporated many of the now recognised characteristics of a crisis intervention approach: active therapists; initial contracts; time-limited approach; early intervention with a service easily accessible to clients; teaching new coping skills useful beyond a resolution or abatement of the immediate situation; restoration of client to at least the ordinary level of functioning prior to the crisis.

Finally, experience at the Crisis Centre has suggested that clients who are accustomed to a psychiatric admission when problems loom large are often resistant to a crisis approach; but those who have never been admitted are usually anxious to try and avoid the stigma of a psychiatric admission. The apparent success of this case could be attributed to many factors, one of which may well be such additional sources of motivation as this.

11 Mr L.:

casework with a dementia sufferer

CASE HISTORY

Mr L. was eighty-one years old when he was referred by his general practitioner to one of the consultants in the dementia service run by the district health authority. He was a large man with a tendency to become breathless and a sweet expression when well. Mr L. came from a farming family and was the second of nine children. He left school early, during the First World War, to help out on the farm. In the 1930s he married and became a tenant farmer himself. The couple had three children, one of whom died as a child. The son became a farmer and brass band player like his father. The daughter married and left home but still lives locally; she is a grandmother herself now, making Mr L. a great-grandfather. Mr L. had always been keen on music, especially church music and brass bands. He used to play the euphonium. He was described as having been a 'jolly' person and very kind.

Mr L.'s wife developed kidney trouble, so he gave up farming, when he was aged about sixty. His wife died in 1965. Afterwards, he lived with his son and daughter-in-law for a short time until meeting a forty- year-old spinster at the local church. She had stayed at home to care for her parents who, at the time that she met Mr L., had both recently died, leaving her on her own for the first time in her life. She and Mr L. were married; they lived in two different parts of the same rural area before moving to a modern bungalow on a large estate in a busy village. They had a car and Mrs L. drove. She said that they had a happy marriage.

Mrs L. had a sister whose husband, also a farmer, had also developed dementia, and this brother-in-law had already begun attending the day hospital.

Mr L.'s health had begun to decline when he was in his seventies. In 1978 heart trouble was diagnosed and in 1978 he also had an operation for gallstones. He tended to be very hypochondriacal, especially on these occasions.

Late in 1983 Mr L. developed ideas that his wife was being unfaithful to him, based on some real incidents which he misconstrued. He tried to leave home by going to stay with his son, but his son would not condone this behaviour. Over the next two years, Mr L. would occasionally say 'nasty things' to his wife. When speaking, he began to leave his sentences unfinished and had to search for the right word; Mrs L. was correcting him and 'filling in the gaps' without being conscious of what was happening. He lost his sense of the value of money. In 1984 Mr and Mrs L. went away on holiday to Blackpool. The place was new to them and Mr L. could not find his way about, a fact that made him very irritable. Late in 1985, a chest infection coincided with Mr L.'s experimenting with the medication that had been prescribed for his heart condition; by trying to do without it, and he developed a toxic confusional state. He was very disturbed at night, stripping off his clothes and lying on the floor; twice his wife sent for his son to help her with him in the night. Mr L. expressed ideas about being 'guilty of sin', not a religious sentiment which was usual for him.

At that time, Mr L. was admitted for three weeks to the assessment unit for the confused elderly. The diagnosis made was of underlying dementia, exacerbated by physical illnesses causing acute confusion. At this time, the social history was taken by the social worker. After treatment Mr L.'s orientation was fairly good, but his short-term memory was impaired. His delusions had not disappeared completely. Otherwise, his functioning was good; he was able to dress himself and was not incontinent. As the basic condition was likely to deteriorate and infections were likely to recur, Mrs L. was offered a day care place for her husband at the unit's day hospital on two days a week. She accepted this form of respite care, but was very anxious and fearful of the future.

Mr L. attended for just over a month. He grumbled about going but socialised well once he arrived at the unit. He enjoyed group activities and reminiscence activities, and contributed the tenor harmony in the hymns during the religious services held regularly on the unit. Then he developed a pneumonia which was slow to respond to treatment and had to be readmitted as an in-patient because he became aggressive.

Mrs L. took the opportunity to go away for a few days. After four weeks Mr L. returned home with the recommendation that he attend day care for three days a week in future, but Mrs L. was so distressed by his objections to attending that she, in effect, sabotaged efforts to provide respite in this way. Advice by both the day hospital staff and the CPN did not seem able to overcome her fears.

During the summer Mr L. did not attend. He was visited at home but Mrs L. did not feel free to speak in front of her husband about the problems that she was having. However, the CPN did report that Mr L. was experiencing aggressive outbursts which were not helped by medication, and he still made accusations against his wife. In July he was persuaded to go into the unit for two weeks, and was taken in by his son in order to give Mrs L. a break. She went away for a week's holiday. Upon her return, the social worker took the opportunity to visit her at home while Mr L. was not present.

Mrs L. described herself as being 'no nurse', and had a certain reserve about the intimate side of marriage. She was also anxious in a way that tended to precipitate trouble rather than forestall it. She felt that in not being able to care for her husband herself, she had failed as a wife and that she had let him down in delivering him into the hands of strangers. She had had problems in accepting his illnesses, and his real physical and mental limitations, partly due to his past hypochondriasis. His mental state was very variable, as it was influenced by both chronic and acute conditions, so that Mrs L. had difficulty in believing that the general overall course would be towards deterioration. She had been told this formally by the consultant and informally by other professionals on various occasions and had, briefly, attended a relatives' support group. She understood the situation at an intellectual level, but had not come to terms with it emotionally.

In their marriage, Mr L. had always taken the lead and it required a tremendous effort for her to assert herself against him if he chose not to do something. The social worker assured her that her reluctance to get him to attend as a day client was an understandable and, in fact, a common problem and one that the escort staff who travel with the unit transport were familiar. The social worker and Mrs L. not only discussed her feelings about her husband's reservations about attending, but also rehearsed how she might react. It was decided that Mrs L. should not anticipate trouble by rushing about trying to get her husband ready, but should behave as if it were any other day until the moment the transport arrived. If Mr L. shut himself in the bedroom on seeing the vehicle, she should leave it to 'the girls' to coax him out. Mrs L. had to face the question and decide whether it was worth bearing the pain of occasional temporary distress in order to gain longer term relief. She needed to be assured that he joined in well at the unit and spent a pleasant day when he was there. She also needed to understand that there was nothing special in the attention being paid to her, as if she were creating the problem, but that the service exists because the problems are common. The underlying aim of the service is to offer respite and support to the carers so that they can continue caring for longer. This benefits the sufferer in the long run, which is an intention that the professionals share with her and other 'informal' carers. Mrs L. was helped to see that her guilt was obstructing the provision of resources to help her go on caring, and not to come to a point of exhaustion and rejection.

After some consideration, Mrs L. finally accepted the reinstatement of the day care. A change of medication helped Mr L. to be more pleasant and he attended fairly well with only the occasional refusal. He did continue to be suspicious of his wife, especially at night, and when leaving for day care would say loudly in the street that he knew she would have another man in the house the minute his back was turned. Despite this, the principle was established that he would attend and a sound basis was laid for future increases in the level of care provided. Mrs L. was helped too by her sister who was better at being firm than she was. Mrs L. appreciated the respite very much, having been without any relief for several months. She declined to attend the relatives' support group, preferring, instead, to use the time 'to do her own thing'. She appeared able to use the relief well to 'recharge her batteries', often in the company of her sister.

COMMENT

At first sight, this would appear to be a case with relatively little social work interest. Indeed, the social worker did have only two long interviews with the carer. However, this intervention made an important contribution to the work of the multi-disciplinary team in this case, which illustrates some of the principles common to work with this client group.

Mental Health Aspects

Mr L. suffered from senile dementia, which is one of a number of types of organic brain disorder which affect the elderly. In particular, it is marked by a gradual, global and irreversible deterioration in the brain's structure, which leads, in varying degrees, to resultant changes in the physiology and psychology (particularly the personality, intellect and memory) of the person. This disease is varied in form and how it affects individuals depends very much on individual factors such as physical health, heredity, pre-morbid personality, age of onset and previous life experiences. In this particular case the disorder appears to have emerged 'endogenously', from within, quite late in life, but was influenced by extrinsic factors such as disease. Of the characteristics of dementia which are most common, by the time this point in the case had been reached Mr L. already clearly displayed several, including a gradual loss of memory; changes in his personality, highlighted by his increasing unco-operativeness; disinhibition and suspicion; changes in mood, marked by agitation, irritability and, perhaps, depression; changes in intellect, such as inability to adapt to new circumstances and confusion, including disorientation to time and place. Also, the social factors are many, but in this case include a change of status within the family; damage in personal relationship with spouse and, potentially, children; and loss of independence (see Gray and Isaacs, 1979).

Casework Aspects

The social history provided a framework for understanding the relationships and attitudes in the family and the wider support supplied by them to the chief carer, within which the team could offer formal services. Such a history forms part of the assessment process which decides what are the needs in any case and what services it is appropriate to offer. Also, during the information gathering, a relationship is built up between the social worker and the carer which can become the basis for a future therapeutic intervention (see Sullivan, 1954, for an old, but highly valuable, exposition of the principles involved).

The second interview was essential in getting the carer to accept the services she needed to enable her to continue caring. There were several principles at work here which can typically be applied to various aspects of such cases.

1. The social worker treats the principal carer as the client. In a very similar way to child guidance practice, the patient is in the hands of doctors, nurses, occupational therapists, physiotherapists, etc. The social worker is usually unable to build a therapeutic relationship with the dementia sufferer. Instead, because of the patient's loss of short-term memory, a superficial relationship is all that is possible. Work with the carer, however, benefits the patient indirectly. If the carer can be helped to modify his or her attitude to, and behaviour with, the dementia sufferer, this can be of great benefit to them

both. This distinction is akin to that between 'client' and 'target' described by Pincus and Minahan (1973). Information and advice are also provided to the carers by CPNs and other members of the team but, as has been illustrated, their intervention has real limitations because they must also focus directly on the client.

2. Carers, almost universally, feel guilty. Actually, official efforts to intervene may make them feel even more so. There seems to be a direct relationship between guilt and degree of caring. It seems frequently that those who have tried hardest and longest, and done most for the sufferer, are those who feel the most guilt. Professional training equips the social worker to address these emotional conflicts. This is, perhaps, the main reason why it is so unsatisfactory that untrained staff are so often left by Social Services departments to deal with cases involving the elderly. In contrast to the situation where a refusal to accept the services offered meets with a sigh of relief and an entry of 'no further action' on the referral form, good practice indicates that positive efforts should be made to overcome the emotional barriers to the acceptance of help. Social workers are in the business of trying to bring about change to the benefit of the client (and the benefit of those for whom the client is caring).

3. Acceptance of the illness and its downward course is hard. Facing the reality of the disease and its poor prognosis brings much emotional pain to those emotionally attached to the sufferer. Here again, training prepares social workers to face pain with their clients. Experience suggests that it is a good indicator of success in this area if the carer cries and is allowed by the social worker to do so. Other professionals can also be good at this, but this is usually by grace of temperament and experience rather than training and education. The principle behind this process is that constant denial leads to inappropriate behaviour on the part of the carer, and prevents them from living with any understanding through what can be a long, drawn-out experience. It is fundamental to human well-being that man is able to make sense of what is happening to him. If carers cannot, or will not, do so, the consequent distress over a long period can lead to a rapid rejection of the situation in the shape of a sudden refusal to go on caring. Denial is another factor in the refusal of services.

4. There is a real need for social workers to understand that assessment is not simply for the benefit of themselves and their professional colleagues. In cases such as this, it is to be shared with the client/carer so that realistic goals can be agreed.

5. The majority of families wish to go on caring and, therefore, the patient's interests and those of the carer are the same. This is confirmed by research (Levin et al., forthcoming). Sometimes, of course, there are conflicts of interest and, again, these should be made explicit.

6. There are limits to client self-determination. A person with anything

more than mild dementia lacks judgement. Because short-term memory and orientation are impaired, he or she lacks the basic factual information on which to make an informed choice. Dementia sufferers often demonstrate this by becoming disturbed if put under pressure to make a decision. The professional team generally supports the carers in making decisions and choices for people previously capable of making their own.

7. The whole approach illustrated by this case is based on the assumption that the provision of services in support of carers at home leads to later admissions to residential care. This is not necessarily confirmed by the research which has been done so far. Levin *et al.*, for example, have found that the major determinant in date of entry to residential care was the carer's previous attitude to institutional care. Nevertheless, Mr L. was an appropriate admission to day care and fulfilled three of the five criteria in the profile of 'best candidates' outlined by Gilleard (1985): some degree of impairment in self-care; continent; supporters are supported by the family.

12 Mrs D.:

an integrated casework approach

CASE HISTORY

Mrs D. was referred to me (hospital social worker) by the paediatrician, as she appeared depressed following the death of her youngest child who had been handicapped. She was thirty-five years old at the time and her religion was Muslim. She and Mr D. came to the UK from Bangladesh; and they had been living in this country for the previous eight to nine years, with Mr D. working for a local authority.

Mrs D. got married at the age of twelve and gave birth to a son a year later when she was thirteen years old. It is often the custom in Bangladesh that when a woman is in labour she is put in a separate room away from the other members of the family. The mother and newly born baby are then kept there for ten or twelve days. While in confinement, Mrs D.'s son had died and she was sure that it must have been her mishandling of the baby that caused his death.

However, in spite of this early loss, Mr and Mrs D. had five children, the eldest being a daughter, sixteen years of age, and the youngest, who had just died, having been born handicapped. Mrs D. felt that she was responsible for the child's handicap. When she became pregnant she had wanted a termination. According to her, she used to have hot baths and did things that she had learned from 'old wives' to have a natural abortion. She was convinced that these actions might have caused the child's handicap. Since the birth of the child, Mrs D. withdrew herself totally from everybody including the other children and her husband. She devoted herself exclusively to caring for the baby. She said she had loved him so very much that she could not bear to part from him for more than an hour. She told the other children that she loved only the youngest child. Both her husband and the other children accepted this and the eldest girl more or less took over the mother's role in the family by looking after her younger siblings, doing the housework, etc.

During the first two weeks of my visiting, I could hardly carry out any conversation with Mrs D., who refused to eat, drink or sleep. She didn't want to talk to anyone; either she was wailing, calling her child's name, or she kept silent. It appeared to be an 'acute grief reaction' and I planned for long-term bereavement counselling. Mentally, I reviewed the mountain of literature, especially Parkes (1972, 1978), Kubler-Ross (1973), Hinton (1973), Freud (1925), to name a few. It seemed that the likely methods to try and apply were crisis intervention and the problem solving model.

However, within a few weeks some issues became so evident that they necessitated a review of the situation. These raised dilemmas that demanded I rethink any number of assumptions which I had previously made in respect of social casework as I had known and practised it.

To begin with Mrs D.'s grief over the first child she lost was far from being resolved. She was more or less convinced that her handling of the baby had been responsible for his death. The fifth child, then, having been born handicapped and subsequently dying, was, to her, the punishment she deserved. Crisis intervention seemed inappropriate for three reasons. Firstly, her prolonged grief over the death of her first child had become 'chronic' and had been revived by the recent death. Secondly, recent research studies on grief and bereavement lead us to see such things less as a life crisis as described by Lindemann (1944), and more as a life transition (Glick *et al.*, 1974). Thirdly, to people of the Indian subcontinent, suffering is seen as part of life; unhappiness, sadness are all normal life events, like health and illness (Currer, 1983). Suffering is an an act of God. The expectation of clients motivated by the 'relief of suffering' (Rapaport, 1970) seemed inappropriate.

My visiting of Mrs D. and her family made me reflect again on the nature of the family. In spite of having lived here for several years, they were, in customs, religion and language, still strongly dominated by Indian culture. The family as an institution plays such an integral part in every aspect of life in the Indian subcontinent, that individualism, the right to be an individual, is seen as secondary to the duty of being a good member of the family. To Mr and Mrs D.

and their children, to be a dutiful son or daughter, father or mother, husband or wife was regarded as being of crucial importance. The problem solving casework process (Perlman, 1970), so heavily based on the functional school of ego psychology and so Western in its emphasis on the individual, his instinctual drives towards pleasure and such, again seemed inadequate.

Again, with Mr and Mrs D., as with other people from the Indian subcontinent, the idea of a 'professional friend' was bewildering. They were used to the professionalism of doctors, nurses, teachers, etc., but not someone who appears as caring as a 'sister'. The vibrating force of family life goes beyond the nuclear and extended family. When anyone becomes close to such a family, the sign of acceptance is shown by treating him/her as a member of that family such as an uncle, aunt, sister or brother. Hence, as I began to know the D. family better, I became aware of the conflict between the concept of a 'professional friend' adopted from my living in this country and the unconscious acceptance of being a member of the family of the client. Yet, helping clients through a relationship is paramount in casework, regardless of the various methods or models employed. This ambiguity struck at the heart of my ability to help because of the danger that it may have hampered the objectivity one needs to have.

May I point out that it took me nearly six months to elicit these factors. As mentioned before, having been trained here and practising casework so far with the native clients, I had never yet questioned the cultural validity of the casework process. I assumed that it would work out with clients irrespective of race, sex and age.

When working with Mrs D., the advantage I had over a native British social worker was that I was familiar and accustomed to the cultural values for the Indian subcontinent. I could be quite at ease negotiating and comparing the norms between the two cultures, and in assessing what was normal or abnormal behaviour for that culture. In trying to help Mrs D. to resolve her grief, I made an attempt to try and use an 'integrated method' of casework, i.e. some of the processes from casework with an Eastern philosophical perspective on life. For example, it seemed that some of the ideas from systems theory would be helpful to reduce stress in the family. Systems theory is about the relationship between the one and the many, between man and society, between the minority and the majority. It gives greater emphasis to the contemporary environment, particularly in attending to the person's social interactions, as both an enabling and constraining factor.

Informing my casework this way made the process seem changed from what one normally experiences in the British context. Mrs D. and I discussed things like the meaning of life, our perceptions of God, the question of life after death, the compatibility of so much suffering in this world with the existence of God as a compassionate creature, etc. The discussion was very much two way—coming from a Hindu background I was challenged by Mrs D., a Muslim, about my beliefs, my ideas.

Also, I took an active interest in finding out how members of the D. family saw their role in a contemporary multiracial British society. This was particularly relevant with this case due to the grievances expressed by Mr D. and his elder children about being racially discriminated against. While discussing this issue, they also felt relaxed, talking about the death of the handicapped child and the impact of having a handicapped child in the family. Mrs D. was sympathetic to this issue of race, somehow it cemented the gap between her and others which had been created since the birth of the handicapped child.

I liaised with all the schools the children attended and the general practitioner to put them in the picture as to what was happening in this family, and to dispel some of their assumptions (rather stereotyped) about the family.

I terminated the case when, after a year, Mrs D. said that she was looking for a job and complained more of her marital relationship than her grief.

COMMENT

Mental Health Aspects

Depression, like many psychiatric disorders, is to a great degree a culture-bound concept and the case of Mrs D. highlights some of the distinctions to be found in its presentation across cultures. The symptoms which she displayed were not so much affective as somatic. That is to say that she displayed sleep disturbance, loss of appetite and socially withdrawn behaviour. Later, it became apparent that she harboured a deep-seated sense of guilt for the death of her first child, and ideas of retribution concerning the handicap and death of her youngest child. She did not present me with feelings of tearfulness or loneliness which so characterise the complaint among Westerners. As Rack (1981) says, 'The English woman produces her emotional distress first, and her physical complaints as an afterthought, whereas the Pakistani woman produces physical symptoms and makes no reference to her mood. Indeed, she may not say that she is depressed even when asked directly about this' (pp. 91-2). There are many potential explanations for this phenomenon, but many authors point to the fact that in many parts of the world, internal distress is not equated with illness as frequently as it is in the West, and that familiar constellations of symptoms are not linked together into disorders in the same fashion as they are here (Cochrane, 1983, p. 84). A lot of reactions are not culturally dependent but are merely expressed differently according to their cultural context. For example, an overprotective attitude to children is common in the West and not a function of this client's ethnicity. Experiencing grief in such circumstances is normal though, perhaps, experienced differently regardless of background. Nevertheless, it is important that health and Social Services professionals are aware of these differences so that accurate assessments can be made and appropriate help offered.

Casework Aspects

It is interesting to note that as early as 1958, Heimler wrote, 'It was very important that anyone dealing with immigrants or refugees should have a thorough knowledge of previous cultural influences, otherwise misunderstanding and misjudgements may occur in handling with immigrants ... Beyond the past the refugees also had to forget their deeply unconscious reaction to adapting to this culture. Particularly those who are middle-aged and over, often felt that by doing so they would be unfaithful to their greatest love, their home. They didn't want to be unfaithful, but at the same time they would not want to remain the odd man out either.' As can be so clearly seen, here, cultural factors were very important in both the genesis of the client's predicament and the style of help offered to Mrs D. These 'cultural factors' were not mere empty abstractions which we have all grown weary of hearing bandied about in social work circles, but real issues such as child management customs, race, religion, the psychological nature of individuals, the influence of family, the perception of the professionals, language, etc. To deal with such cases as this, all of these things may, to some varying degree, need to be understood and dealt with effectively in addition to the psychiatric aspects mentioned above.

During the case what dawned on me was the degree to which social work, in its attempt to become 'secular', was becoming reluctant to bring religious or philosophical dimensions into the work. What this means is that we possibly feel uncomfortable working from this perspective, the ideas having become part of an unfamiliar framework. However, to people from the Indian subcontinent, whether Muslim, Hindu or Sikh, whether educated or not, religious belief is a blueprint for living and dying. Therefore, to avoid the issue of religion is to create a deep void in communication between onself and the client. This void serves as a barrier, preventing the formation of a useful relationship with him or her and, hence, would likewise prevent casework from being of any use.

As I am from India myself, I was able to communicate with Mrs D. and with the members of her family in her native language. This was, no doubt, a great advantage in view of the fact that as recently as 1976 (Roberts, 1978) it was widely reported that as few as forty per cent of Asian women could speak English. Also, having been part of that culture, I was able to see areas of stress which were confronting the family and address them. For example, it seems that social workers dealing with families from the Indian subcontinent or Afro-Caribbean countries must be prepared to tackle the issue of race, even if it is not the presenting problem. According to a recent review, it may be argued that racism engenders depression by 'denying its victim any control over

external events. Poor self esteem, rejection and loss exacerbate the phenomenon' (London, 1986, p. 268). In this case it proved to be of central concern
to the family, though well-hidden at first. It was not until it was tackled,
however, that other feelings, more closely associated with the presenting
problem began to surface.

During the course of seeing Mrs D., I abandoned the more analytic
approach of my training and adopted a more intuitive approach. This seemed
more appropriate to the management of problems associated with loss and
grief for people with the cultural background of the D. family. The wisdom of
this is, no doubt, something that workers will wish to consider. Nevertheless, it
does appear that one must consider the manner in which culture actually
affects the intellectual and emotional structures through which people interact
when trying to engage with them. To attempt to maintain the proper 'professional distance' in circumstances, when to do so would exclude one from
making a workable relationship with an individual (because from within their
perspective one needs to be able to place a helper within one's kinship
network), all seems rather futile. This seems especially true of Muslims, where
the strong familial tradition makes it unlikely that personal difficulties will be
brought to the attention of outsiders (Cochrane, 1983, p. 103).

This case study is likely to be the 'odd one out' in relation to others
illustrating the application of casework methods in practice. The aim of
choosing Mrs D., a client from Bangladesh, was to highlight issues which arise
when applying a casework process based on Western, Anglo-Saxon values,
which may be very different and alien to those from the Indian subcontinent.
The reporting of work, such as this, is particularly important in that we cannot
even begin to progress from our most rudimentary state of practice knowledge
in this area, 'until psychiatry and related disciplines have built up a substantial
volume of caselore on different (ethnic) groups' (Rack, 1981, p.88). Hopefully
it will give food for thought and stimulate much needed research.

13 Mrs E.:

on managing our own fears of madness

CASE HISTORY

The E. family were referred to the area Social Services team by the police
as a case of matrimonial difficulties. Mrs E. had complained of her husband's

drinking and physical cruelty to her, alleging that he beat her when he was drunk. Mr E. described his wife as being cold. He said that she showed little affection either for him or for the children. She denied him sexual intercourse, neglected the household, never prepared meals, etc. Mrs. E. agreed to be seen by a social worker who contacted her, and later her husband, with a view to finding out more about the marriage and whether they both could be helped to make a better adjustment to each other.

After nine interviews (six with Mrs E., one with Mr E. and two joint interviews), Mrs E. decided to divorce her husband. She had tried to do so earlier but did not carry through. By this time, both partners felt that they had nothing more in common. Mrs E. said that she had married her husband only because she had been pregnant and because he had been willing to accept Betty, her daughter.

Mrs E. was born in a small village, her parents being farmers who grew fruit. She lost her mother, whom she adored, when she was sixteen, and subsequently experienced her father as being very strict. One year after her mother's death, her father got married for the second time. Mrs E. could not 'get on' with her stepmother and left home to take up work in a factory. She became pregnant at the age of twenty-four and lost her work in the factory because of the pregnancy, but felt too ashamed to return to her family. Instead, she took up work in a hospital and Betty was born. Immediately after the birth, she placed the child in care where Betty stayed for three months, the mother working, paying for the child and visiting regularly. She met her present husband and took up work in the town where he lived, soon becoming pregnant again. They married shortly before Michael was born.

Mrs E. was described as a tall, slim, dark-haired young woman of rather unkempt appearance with restless movements. Mr E. gave the impression of a quiet, good-natured, somewhat boyish person who had temper tantrums when he became angry. He wanted, above all, cosiness in the home and someone to look after and care for him. When they had agreed upon the divorce, Mr E. decided to return to his mother's home and took Michael with him. He left the flat to Mrs E., who kept Betty with her. She felt that she could not cope with two children and wanted, above all, to go out to work, to earn money and to clear their debts and to 'get on with life'.

The social worker felt some doubts about whether Mrs E. would be able to stand on her feet alone and whether she would be capable of being an adequate mother for Betty. Mrs E. felt it had been very difficult to begin married life with two children and had felt more affection for Michael than Betty. The little girl got on her nerves because she was restless, greedy with food and longed for tenderness which the mother felt she was not really able to give. After the divorce was granted, Mrs E. found herself a job as a kitchen maid in a restaurant and with the social worker's help, Betty was placed in a nearby nursery where the child received warm and careful attention. Mrs E. gladly accepted the social worker's offer to keep in regular touch with her. She never came to the office, but home visits were arranged every fortnight and announced beforehand by letter.

The social worker's supervisor felt that there were strong indications that Mrs E. was becoming a seriously disturbed person. There was a note in the case record that shortly after the marriage, Mrs E. had asked for help because the flat, clothes and underwear were full of vermin. The Environmental Health Officer, however, could find nothing. Several times during the first nine interviews Mrs E. had expressed fears that living with her husband would make her 'go mad' like her sister-in-law who was in a mental hospital.

The supervisor expressed his concerns to the social worker in one of their regular supervison sessions, asking what she felt about Mrs E.'s remarks. The social worker reacted with some resistance. She felt that one should not place too much weight on what Mrs E. had said, and felt that there was danger in interpreting something into a case. She recounted how she had once brought a case to the attention of a psychiatrist who had laughed at her and belittled what she described as signs of a possible disturbance. The supervisor agreed that assumptions should be based on sufficient factual material. Nevertheless, the supervisor wondered if they could, for instance, look a little more closely at the kind of relationship which the social worker had with Mrs E.? How would the social worker characterise it?

The social worker said that she felt that Mrs E. trusted her, and often spoke freely and openly, though she was always restless and went up and down in the flat, sometimes doing housework during their discussion and almost never sitting quietly on a chair. But the relationship sort of broke down after each contact and had to be built up anew each time that they met. It was discussed that this kind of brittle, fragile relationship was something which one finds, for instance, in cases of schizophrenia, and therefore was something to be noted. The supervisor and social worker agreed upon the fact that Mrs E. would need the experience of feeling accepted with whatever she wanted to express so that the social worker might be able to get a fuller understanding of what was happening within the client.

It was only after nine more interviews that Mrs E. was able to express her fears more fully. She said that she sometimes got 'ideas' in her head which made her so restless. She felt an itching rash all over her body, but the general practitioner had told her that he could not find anything irregular. She saw vermin on clothes, curtains and mattresses and therefore had to wash and scrub all of the time. She had taken everything to the cleaner and had thrown away many things so that she got herself into financial difficulties because she then had to replace everything with new. According to Mrs E. it had been her husband who had dragged in the vermin first—she had told him so—and this was the reason why she had felt unable to live with him any longer. An inner voice had told her that she ought to leave him. She projected her fears into the flat which she felt had brought her 'bad luck'. She had started going out every night from fear of being alone in the flat and had casual sexual intercourse with numerous different men whom she had just met. When she got pregnant again and had a miscarriage, she felt that people in the house might have practised witchcraft on her. She consulted several of the general practitioners at the surgery with whom she was registered but carefully avoided seeing a psychiatrist.

The supervisor suggested that the social worker discuss the case with a psychiatrist to get diagnostic help and to discuss treatment aspects and possible prognosis, etc., so that the social worker might be better able to make plans with Mrs E. for herself and the child. This would have entailed the social worker making contact with the psychiatric services at the local hospital. When the social worker was a little reluctant, the supervisor asked whether perhaps she felt afraid that asking for a precise diagnosis meant 'labelling' people and thus doing an injustice to them? (During the course of her work with the agency, the newly qualified worker had, more than once, expressed her ambivalance about so 'labelling' people and thus committing them to a 'career as a psychiatric patient'.) To this the social worker replied with some feeling that when she was a young girl she had great difficulties with her stepmother. She had resented very much that her own father had married a second time and took a young girl not much older than she. Out of rivalry and opposition she had behaved badly herself. As a consequence, her father and stepmother had decided that she should see an psychiatrist because they felt she was 'mad' and even spoke of sending her to a mental hospital. This had deeply shocked her. Since then she had been afraid of having people 'labelled' like that.

The supervisor agreed that this must have come rather as a shock to her in her rivalry with her parents. But she was then an adolescent girl who reacted violently against what she might have experienced as loss of her father—especially when, as she had told, she had looked after the younger siblings for most of the year following her mother's death. The supervisor reminded the social worker that we were all prone to carry over some of our feelings into later life and also into professional situations which touch on past experiences. The hallmark of professional work was the ability to face up to, and understand, such influences and then to act objectively in spite of them.

After that conference, the social worker no longer had any difficulty in consulting a specialist on that case. He was uncertain as to an exact diagnosis without having seen the client personally, but said that it sounded like obsessive-compulsive neurosis, or a transitional state between neurosis and schizophrenia. He felt that the case had a poor prognosis because of its slow onset and because this kind of patient would not easily accept treatment. The sincere interest which the psychiatrist took in the case proved to be a positive and helpful experience for the social worker. She has since made use of expert opinion in various cases.

Mrs E.'s condition continued to deteriorate. She developed the idea of having contracted Aids during her last intercourse and felt that Betty might also be infected. She eventually lost her job because she had missed so many days due to illness. She asked the social worker to help her to find a good home for Betty as she no longer felt able to cope with work, the household and child. Fortunately it was possible to find very understanding foster parents and Mrs E. and the social worker brought Betty to them. The child eventually settled down happily and has since made up a great deal of her retarded development. Mrs E. gave up her flat and found a job on a hospital ward, living in staff accommodation. This kind of 'sheltered employment' satisfied some of her strong dependency needs. She was able to keep regular contact over the telephone with Betty, the foster parents and the social worker who tried to give her every support and helped her to overcome her feelings of separation.

For a number of weeks she was able to work steadily. Then, after an attempted suicide with an overdose of sleeping pills she was referred to the psychiatric department of the same district general hospital and has been under psychiatric treatment since.

COMMENT

Mental Health Aspects

As with many individuals who eventually find their way into the psychiatric network, Mrs E.'s condition was difficult to describe exactly and developed insidiously over a long period of time. It might have been appropriate to term her as having a 'borderline state', 'borderline personality', or 'latent' or 'borderline' schizophrenia. The key point was that while she was not usually frankly psychotic she frequently 'bordered' on it with her thinking (i.e. irrational, overvalued and unusual 'ideas' eventually moving into delusions); perceptions (i.e. what were perhaps misperceptions and misinterpretations, but certainly obsessions eventually approaching the level of hallucinations); affect (i.e. rather cold with a 'brittleness' to personal relationships); and behaviour (poorly motivated, unkempt appearance, promiscuous, fairly self-centred and eventually self-destructive).

Casework Aspects

This case raises many issues relevant to both social work theory and practice of which I shall deal with just two.

Psychodynamic theory, borderline personality and casework practice
The various competing theories of borderline personality all agree that in such individuals there is a structural inadequacy in the ego, particularly in the area of identification. This results in the individual sometimes displaying various

defences designed to protect the fragile structure, and sometimes displaying frankly psychotic behaviour, acting out as the defences break down. Mrs E. surely did both and without a great deal of supposition as to her experiences and possible psychological development during early life, her case presents some rather clear examples. For instance, she showed a strongly neurotic defence of obsessionality which sometimes reached psychotic proportions. Here, Mrs E.'s state this may well have been related to her loss of mother during the critical adolescent period and her subsequent conflict with her stepmother. Certainly, she seemed to transfer unresolved portions of her childhood into her adult life, and did not easily identify with the adult role of parent as she found the subsequent challenge of establishing an intimate relationship very daunting (i.e. divorce, followed by continued promiscuity). It is thought that such individuals have a marked ambivalence to close emotional relationships, making them at once feared but sought after. This was increasingly true in this case as demonstrated by Mrs E.'s relationships with men (her husband and those who followed after their divorce) and with her children, which always broke down under the stress of living in close emotional proximity to another human and having to meet their dependency needs.

There is a great degree of controversy concerning as to what is the best approach to treatment for such persons. In this instance, the worker chose an 'ego supportive', rather than an 'insight' approach. No doubt this was based on an assessment of the positive strengths of the client's ego and the relative strength of unconscious (particularly ID) impulses which challenged the ego's integrity. Consistent with this approach is the creation of a 'holding environment' by the therapist, who serves as a continuous, stable, reality-based object to which the patient can anchor him or herself. A recent review of psycho-dymanic therapy in this area (Waldinger, 1987) points out that there are several principles for work with such individuals, many of which were exemplified by the social worker in this case. These include: providing a stable framework for treatment; an increased level activity by the therapist during periods of contact; tolerance, especially of the client's hostility; being aware, and making the client aware of the self-destructive nature of their behaviour; helping to establish a bridge between the client's actions and their feelings in the present; setting limits and blocking acting out behaviours; focusing early clarifications and interpretations on the here and now; and careful attention to countertransference feelings (p. 268).

Supervision and modifying a worker's defences

As one would anticipate, working with psychiatric patients is one of the most challenging areas of social work precisely because, as Harry S. Sullivan said, 'we are all more human than otherwise'. The more closely that we come to identify with the situation of the client, the more likely this is to be so as the boundaries between ourselves and our clients can easily become blurred. In this case, the basic 'humanity' of the beginning social worker was revealed by the way in which working with Mrs E. brought to the surface conflicts of her own which lay below the surface, unresolved.

This case raises the classic example of the new worker, taken by surprise by testing, and unfamiliar demands, 'who at the beginning finds social work material and the requirements of field practice so anxiety-provoking and threatening that he/she must cope with the situation by clinging dogmatically to old standards and beliefs, closing the door to new experience and ideas' (Selby, 1955). The task of the supervisor was not to 'psychoanalyse' the worker, developing a detailed account of the worker's personality and motivations. Indeed, far from it. Rather the problem was properly addressed in professional terms by encouraging the social worker to reflect on how her own personality was influencing the quality of her performance (i.e. her casework). The supervisor's objective for staff-development with this social worker was much the same as with most learning associated with psycho-social casework: 'self-assurance and independent functioning in the professional role and the ability to operate as a skilful and competent helper in the field of human relations without tripping over his/her own unconscious reactions, his/her personal value judgements or his own defences' (Selby, 1955).

If nothing else, this case shows the absolute necessity of supervisors having a clear grasp of the theoretical and practical aspects of the casework required of the staff whom they supervise. This is particularly important in an era during which it has become fashionable to see the supervision role increasingly only in 'line management' terms. Here, only because adequate professional knowledge was present, the supervisor was quick to recognise 'blocks' in the form of the social worker's self-protective responses. The supervisor made an appropriate assessment both of Mrs E.'s irrational behaviour and of the social worker's resistance to recognising it. The supervisor also understood that simply allowing nature to take its course and waiting for the social worker to change her attitude herself was inadequate. Instead, within the context of a safe climate of basic trust but without probing, the social worker was encouraged to examine her feelings for Mrs E. This eventually led to relevant information (i.e. the social worker's own adolescent crisis and the source of the 'counter-transference') surfacing. The supervisor dealt effectively with this material once it had become conscious, allowing for appropriate ventilation, focusing on the 'here and now' and helping to reinforce the worker's ego by drawing boundaries between her and the client.

Though a good example, this case is, probably, somewhat unusual. Research demonstrates, sadly, that such an effective approach to counter-transference as this is, in practice, likely to be taken by only a minority of supervisors even in psychotherapy, which places at least as high a premium on therapist self-awareness as social work (Goin and Kline, 1976). This process allowed the social worker to separate her own past from the present and to gain self-control in a manner which was both professionally developmental and emotionally healing.

14 Mrs Finley:
joint work with a neurotic client

CASE HISTORY

The situation at referral

Mrs Finley was a forty-four-year-old married woman who was originally from a remote area of rural Wales, living, at referral, in a large English city. She was referred to out-patients where, in accordance with the usual practice of the clinic, she was seen initially by a social worker and a psychiatrist (in this case, a junior registrar) together. The general practitioner's letter referred to a three-year history of various physical symptoms about which the patient was 'desperately worried'; to investigation at a nearby teaching hospital with normal results and; to failure to respond to a variety of medication. The patient complained of panic attacks, a feeling of choking, palpitations and breathlessness, and tremor occurring three to four times daily during the preceding eight months, and lasting for several hours. The attacks occurred at any time; when watching TV or even in her sleep (she claimed they woke her at night), as well as outside the home. She was frightened to go out, and had given up her job as a part-time secretary in industry because of attacks at work.

Previously, she had not regarded herself as a nervous person, but was always rather 'happy-go-lucky'; there were no obvious precipitating factors. Both her parents and all her siblings were reported to be alive and well in Wales; her husband was in secure semi-skilled work and the marriage was happy. Her son (aged nineteen) was also in work and her teenage daughter was at college. Both lived at home and neither had made any plans to leave.

In discussion with the consultant, a provisional diagnosis of anxiety state was made; the fact that she denied any problems in life '... to an almost absurd degree' was noted, and arrangements were made for her to be seen again with her husband. A mild anxiolytic drug, which Mrs Finley had previously taken and found to be helpful but which had been stopped by her general practitioner because of concern about its habit-forming potential, was again prescribed. The consultant's view was that patients of sound previous personality who are reluctant to accept medication, but who have severe anxiety symptoms, generally take minimal quantities.

Subsequent management: phase I

During the next three months, the patient had four appointments. At the first, she and her husband were seen as arranged by the social worker and registrar together. Thereafter, because the registrar left, the psychiatric management passed to the consultant who, except on one occasion when the patient requested an emergency appointment, continued to work with the social worker.

At the first follow-up interview, the panic attacks and somatic symptoms of anxiety had subsided, but Mrs Finley appeared somewhat more depressed. She was also extremely worried about the possibility of recurrence; specifically, that she would have a breakdown, lose control and become like one of the very disturbed people she had seen in the reception area. Her husband, like Mrs Finley, described their family relationship as very happy and denied the existence of any problems. She had not been like this previously, and was bewildered and totally shattered by these feelings. There were some problems—the husband was to have a minor operation, and builders at their home had done some unsatisfactory work—but both partners denied any anxiety related to these matters.

The team began to think that Mrs Finley had always been a person who could not acknowledge feelings of worry and had somehow now collapsed under the strain. She was asked to keep a note of any particular worries during the next two weeks to see if some pattern relating to her symptoms could be discovered.

When next seen (by the consultant) she was worse, and her symptoms were much more clearly those of depression. Her mood was low, with feelings of hopelessness and tearfulness; the previous somatic symptoms were showing a marked diurnal variation; she was waking early. Despite previous unsuccessful trials of antidepressant medicine, the consultant thought it necessary to make another attempt and the prescription was changed to a tricyclic antidepressant. A diagnosis of depression seemed more consistent with the absence of any clear environmental stress. Her husband's minor surgery had been completed successfully and the problem with the builders resolved.

At the next couple of interviews, she said she felt no better at all (although more objective measures, such as the reports of the time of awakening, suggested limited improvement). On each occasion a further careful enquiry was conducted for possible leads towards social or psychological factors which might underly what was clearly a quite distressing and disabling illness. The consultant felt strongly that a simple drug-responsive depression should have responded better (dose levels and the patient's compliance appeared perfectly adequate) and, thus, more must be going on. In a lengthy interview, the social worker and psychiatrist tried to unpick some of the dynamics of the situation.

Despite some difficulty in participating in this kind of discussion (psy-chodynamically, 'resistance'), it gradually became clear that she did not get angry very often and clearly had the self-image of being a placid, competent and pleasant mother. In situations when she might be legitimately cross, for example, with the children, they would jolly her out of it and she had all the while to internalise her aggression. Thoughts of this kind seemed relatively new to her, but she was encouraged to consider them and a further appointment was arranged for six weeks.

Generally, throughout this initial phase, Mrs Finley presented as an extremely passive patient awaiting a cure for her illness, whilst the therapists searched diligently for the solution. In the process, however, Mrs Finley was often experienced by therapists as being quite powerful, invoking feelings of impotence, frustration and some annoyance in the fact of sustained and worsening complaints. It was, then, at this point that the idea of shifting to a family therapy approach was suggested.

Management: phase II

During the subsequent three months, Mrs Finley attended on a further four occasions—the more salient two of which were conjoint family sessions including Mr and Mrs Finley and, on one occasion, their daughter, together with the psychiatrist and the social worker.

At the first of these, Mrs Finley's clinical condition was essentially unchanged. Some degree of improvement in the depressive symptoms had occurred, but she now had a new and prominent complaint of severe head-ache. The family dynamics were reviewed in the presence of her husband. It was decided at this stage to withdraw the antidepressant medication, leaving her only a small dose of anxiolytic.

At the following appointment (when Mrs Finley was seen alone) it was found that the depressive symptoms had substantially remitted; the headache, however, remained troublesome and severe. In addition, there was a further letter from the general practitioner expressing anxiety about this and suggest-ing re-referral to the teaching hospital neurologist she had seen previously. This was arranged, and at the subsequent appointment the report confirmed the opinion that no significant organic pathology existed and no further neurological investigation was required. The headache had, in fact, cleared up, but there was a return of minor symptoms of anxiety and depression.

The final appointment of this phase was a further conjoint family session. Mrs Finley felt unable to invite her son and, in the presence of the daughter, the session made a slow start. Eventually, the group 'thawed' as the family turned with some enthusiasm to the discussion of their dynamics. Ultimately, some-what to Mrs Finley's surprise, both her husband and daughter expressed a good deal of sympathy and support, and a willingness to share with her the everyday frustrations and unhappiness as she experienced them. The co-therapists thought Mrs Finley was sufficiently aware of her tendency to use denial and symptom-formation (including somatisation) as a coping mechanism, particularly in respect of feelings of anger, to suggest that the future management should consist of more intensive (weekly) psychotherapy with the social worker. Additionally, a small dose of mono-amine oxidase inhibitor (MAOI) was prescribed, to be supervised by the general practitioner.

Management: phase III

Beginning the following week, Mrs Finley saw the social worker, initially weekly but later at more spaced intervals, for a total of ten occasions over the next four months. During the first individual session she talked (for the first time) with feeling about the loss of two best friends of twenty years' standing, who had returned to Wales a few weeks before the onset of the original anxiety symptoms. In subsequent sessions (also contrary to previous statements that her family life had been uncomplicated) she recalled that her son had been premature, that he had suffered with an infantile hiatus hernia and had required to be fed hourly for the first six months of life. Her husband was unable to help much at this time because he was depressed following the death of both his father and brother, and that the boy had been a very delicate child who had vomited virtually daily to the age of about ten years and was also asthmatic. Also, her own father (whom she had reported to be in good health) was, in fact, severley demented. He had had a fall between her initial and second appointments and, at about the end of phase I (above), had been admitted to an old persons' home; he had failed to recognise her on her last visit. Further, at about the middle of phase II, she had obtained a new job which she liked, and she talked at considerable length about how strongly she had disliked her old job (again, contrary to her previous report).

During this period, her clinical condition steadily improved and she progressively reduced her level of antidepressant medication. She made arrangements to visit her old friends. Her appearance became smarter, she had her hair done. Later the family had a successful holiday together, and she was able to talk realistically about her worries about her father dying. She said she thought that the condition had become more serious at the point at which the general practitioner had suggested that she should see a psychiatrist, because 'it meant I was a nutcase!' By the end of four months in phase II (i.e. ten months from the initial referral), she was 'back to her old self'.

Regular contact was terminated at this point. A review appointment two months later revealed that she had remained well, was socially active and (with the general practitioner's agreement) had taken no medication for some weeks. Telephone follow-up four months later confimed that she had remained symptom-free.

COMMENT

Mental Health Aspects

The clinical picture presented by Mrs Finley was clouded by a mixture of neurotic features of an affective nature. She was initially diagnosed as having 'anxiety state' due to the combination of panic and somatic symptoms which she showed. Later, she displayed clear signs of depression, including lowered mood, feelings of helplessness and sleep difficulty. The fact that these appeared in a person of previously sound personality, and in the apparent absence of either organic or social precipitants, made her condition initially perplexing. This mixture of signs and symptoms and even the presentation is one commonly encountered by clinicians in practice. Also, drug-based treatment alone was not sufficient to resolve the acute episode. Improvement was not hampered by organic factors so much as psychological ones (e.g. denial and repression). The combination of mild drug regime and psychologically orientated treatment, prepared to look both at historical and situational antecedents, eventually produced the best result which, in reality, is very often the case.

Casework Aspects

There is nothing particularly unusual about this client and her problems. The case is described as an example of out-patient work in a District General Hospital unit where close disciplinary collaboration is the everyday routine. The management fell into three fairly distinct phases which illustrate aspects of the different, but overlapping, contributions of the social worker and psychiatrist.

In thinking about teamwork, clear 'role definition' among team members allows for rational decisions about 'role differentiation' and 'role blurring' (neither of which alone is, of course, a universal panacea).

Role differentiation is illustrated in this case in the following ways. Certain aspects have fairly strong medical implications (e.g. the assessment of somatic symptoms, referral to a neurologist, the management of a drug regime) and the input is by a psychiatrist. Other aspects, most obviously in phase III, require the input of the social worker. Note the patient's suggestion that her anxiety was increased by psychiatric referral, and the inference that her use of denial was enhanced in the sessions in which the psychiatrist participated, whereas the individual relationship with the social worker was easier and more productive. This highlights an important difference in roles concerning insanity ascriptions, for it is normally the psychiatrist alone who has the authority to uphold or refute formally those informal pronouncements of madness which have already been made or assumed by the lay person (and her family). The social worker does not legitimately have this power. We may speculate that the absence of such power was itself helpful in relieving Mrs

Finley's anxiety. Furthermore, the role of the social worker carries with it the implication that the problem is not necessarily or solely a medical one, but is susceptible to a non-medical solution in which the client participates actively.

In addition, whether we like it or not, in most out-patient settings it is easier for weekly sessions to be provided by a team member other than the psychiatrist (in this case, the social worker); and the intensity of contact during Phase III may well have contributed to the progress being made at this stage. In retrospect, the team has wondered whether even more social work input—perhaps investigation of the patient's social network—could have been helpful; the son was never seen and a home visit (perhaps wrongly) was not contemplated at any time.

Role blurring is evident in the common commitment of psychiatrist and social worker to a patient search for social and psychological determinants of Mrs Finley's troubles, including conjoint assessment (the routine practice at this clinic) and a co-therapy to the patient individually, to the marital pair and the family group. A high level of mutual respect and trust exists between the workers in this case.

The striking contrast between the denial of significant underlying problems in phase I and the material that emerged in phase II cannot, we believe, be accounted for by poor history-taking or by anything obviously threatening in the situation; the interviews throughout were unhurried and conducted with gentleness and sensitivity. Yet it became equally obvious that they were perceived as threatening by the patient.

There is a strong suggestion that this perceived threat derived in part from Mrs Finley's fear of losing control and being pronounced insane (and ultimately hospitalised). It is reasonable, therefore, to speculate that the factors underlying the development of sufficient trust between patient and social worker to permit the disclosure of the putatively significant material in phase III include: the less threatening nature of a social work setting and role (although a similar interview room in the same building was used); the firmer boundaries and structure imposed by regular weekly sessions of a set length, together with a shift in orientation and expectation away from a passive patient/disease metaphor; the sense of 'permission' conveyed by the family meetings in phase II; and (possibly) some sense of reassurance about the absence of physical pathology conveyed in phases I and II.

15 Mrs M.:
Social Services and a 'bag lady'

CASE HISTORY

Phase I: The First Referral

Mrs M. presented herself in the area Social Services office with a bizarre story of eviction from local lodgings. Bizarre enough for me to interview her in depth before referring her to the local Housing Department. Mrs M. was in her middle forties, and until five years previously had been a manageress of a bakers' shop. She gave up the job because she believed everyone had turned against her and, as her flat was tied to the job, she became homeless. She floated between various furnished rooms, gradually losing or leaving behind most of her belongings. Most of what remained she was able to carry about in several plastic bags with the name of a large supermarket chain printed on the sides.

She usually moved because of problems with the landlord or other residents. She had entered a short-lived marriage in which she was seriously physically abused. She had also developed an interest in psychic matters and had become convinced that she was a 'medium'. Indeed, she had taken to dressing in a Romany style although she was of Yorkshire origin. She had no family.

The only constant factor in Mrs M.'s life during this long period was a general practitioner who had been willing to keep her on as a patient despite the frequent moves. The doctor was willing to support my assessment of her as a single 'vulnerable' person in order to establish her eligibility for accommodation with the local Housing Department. He also confirmed that Mrs M. had begun to drink heavily. To the best of his knowledge, Mrs M. had not previously had any psychiatric treatment.

She lasted only three days in the bed and breakfast accommodation provided by the Housing Department but they continued to view her as both homeless and 'vulnerable' as she moved through a succession of brief stays in the spare room or on living-room floors of friends and acquaintances. Throughout this period, I acted as a befriender and negotiated with the

Housing Department, where necessary and occasionally with some of the people with whom she stayed. I often ended up storing her belongings for a few days in the office storeroom.

Eventually, after nine months of waiting, she was rehoused in her own one-bed maisonette with its own entrance. I assisted her in getting a grant from the Department of Health and Social Security (DHSS) for furnishings. Soon, Mrs M. had furnished her flat, mostly from local secondhand furniture stores, and in very much her own style. Now that she had her own housing, her drinking reduced significantly. Five months after she had moved into the flat, I withdrew from working with her.

Phase II: Re-referral

I had occasionally seen Mrs M. in the street, but not for over a year. I became reinvolved because she began calling at the office regularly, making bizarre complaints about her neighbours.

Her physical condition and appearance seemed to have deteriorated over the previous six months and I agreed to work with her again. This entailed initially seeing her in the office. Mrs M. told me convoluted stories which seemed to vary in complexity, being sometimes more and sometimes less understandable. The main difficulties were that Mrs M. felt unable to go out and about as she had done in the past, because she believed that the whole of London was involved in a war. She believed that she was receiving messages telepathically from Saudi Arabia and would stop in mid-sentence to listen to them. She also maintained that her downstairs neighbour was entering her house at night and changing her clothing for identical items which were then giving her evil messages. I was surprised to find, on visiting her house, that all of her belongings had disappeared and she literally had only the cooker, her bed and the clothes she stood up in. She told me she had given the rest away to prevent them from being exchanged.

I tried to work with her at this stage by making clear the things I could not accept, for instance, that all of London was at war, and to deal instead with the more rational problems which I could accept. Over the course of three months working with her, I became convinced that she was suffering from a psychiatric illness which would only respond to medication. I arranged a joint visit with the local consultant psychiatrist and we agreed that she needed treatment. Mrs M. was not willing to accept the proposed treatment as an out-patient. We considered compulsory hospital admission but decided against it, however, and agreed that I should continue working with her, trying to get her to accept a voluntary admission.

Mrs M. was asking for help from me to deal with the delusional and halllucinatory aspects of her illness since I had offered practical help in other areas. I made it clear that the only help I felt able to offer at the time was to get her to hospital. Nevertheless, I continued to be willing to see her in the office or, if necessary, at home to listen to her. Mrs M. agreed to visit the local psychiatric hospital with me on the understanding that if she did not wish to stay I would bring her back home again. This we did, but she decided, after an hour and a half, that she did not want to stay there and I returned her home.

Within three days Mrs M. had come to the office early in the morning in a crisis. She was extremely scared and very distressed, believing that her skin was falling from her body in strips. She was amazed that I could not see it too, and was desperately pleading for help. I suggested that the only help I could offer was admission to the ward we had visited. This time she agreed and I arranged informal admission through the consultant psychiatrist. This time, however, I would have been prepared to use compulsion if she had refused an informal admission.

I visited Mrs M. in hospital. She was not happy there, but quickly responded to medication and lost her more obvious psychiatric symptoms. She was discharged after six weeks. Although still blaming me for her admission, Mrs M. chose not to be discharged until I returned from a short period of leave.

Phase III: Rehabilitation and Resettlement

Following her discharge, Mrs M. went through a period of gradually building depression as she realised that she had no belongings. She still had some hints of delusional thinking, but worked with me to get DHSS grants for clothing and furniture (this time supplied on the understanding that I would supervise the expenditure). Mrs M. gradually stopped attending out-patients appointments and stopped taking any medication. I tried to link Mrs M. with the local day centre for the mentally ill. She felt angry that I saw her as 'mad' and felt that she did not need to use the centre.

Mrs M. became gradually more withdrawn, not venturing out much. I challenged her again over the use of the centre and pointed out that in the past she was always out and about and never had enough time; now she was just sitting (literally) doing nothing. She agreed to start attending the centre on the principle that she would know when she no longer needed it.

Mrs M.'s depression reached a crisis about two months after discharge from hospital. She was now eating virtually nothing and taking very little fluid. I convinced Mrs M. to go with me to an out-patient appointment with her consultant psychiatrist. Mrs M.'s blood pressure was very high due to her reduced fluid intake. We considered compulsory admission on the grounds that Mrs M.'s depression was seriously endangering her physical health.

We decided against admission. Instead, we decided to take the risk and leave the client at home with support from me. I was able to offer visits three times a week to do shopping with her and check on her fluid intake—Mrs M. used to keep her used tea bags to show me!

We maintained Mrs M. at home for three months like this with gradual reduction in my visiting and a gradual increase in Mrs M.'s attendance at the day centre. I also arranged home visits from the specialist occupational therapist (OT) aimed at reviving Mrs M.'s cooking and home care skills.

The first positive signs were Mrs M. becoming involved at the centre in the pottery classes and beginning to refurnish her home with bits and pieces from the local junk shops. She remained depressed, however, and my own work with her largely consisted of reassuring her that the depression would eventually lift, being hopeful for her as she was not hopeful for herself.

The breakthrough seemed to come during a review at the day centre when Mrs M. expressed her great anger at us all (and me in particular), feeling we were pushing her to do things she did not want to do, interfering in her life. She told us she did not want any of us to visit again until she invited us. We all agreed to abide by her request, seeing her anger as a positive sign.

Within a week there was a significant, almost startling, change for the better and her depression lifted. Shortly afterwards, I was invited back to work with Mrs M. and within six weeks she no longer had any time in her life for the day centre or need to work with me.

COMMENT

Mental Health Aspects

In many respects this case is an excellent example of the difficulties and pitfalls of arriving at a clear diagnosis in psychiatry. Probably the best rule of thumb seems to be, in practice, that one simply has to wait and see how the patient's condition unfolds over time.

The most significant facts in respect of her mental disorder were as follows. Mrs M. coped into her late thirties and then developed a condition which appears to have been most clearly marked by delusions of persecution (these delusions were also accompanied by auditory hallucinations and formal thought disorder, i.e. thought blocking). She was known, and we can presume seen, by her general practitioner over this period, and also examined in hospital with no organic factors being identified. There was gradual, insidious onset with personality still very much intact and increasingly eccentric behaviour. These signs tend to confirm the condition of paranoid schizophrenia, a major functional mental illness particularly associated with middle age onset. Nevertheless, as is all to often the case, other factors emerged over time. Her depression could have argued for a mixed, 'schizo-affective' disorder (i.e. schizophrenia with an affective component). Finally, the fact that she was known to drink heavily could, in fact, have been either a causal factor (i.e. depression and psychotic symptoms as a result of alcohol abuse) or an effect (i.e. 'symptomatic' alcoholism) and, although unlikely to be undetected in the face of so much psychiatric investigation, could have confused the picture at various points in the case.

Casework Aspects

Establishing a positive casework relationship

This case illustrates that the basic principles of good counselling and casework are no different for mentally disordered clients than they are for any other client group, though the mental health social worker requires specific skills in applying these basic principles to her or his clients.

Empathy, genuineness and respect are widely recognised as key ingredients in establishing effective helping relationships. One of the more difficult tasks of the mental health social worker is to communicate these attitudes effectively to a client who is acutely psychotic. The worker's challenge is to communicate concern and empathy regarding the distress the psychotic patient is experiencing, demonstrate respect for the client by accepting that for the client the psychotic experience is very real, while being honest with client about the worker's different perception of reality. That the social worker in this case was effectively able to meet this challenge, probably had much to do with his ability to maintain an ongoing relationship with his client, and the positive outcome of his work.

Risk assessment and management

Throughout the social worker's involvement in this case, he was required continually to assess and reassess the risks presented, and decide on how to manage these risks. The worker's knowledge of the client and his positive relationship with her enabled him to support his client in the community through quite high-risk circumstances that may have resulted in compulsory hospital admission of a less well-known client. This was particularly so during Mrs M.'s period of depression. At this point, the social worker identified that there was a significant risk to this client's physical health due to her reduced fluid intake and was able to intervene, in a very practical way, to lessen this risk without admitting her to hospital. This illustrated the importance of specifically and clearly identifying risks in order to make equally specific and clear plans of intervention to lessen risks effectively.

Practical support as part of the casework relationship

Mrs M.'s social worker offered her very practical support on a number of occasions, something which he viewed as an integral part of his role as a mental health worker. He helped her to obtain suitable accommodation and furniture, and was willing, when necessary, to offer his office for the storage of some of his client's belongings. During Mrs M.'s period of depression, the social worker's practical help included such basic activities as helping her with shopping. Some might argue that it is inappropriate for trained and experienced social work staff to carry out such practical tasks, and that such things are better delegated to others. Certainly, such work does not obviate the need for the direct, therapeutic work for which social workers are professionally trained. Rather it supplements it, for example, helping to sustain clients over difficult periods when they are not in a mental state suitable for insight-oriented work. The offer and provision of practical support is sometimes the most effective way a worker can establish or maintain a positive working relationship with a client, and this is particularly so in cases of very long-term work involving clients with chronic mental health problems.

Ongoing involvement

This case details work carried out by one worker over a five-year period. Although the social worker concerned was not continually involved with the client for the entire period, he was available to offer support to Mrs M., and sometimes very intensive support, as and when necessary. In looking at the case, it would appear that the relationship the worker was able to build with client over a lengthy period of time both allowed more risks to be taken and made them more likely to be successful.

This highlights the need for continuity of care for people with mental health problems. Here the worker was involved prior to her first psychiatric treatment (phase I), remained in contact while the client was hospitalised (phase II) and finally, was a significant factor in the process of rehabilitation (phase III). Other professionals, as in this case was true of the client's general practitioner, may have been involved for even longer. It is essential to recognise that for many clients, the disabilities imposed by their mental health problems mean they will require professional support over a significant proportion of their life, rather than merely one-off work during a crisis. Moreover, the more we can develop ongoing support networks for clients, the more effectively we will be able to intervene when they experience a crisis.

Taking and giving back control

This case illustrates well a dilemma involved in much of social work, particularly in mental health social work where the worker has been appointed by a local authority to carry out the functions of an 'approved' social worker under the provisions of the *Mental Health Act* 1983 for England and Wales. A general aim in social work is to enable clients to take control of their own lives more effectively. Paradoxically, sometimes to achieve this aim we need, at least for a time, to do the opposite, that is to take control from the clients. In mental health work it is sometimes necessary, through the use of mental health legislation and/or forceful persuasion, to insist that a client receive help or treatment they have neither requested nor want. It is equally important for the worker to know when to return control to the client.

In the case of Mrs M., the social worker persuaded her to accept voluntary admission to hospital, but was prepared to use compulsion if necessary. He also persuaded Mrs M. to attend out-patient appointments and the day centre when she was otherwise inclined. Nonetheless, a major breakthrough for Mrs M. was when she was able to assert control over her own life by successfully persuading workers that they could visit only on her invitation. As stated above, an assessment of potential risk, based on detailed knowledge of the client's past behaviour and present condition, made this 'ego enhancing' work possible.

16 Mrs R.:
depression following a delayed grief reaction

CASE HISTORY

Mrs R. is a thirty-two-year old woman who was referred to the psychotherapy unit with depression. Her husband had died five years earlier. At the time of the referral, Mrs R. was feeling very miserable and unable to cope with her two children, Clive, aged seven, and Michael, aged five. Medical examinations had revealed no organic pathology related to her condition. Her general practitioner had been treating her with antidepressant medication with no effect. She was feeling particularly low in the evenings and had taken to using alcohol and abusing her medication in order to sleep.

Mrs R. had married when she was only eighteen, seeing this as a means of getting away from her family. Her husband had a cardiac problem which was familial in origin but, interestingly enough, she had gained very little knowledge of his condition and seems to have misunderstood or denied its probable outcome throughout her married life. Her husband had been reluctant to discuss his health with her and, as if this had not been sufficient to keep her poorly prepared for the eventuality of his death, she had felt further excluded by Mr R.'s brother, a doctor, who appears to have assumed authority in this area. Although Mr R. had managed to maintain a job, their activities had been considerably restricted due to his health. Nevertheless, Mrs R. recalled having had a good marriage with minimal conflict.

Mr R. died when Clive was two years old and Michael six months. Mrs R. had received considerable support from her parents and an uncle at this time and, at first, appeared to cope remarkably well. She had maintained an independent home and cared for the children. At about the time that Clive started school, she began to experience difficulties and the problems increased in severity over the following two-year period. Initially, her parents and friends had been sympathetic and supportive. As her mood deteriorated, however, she began to feel that she had pushed people away. Her parents became unable to deal with her and finally withdrew from contact, thus increasing the stress on her. The younger child, Michael, was showing behaviour problems by the time of the mother's referral.

The casework with Mrs R. fell into three phases and lasted over an eight-month period. The initial plan was to see Mrs R. on an individual basis. The impression was that her depression coincided with a developmental stage in the family (that of the children beginning school and becoming less dependent on her), and that her depression reflected her difficulty in adjusting to this, compounded by her status as a widow. In fact, as can be seen, two further stages of the casework were required.

Stage I—Individual Work (0-5 months)

The initial contract was to see Mrs R. for six weeks in order to determine whether or not individual casework was going to be useful to her. In the first session, Mrs R. presented her feelings of depression and isolation, seeing them as related to her current circumstances as a single-parent family. She also spent time describing her difficulties with Michael. Michael was often beyond her control and seemed irritable and miserable, particularly in the mornings. Mrs R. thought her own moodiness and irritability with Michael were causing some of his problems. She was resistant to talking about the past and maintained that she could not remember much about her own childhood.

Over the next five sessions Mrs R. was able to become more reflective and used the time to look at her marriage. In part this was due to having an opportunity to talk on a regular basis. Also, it was due, in part, to the fact that for the first time since her husband had died, she had begun a relationship with a man. She was extremely surprised by the well of sadness still inside her. She was also surprised at the acute feelings of disloyalty she was experiencing in beginning to see another man.

After the first six sessions, progress was reviewed and it was agreed to continue on for a further six months to look at the unresolved grief and deal with the presenting problems.

It was very difficult for Mrs R. to accept how profoundly her husband's death was still affecting her, particularly under social pressure to 'have got it over by now'. She felt that there must be something wrong with her to still have been feeling that way. Gradually, she realised that the initial 'coping well' had been adaptive to the needs of her new baby at that time. Likewise, she concluded, 'rejoicing at birth' and 'grieving a death' cannot proceed simultaneously. This helped her to recognise that her current depression was understandable and could, therefore, be dealt with. During this time some of Mrs R.'s symptoms became worse as she became more in touch with her feelings rather than repressing them. Coinciding with this, Michael's behaviour deteriorated and some family sessions were arranged.

Stage II—Family Work (Month 6)

When his mother had taken him to school in the morning, Michael was running back out after her and was later tearful in school. At home, when disciplined, he ran from the house and into the street returning up to half an hour later. Clearly these behaviours were both distressing to Mrs R. and dangerous to himself.

Two family interviews were arranged. The first looked at the problems as seen by each of the three family members. It was apparent that the children were concerned about their mother, particularly when she was sad, and were fearful lest something should happen to her. They were both anxious about her being alone, and this was reflected, at least in part, in Michael's reluctance to go to school. The family all agreed that there were lots of arguments and the children were not clear about the limits to their behaviour. Mrs R. agreed that she was often inconsistent and felt a great burden in having to carry all of the discipline as well as all of the nurturing alone.

At the second meeting, we constructed a family tree to ascertain from where support might come. The exercise showed another death (a year previously) of an uncle. This uncle had been unmarried and had lived with the maternal grandparents, offering a male figure of importance for the children. On the parental side, there were other siblings of their father who had died as well. The use of the family tree enabled the issue of death to be raised between the three. This freed the children to express their anxieties. Also, at this meeting we worked out strategies for discipline to which they all agreed.

These two meetings allowed the family to verbalise their anxieties and had the effect of freeing Michael from acting these out. They were also able to tackle the presenting problem of discipline as a family.

Stage III—Assistance with Parenting Skills (months 7 and 8)

During this stage casework continued with Mrs R. with meetings every two to three weeks. The increased time between meetings reinforced the fact that Mrs R. was gradually gaining control. Mrs R.'s depressive symptoms were decreasing and although she was prone to 'bad days' these were increasingly less frequent.

The casework up to this point had enabled her to explore her grief and some of her past. The last stage was more task-orientated and aimed at dealing with specific problems in relation to her roles with the children. A particular stress point in this area was associated with getting the children off to school in the mornings. Normally they would wake in an irritable mood and before even getting dressed, Mrs R. found herself shouting at them. This would continue until they left for school and Mrs R. would be left feeling terrible. We spent time working out different strategies for dealing with this time of day with rewards like playing a game together for increased co-operation. This approach to problems was successful and dramatically altered the mood in the home. It also enabled Mrs R. to gain confidence.

At the outcome, the case showed some degree of success in two important respects. First, Mrs R.'s depression lifted through the period of intervention and she was not hospitalised. She was able to gain some understanding of why she had become so depressed and to identify warning signals of any recurrence. Second, she was able to handle the children more consistently and confidently. Michael's behaviour improved rapidly as a result.

COMMENT

Mental Health Aspects

Mrs R.'s condition was a very common one, encountered often in clinical practice. Her symptoms, though distressing to her, achieved neither the quality nor intensity of a major depressive illness. For example, she did not suffer from delusions, intense suicidal ideation or the many biological features of a psychotic condition. Her neurotic or reactive condition can be closely related to loss, a common aetiological factor in such conditions. The irritability, difficulty in getting off to sleep and abuse of prescribed medication or alcohol shown by Mrs R. are factors often encountered in such cases. The psychological feelings of guilt, however, were quite real, as were the depressed mood and threatened self-confidence. There is often a temptation to underestimate the seriousness of such conditions. Experience, however, teaches that people with 'mild' depressions should never be dismissed as they are perfectly capable of suddenly and dramatically ending their own life or becoming a danger to others, such as young dependent children (Hudson, 1982, p. 37). Mrs R.'s proclivity for mixing drugs and alcohol, and the conflict she was having with her young children were both causes of concern throughout treatment.

In the case of loss and subsequent grief, it is sometimes difficult to distinguish between the normal and pathological. Here, depression emerged many years after the loss, long after one might have anticipated that the feelings of grief would have been satisfactorily resolved. This may well have happened when it did for several reasons, though the reawakening of sexual feelings, as with Mrs R., sometimes long suppressed, appears a strong possible cause here. When such reactions happen, both the psychological sources of the depression and its social consequences can (if the client has a suitably stable personality) be dealt with by casework or psychotherapy as opposed to a simple reliance on drug therapy which, in this instance, appears not to have been effective anyway. (For a more complete consideration of the effectiveness of psychotherapy under such conditions see Hudson, 1982, Chapter 4.)

Casework Aspects

Mrs R.'s case demonstrates a number of learning points for casework with clients whose conditions are similar. Perhaps, the most salient are as follows.

First, problems, as they were presented by Mrs R. and clients like her, may need to be redefined before work can begin. In this case, Mrs R. did not perceive her husband's death as part of her current predicament. It took time and patience for it to emerege and the client needed to come to a point where she could consciously accept her husband's loss as a source of distress. The task of the professional worker was to facilitate this in the light of a good history and a sound initial assessment.

Second, workers must be prepared to reassess a case. Here, the family needed attention during the casework described and the focus of work altered accordingly. This necessitated the use of different methods of intervention at different points in casework. Hence, individual psychodynamic casework, family intervention and task-centred casework were all utilised. Each method was different from, but built on to what had emerged from, the previous stage. Experience suggests that there is value in a degree of 'eclecticism' (i.e. a worker possessing knowledge of how to apply various methods) as it is sometimes required by circumstances. In the case of Mrs R., the principal alternatives seem to have been either to have used the same method in every instance, no matter how inappropriate it may have seemed (i.e. to have taken on both of the children independently as casework clients), or to have risked referring some parts of the work to other professionals.

Third, the frequency of sessions can be used to locate control and responsibility clearly back with the client. The shift in emphasis was clearly signalled by this technique between stages II and III.

17 Sarah and John:
a case of 'who's the client?'

CASE HISTORY

The psychiatrist with whom I worked recently believes strongly in the value of social assessments for psychiatric patients. At his weekly out-patient clinic, he routinely asked the social worker to interview the relative who usually accompanies each new patient; it was through one such interview that I met John and his wife Sarah.

Sarah had been referred by her general practitioner for 'the failure to cope' syndrome, together with poor sleep, considerable weight loss, bouts of crying and mild agoraphobia. She was a twenty-six year-old health visitor, who had been off work for the previous three months. I was asked to see her husband John, a thirty-one-year-old engineer who had accompanied Sarah to the clinic.

John had made copious notes about his wife's problems, and it was difficult to separate him sufficiently from these in order to get a more spontaneous account of the situation. He appeared to lack confidence, but at the same time to have put himself in the role of therapist who seeks guidance on managing a problematic client. I learnt that Sarah was normally a person with high standards but little confidence, that her father had had a depressive breakdown some years previously, and that she viewed both parents as rather cold and critical. She did not feel close to either of her parents or her two younger brothers. John described several possible precipitating factors in the six months before her symptoms became so severe that she had to stop work. She had changed her job and felt that her new nursing officer was critical of her; partly because of this she had suggested giving up work to start a family, but John had disagreed. Her father had become ill and she worried about him. On her way to visit him she had had a minor car accident and had not been back to work since then.

Whilst the history was emerging from John, the psychiatrist was obtaining a similar story from Sarah. However, their accounts differed significantly in the emphasis that Sarah placed on wanting to start a family. The general practitioner had prescribed antidepressant medication which was already taking effect; the psychiatrist's diagnosis was that she was suffering from mild agoraphobia, that she had had a depressive illness which was responding to medication, and that the main precipitating factor had been disagreements in the marriage over whether to start a family. Marital therapy was prescribed and the couple agreed to see me weekly, initially for six sessions.

In the first joint interview, Sarah appreared rather quiet, allowing John to do much of the talking. They agreed, however, that both lacked confidence and that because of John's dogmatism and Sarah's sensitivity to criticism, it was difficult for them to discuss their difficulties. They focused on Sarah's agoraphobia which contributed to her problems in getting back to work. Both seemed eager for 'homework' and we agreed that they would make a list of phobic situations in ascending order of difficulty. The question of starting a family was briefly raised, with John saying flatly that they could not afford it and Sarah indicating that she did not feel emotionally secure enough to cope with the responsibility.

During the next five sessions, John took a delight in describing his supervision of Sarah's graded exposure to the phobic situations that she had listed, and it was noticeable how her confidence and mood level improved to the point where she began to make arrangements to return to work. She role-played what she wanted to say to her nursing officer, talked of making more friends and possibly occasionally having an evening out with 'the girls' from work. In contrast, John admitted that he found it hard to give up the role of 'therapist', that he liked having Sarah at home and that he was not sure he could cope with her new-found confidence and wish for more independence. He began to describe problems that he had both at work, in being appropriately assertive, and with his own family, whom he felt to be critical of him, continually undermining any confidence that he had. In the sixth session, he was on the verge of tears. He described his fear that he could not cope if they started a family, as Sarah would give a baby all her attention, and he would be unable to be a good enough father. He talked at length about his unhappiness as a child and how he feared that he would turn out like his own critical, rejecting parents. He could see that it had been easier for him to focus on his wife's problems rather than his own, but that as Sarah became more independent he was left facing his own insecurity.

Both felt that they would benefit from more sessions, focusing particularly on the problems described by John, and on communication in the marriage. We agreed to continue to meet weekly for an hour, for as long as appeared to be useful.

For several months the discussions were stormy, with one or the other frequently in tears. Sarah did not particularly want to listen to John's difficulties, so similar to the ones that she had recently been discussing herself. She could not readily understand that he felt threatened by the independence that she was beginning to enjoy. At times they seemed like a squabbling brother and sister, treating me like the parent who was expected to arbitrate. When this was suggested to them, they agreed that this was, perhaps, the case.

They began to mention sexual difficulties, problems in describing what each wanted of the other, what words to use, fear that the other would ignore what was being requested. We again had homework at the end of each session, a method that both appreciated, joining in with some enthusiasm to decide on the tasks. The latter varied from setting aside time each evening (instead of watching television) to listen to each other, to some techniques related more specifically to their sexual difficulties, e.g. sensate focus as described by Masters and Johnson in *Human Sexual Inadequacy*. The sexual problems, however, were not the main area of difficulty, but rather illustrative of how far each could express their needs and have them met. John emphasised his need for reassurance that Sarah would appreciate him. Sarah wanted John to be more adventurous in the way they spent their free time. She persuaded him to go out more often with her; they joined a dancing class, went to the cinema and, gradually, began to enjoy life more.

Nine months after the initial referral from the general practitioner, Sarah announced that she was pregnant. The pregnancy had been 'unplanned', but John, though apprehensive, appeared to be pleased. The sessions continued until three weeks before the baby's birth, often focusing on John's fears, how he felt his own father had been a very poor role model, how he would need reassurance from Sarah that he still mattered to her.

Postscript

Three weeks later I received a telephone call from John announcing the birth of their son, saying that all was well, and that they would contact me should they need further help. He sounded very pleased about the baby, though still apprehensive. Five months later, Sarah wrote in response to a letter from me inquiring how they were. She said that the baby had strengthened the relationship, that John was enjoying fatherhood, that with her help he had coped with redundancy, and had now found a job. A successful Christening party had been held (an event that both had been dreading), and they were now looking forward to the future. Sarah expressed thanks for the help received and said that she would contact me should difficulties arise in the future.

COMMENT

A number of useful links between theory and practice emerge from this case. Some of these concern Sarah's illness, some concern assessment, and more particularly treatment.

Mental Health Aspects

Sarah's major diagnosis was that she suffered from a depressive illness and, as is common, we found possible predisposing factors (a family history of depression), personality factors (high standards, a great sensitivity towards any criticism) and social stresses, several of which immediately preceded the breakdown (problems at work and in the marriage). In addition it is common for people presenting with depressive symptoms to have problems of anxiety, which may manifest themselves in agoraphobia. The social history was a valuable aid to diagnosis and revealed more social stresses than would have arisen solely from the psychiatrist's interview. By involving the husband at the outset, we not only obtained useful information, but also acknowledged the important role of the relative in our understanding of the case.

Medication played a major part in lifting the depression sufficiently to allow us to work on precipitating factors. This had been initiated by the general practitioner and was already showing results by the time that Sarah was seen at the clinic. Had she still been severely depressed, then the involvement of the couple in marital work might well have been inappropriate.

Casework Aspects

Why was the marital relationship chosen as the appropriate focus for treatment? This was partly because of Sarah's emphasis on the importance of her starting a family, partly because John presented initially as having some problems of his own but also as being keen to be involved. I felt from meeting both in the out-patient clinic that there was a rapport between us, that a useful working relationship could be created. Having decided to see them together, the focus became their interaction in the present, and some of the most useful interpretations were made about their behaviour during interviews.

Research has indicated that clients prefer a task-centred approach, and this couple confirmed this by indicating at the end of the seventeen months that they felt that the 'homework' had been the single most helpful factor. One could, of course, argue that is simply that they were unaware of other levels of work, e.g. that through seeing me as a parental figure, they were able to internalise an image of parenthood that enabled them to mature sufficiently to face the task of parenthood themselves.

Literature on casework helps us to distinguish between the presenting problem and what lies underneath. In the case of Sarah and John, Sarah was presented as the client. In taking on this role, she was both expressing and masking the problems experienced by her husband. Her recovery exposed his difficulties and the underlying problems in the relationship.

American writing on psychotherapy indicates that those clients who benefit most from this method are young, attractive, rich, verbal, intelligent and successful (YARVIS). The third of these attributes is less relevant when one does not have to pay directly for treatment, but maybe the other attributes have some relevance in this case. Some would argue that social work should not be taken up with cases like theirs; as the medication was working, why see Sarah and John at all? I would argue that the time spent was a good investment. Sarah was helped to return to work more quickly than might otherwise have happened; without insight into the underlying problems, and under pressure from the marriage, relapse might well have occurred, or John might have become a patient himself. So far, several years further on, there has been no referral.

One final point concerns the value of supervision. I had the opportunity to discuss this case regularly in a supervision group. This was of great benefit in clarifying aims and methods, looking at transference relationships, and generally enabled me to become more objective in my work.

18 Sheila:

a 'suicide' attempt

CASE HISTORY

Sheila tried to kill herself; to be accurate she took an overdose. She spent one night in hospital where she was 'pumped out' by casualty staff. By all accounts they are the ones who try to make the experience as unpleasant as possible—to deter time-wasters from a repeat attempt. The duty psychiatrist offered her an appointment which she kept (only about one in five of appointments following overdose are actually kept). The psychiatrist referred her to me for help with the financial problems which triggered the overdose. He was reluctant to treat her with medication, but did prescribe an antidepressant when he was sure that her symptoms of anxiety and depression warranted it. The combination of this treatment with supportive and occasionally insight-oriented casework ultimately produced a significant improvement in her mental health and her ability to cope with her problems.

When she was referred to me she was already a 'case' of the local social work team. Her eight-year-old son was a problem at school. He misbehaved and was not popular with the teachers. He got into trouble breaking windows with some older children. The case was of low priority in the local office. The social worker and I liaised; she decided that as I was involved they would close the case.

Interviews took place in the front room of a two-up two-down terraced council house in the middle of a derelict inner city area. Remarkably, the interviews were rarely interrupted by other relatives, children or neighbours.

When I first visited Sheila she was worried, and she remained worried in varying degrees for most of the time I knew her. When she was most worried she did not talk to me for long periods. We would sit together through the silence—the interviewing equivalent of a 'black hole'. At other times she reported physical symptoms; she reported a lot of them, to the general practitioner as well, but they were never specifically related to an underlying physical condition. She variously reported eye ache, headache, leg ache, backache. Her preoccupation with her symptoms and her chronic lack of self-confidence did not endear her to those around her, who frequently voiced the opinion that she should 'pull herself together'. At a later stage, and this could be the subject of a whole case study in its own right, she became convinced that her nose was ugly, the wrong shape and badly needed plastic surgery. (This is known as 'dysmorphophobia'—see Goldberg et al., 1987.)

Sheila was divorced and had two children, Mark aged eight and Rebecca aged six. She had no previous history of psychiatric treatment and there was no family history, although her father, a policeman, had had to retire on grounds of ill-health. He soon became a central feature in our conversations. He was an authoritarian and had certainly contributed to her lowered self-esteem, by favouring his sons, being extremely critical and rigid, and by regarding Sheila as an 'incompetent'. Sheila married an attractive man who was very well-liked by her father, but who turned out to be a plausible liar, a wife-beater, a heavy drinker and a womaniser. She said, 'You have to see him when he's with me. He's completely different. They [the family] think he's a great laugh ..... huh! I can't understand him. Maybe he has a dual personality. I hate him. I don't want anything to do with him. He comes on Beccy's birthday and gives her expensive presents. I've told him to stop. How can I get him to stop? The court will have to do something. He can't afford these presents. He must be in enormous debt; or else he is conning "her" [his new girlfriend] out of her money. He's trying to buy the kids' affection.'

Her ex-husband was visiting the house uninvited and she eventually succeeded in keeping him away through her own efforts. At the start she was not confident enough about her own feelings or her ability to be assertive with him. When she was most anxious she found him threatening and frightening.

At the first interview she explained her predicament entirely in terms of her own incapacity. 'I can't cope. I just don't pay the bills. He doesn't give me the maintenance. I haven't got any money. I just pile them up [the bills] over there. I don't know why I can't do anything about them.' I look through them and suggest we try offering a small amount on a weekly basis to start to pay them off. I agree to find a grant towards them if she goes into the electricity, gas and housing offices to make each one an offer. We write all this down. I feel it is important to try to get her started on her own problems, but I don't know her well enough to know how she will respond to having to make the effort or how setbacks and failure might affect her. I hope that some success will help to raise her confidence level. This approach works, but nothing else changes.

She talks a lot about her ex-husband and her father. Her father has been depressed. She wants to know if it runs in families. He refuses to talk to Sheila or to her sister, who has also been divorced. We discuss how the family must have felt about her overdose and how they have responded. She is very ambivalent about her family. We explore her feelings about her father; the first few conversations end in tears. After a time he figures less in the conversation and a new figure appears. She is diffident about this relationship. It is with a much younger man who is single. This relationship began before she took the overdose, but she tells me about it only after several weeks. She describes him as 'obsessed' with her and the beginning of their relationship is certainly odd. I meet him. He is not odd. He is level-headed, mild mannered, and mature.

She is worried. She says, 'He is too young.' She is not convincing; she doesn't convince me, she doesn't convince him and she doesn't convince herself. They decide to marry. She wonders if everything will be all right; will everything work out? She is afraid that he, like others, will find her too much—her feelings about herself are projected onto others. Her boyfriend and to a lesser extent the psychiatrist, the general practitioner and I try to demonstrate to her that we won't be driven away by her 'bad' self.

Before they marry she tells me that her six-year-old daughter has a problem. This has been going on all the time I have been working with her but it is only now, several months later that she decides to tell me. She is soiling her pants. Has her (and our) preoccupation with her own problems led to neglect, or has the child really got a physical problem? Rebecca is seen by a paediatrician; he eliminates any physical problem.

Sheila and I agree to use a behavioural approach to the soiling problem, which is really a developmental delay. Through the use of increased contact between them, no punishment for 'dirty pants', and a system of rewards for clean ones we are able to establish proper control. I have included this final problem for the sake of completeness. It helps to illustrate the way in which she unfolded her problems one by one.

COMMENT

Mental Health Aspects

Sheila had a mixture of personality problems with moderate bouts of anxiety and depression. This combination is not unusual in cases in the community. Symptoms of anxiety and depression frequently coexist (Goldberg *et al.*, 1987) and a so-called 'minor' disorder of this sort is most successfully handled by a combination of drug treatment and simple psychotherapy (Butler and Pritchard, 1983).

The symptoms involving the belief that parts of the body, frequently the nose, are misshapen is not common and can occur in hysterical personality disorder (Goldberg *et al.*, 1987). In her case the idea did not become seriously 'over-valued' and she did not complain openly about it after her other symptoms and her social problems improved.

Relatives, friends and some doctors and social workers are apt to regard what appears to be continual preoccupation with physical symptoms as a nuisance. Members of the family are particularly likely to get fed up with it and to suggest that the client 'snap out of it'. This is not a helpful approach in most cases. Nor is it particularly helpful to regard the symptoms as 'understandable' in the context of the social problems. This rationalisation is sometimes used to refuse or deny responsibility for help. Simply because her circumstances are 'understandable' it does not mean they are untreatable.

Casework Aspects

The social work approach involved mixing several methods; a task-centred approach (in respect of financial problems), supportive and exploratory casework (in respect of her feelings and close relationships) and a behavioural approach (in respect of her daughter's bowel problem). The worker's relationship with Sheila was used to draw attention to her feelings about others, about herself and about the worker, and was used to demonstrate a sense of her own worth, by not accepting her own view of herself as unworthy of help.

Sheila did not present all her problems at once. The initial assessment failed to reveal a lot of the difficulties. She revealed them gradually. This might be called going at the client's pace. She put the problems in order—a practical presenting problem which precipitated an overdose; a chronic lack of self-confidence (as this was revealed the worker acknowledged, but then disregarded, her physical complaints), closely allied to her feelings about her father. Only after work was directed at this was she able to introduce the problem of her ex-husband, followed by the 'problem' of her boyfriend. Her daughter's problem was the last to be revealed.

The case was an open 'prevention' case in the local office, but work was focused exclusively on the son and the school. In such circumstances the case is classified as a child care case, but the main work needing to be done is on the various mental health problems. We know that large numbers of children who progress to care status have parents with serious mental health problems (Isaac et al., 1984).

19 Sue:
a client with personality problems

CASE HISTORY

In October 1982 a woman called Sue was referred to me by a doctor who had been seeing her as an out-patient during a six-month stay as a Senior Registrar at the psychiatric hospital where I work. The doctor, who wondered if psychotherapy was appropriate, asked me if I would assess Sue and decide from there. The brief period during which this psychiatrist had seen her was the first time in her twelve-year contact with local psychiatric services that any sort of regular individual counselling had been offered.

Sue was born in 1947, so was thirty-five at this time. She was bred in

Yorkshire, England of professional parents and has a brother. He is six years younger than Sue, is married with a young baby and has a successful career.

Sue felt that there were high expectations of her by her parents and she initially fulfilled her father's (a teacher) wish by starting teacher training. However, she became pregnant immediately upon beginning training, was abandoned by her boyfriend and her father initially refused her the house or any support. She subsequently had two unsuccessful marriages, the first to a lecturer who beat her and her child, the second to a blind teacher. She and her second husband are now in the process of divorcing at the husband's instigation. Her daughter is now 14 years old.

Her first 'breakdown' and hospital admission was in 1970, following the ending of her first marriage when she was twenty-three years old. Since that time she has had continuous contact with psychiatric services as an out-patient with admissions. Over the years several different diagnoses have been made at various times, including depressive illness (and manic depressive illness), agoraphobia and personality disorder. As might be expected with such varying diagnoses, a range of different treatments has been employed. Various drugs have been used, including lithium carbonate, lorazepam, thyroxine, clomipramine, and amitriptyline. Also, Sue has undergone transactional analysis, group therapy, marital therapy and sex therapy for a problem described as 'frigidity'.

It seemed that, as with many unhappy people who are not mentally ill, but who look for help and get shunted along into the psychiatric net, Sue was not a satisfying patient: she did not respond to treatment. The following comments, made in the medical file, reveal perhaps the frustrations of the practitioners as well as their biases and attitudes. It seems that they may have got caught up in recreating the very family scenario which had resulted in this woman being so psychologically 'stuck'. For example, from a 1976 letter from consultant psychiatrist to general practitioner.:

> My feelings are parallel with yours, that we are dealing with a severe personality disorder and that this is a girl who has always been selfish, irresponsible and difficult to get on with. However, in order to allay her husband's anxieties I would suggest a trial with Lithium.

From the same letter, but regarding the breakdown of her first marriage, 'I suspect he [Sue's first husband] was unable to cope with her personality and took to beating her.' From a similar letter in 1981:

> This is a maladjusted, immature girl ... A lot of work has gone into this case, trying to get her to alter her attitude to her husband and others ... Her own statement that people have not helped her very much may be interpreted as meaning that she wants someone else to solve her problems and still does not recognise that more effort from her is required.

All these comments, made by male figures in charge of her treatment, were replaying and reinforcing Sue's relationship with her father, whom she had experienced as having expectations of her she could never meet and as being highly critical. He also had a vested interest in her 'failure' in case she should challenge him and expose his own vulnerability. As with many people whose personality difficulties are fundamental to their problems, Sue could make people feel uneasy, angry, irritated, frustrated and confused. If they did not think carefully about what was happening, they could collude with Sue's basic sense of inferiority and at the same time punish her for having it.

A more thought-out and useful comment was made in 1977 by two social workers who had run an out-patient psychotherapy group which Sue had joined. They said:

> Sue's participation in the group has been confusing. She is an active, apparently confident and open group member, her behaviour therefore being at odds with her stated psychological and social difficulties outside the group. It would seem that Sue would clearly like to be 'different' but still finds the prospect frightening. She is increasingly entrenched in her view of herself as incapacitated. It may be that at some point she will be more accessible to change.

I have now seen this woman over a span of four years, providing a relationship that has been rigid in some ways and flexible in others. Its rigidity has been in order to remain constant and consistent in the face of her fluctuating neediness, low self-esteem and inner rage. This is an approach which is widely recommended when working with people with the most disordered and chaotic personalities. Our relationship has been expressed from the beginning by a contract in which I said that I would see her fortnightly at a certain time, come what may. By the contract, I was also stating that we would be working with a part of her that wished to recognise and deal with the part that repeatedly left her floundering, helpless and in a sick role.

I have been tested and raged at many times for not seeing her more often, not doing practical social work things for her, not being 'doctorly' in getting her prescribed drug increases and not 'caring' (panicking) when she expressed vague notions of suicide. For some time I also had to handle carrying a lot of uncomfortable feelings myself, finding her, as others had done, a burden, an irritation, constantly undermining any sense of progress. I have had to remind myself, or be reminded, that what I was feeling was likely to be reflecting earlier relationships.

Regularly looking at my work with Sue at a supervision group I attended was essential and most productive. As I learned to understand that the helplessness and frustration I often felt was mirroring a part of her, I was also able to feel how this was a precaution she had taken against a stronger, more capable side which she had not been free to develop. As with many unhappy, underachieving (in the general sense) and dependent people, she needed support and recognition of parts previously seen by her as 'bad' or unlovable in order to develop more autonomy and psychological integration.

So, in time, I was able to make more helpful comments which showed an understanding of her position and let us explore together what was behind her unhappiness and apparent failures. It was noticeable that when I stopped expecting anything from her (i.e. to get better for me like her father, husbands and psychiatrists) and also showed that I would continue seeing her (i.e. not let her down like her mother who, because of her own fear and dependence has not stood up to the father on her behalf), she started to move.

Also, there were various external events that happened during this period which proved essential, albeit painful, sources of learning. Firstly, her husband divorced her, but she asserted herself and fought for a reasonable settlement rather than remaining passive.

Secondly, her daughter gradually separated from her, got a boyfriend and left home. This transitional time was difficult and brought out a lot of Sue's feelings because of her own dependence/independence conflicts. It was hard for her to allow her daughter this freedom but she finally managed despite being quite punishing along the way. This was, doubtless, out of envy and her own sense of personal deprivation. This last point was particularly pertinent as Sue's own mother had never allowed her such growth, continuing to infantilise Sue even to the point of escorting her daughter to our sessions. It was interesting that I had my most difficult feelings towards Sue at this time—when I felt that she was being a 'bad mother' and I was in danger of becoming unhelpful again by harbouring unspoken criticisms.

Thirdly, her parents retired, moved house and found the upheaval difficult. Sue began to see that they were also quite dependent on her.

Fourthly, she eventually gained some unpaid employment at Gingerbread as a sort of social worker! Apart from the obvious signs of identification, this progress was welcome for other reasons. The area of employment had been difficult, for as much as I disliked standing by and seeing her struggle, it had been necessary for me to understand that for her achievement, work and being a capable person were all equivalent to being pushed by father, not meeting expectations and not being free to choose.

Finally, she started a new relationship and it was in this area that Sue showed to both of us the emotional and psychological ground she had covered in the previous couple of years. This time there seemed to be a better emotional 'fit' for her compared to her previous relationships. At the same time she could see realistically, if painfully, that this 'new love' was not going to provide the parental nurturing for which she longed. She took her time, kept her head and explored her 'heart' (i.e. motivations). This relationship, now of two years' standing, is developing steadily.

Sue is coming to see me for the last time next month after a four-month gap. Prior to this we have been cutting down sessions as she chose. She wants to finish rather than have an open-ended arrangement. In this finishing I have taken the same stance as I have all the way through our contact—that she decides, as I believe that only she has the capacity to know what is right for her. The feedback I give her is about different parts of herself and how these might be in conflict and why. At the beginning she hated this, but it has now paid off.

Now, at the end, beause she is more free to be herself, I can be more myself. For example, we sometimes joke about how she used to be and tease each other. She can say, rare for her, how she values me and I can tell her how I admire her, as indeed I do. As she 'to'd and fro'd', testing the waters in terms of giving up the security of our relationship, we have gone over many times the areas in which she remains vulnerable, and discussed what life stresses may cause her to be prone to collapse again.

Her sense of self-esteem is still lightly grounded and therefore can fluctuate. Her needs have been acknowledged and some of them better met, but because they were not met when they should have been, she will remain, to some extent, forever deprived of that experience of being loved as a child and helped to develop at the appropriate times. A consequence of this is that sharing can be difficult and extreme envy can easily be aroused in her. This gets stirred up in relations with her own daughter and her present partner's two children. At one level, she wants them to be cared for and nurtured, at another this can provoke unbearable envy and consequent competitiveness. This area was useful to look at in our work together, where the give and take of the therapeutic relationship reflected these difficulties.

COMMENT

Mental Health Aspects

As with many cases in this series, Sue presents a problem to the diagnostician. In this instance it seems appropriate to suggest that her disorder is basically one of personality. This is to say that her relatively fixed and enduring patterns of perceiving, thinking about and relating to both her environment and herself were relatively maladjusted. Typically, the chief manifestations of her disorder were longstanding, probably with her at least from adolescence and possibly earlier, continuing throughout her adult life and impairing both her social and occupational functioning. As with many individuals presenting with such conditions, Sue's exact form of personality disorder is more difficult to pinpoint because there are several plausible choices, each having something to recommend it. Sue's behaviour certainly strongly resembles the 'avoidant' personality which is characterised by 'hypersensitivity to personal rejection, humiliation or shame; an unwillingness to enter into relationships unless given unusually strong guarantees of uncritical acceptance; social withdrawal in spite of desire for affection and acceptance; and low self-esteem' (American Psychiatric Association, 1980, p. 323). Also, but probably to a lesser degree, she also displays traits of the 'dependent' personality (i.e. passive, demanding reliance on others to make decisions and lacking in self-confidence) and even the 'passive-aggressive' personality (i.e. a strong resistance to situations and people demanding adequate performance, especially authority figures; see American Psychiatric Association, 1980 for a more complete discussion). All of these may be associated or confused with symptoms of depression and anxiety, to name but two.

This display of 'differential' diagnostic possibilities is not just academic, it has serious ramifications in actual life. Personality disorders, alas, are much easier to observe in retrospect that to predict in advance, as was the case here. As a group, their presentation is such that they frequently lead to much uncertainty among clinicians as to which course of intervention to take at any particular time, and experience shows that this often results in such cases being ineffectively dealt with for many years. As with Sue, such failures are almost inevitably to the patient's detriment.

Casework Aspects

This case describes Sue's psychiatric career and her experience in therapy as a means of illustrating the following points about the process.

Psychodynamic casework as 'treatment of choice'
The timing was right for Sue to be helped in this way, but it was haphazard that psychotherapeutic casework was offered. Examining previous responses, it would seem that those were equally haphazard, influenced by the attitude, interest and gender of the person prescribing treatment for her symptoms (or, in one case, a husband's lack of satisfaction with her). Not only were these responses narrow and often over-simplistic, being only symptom-focused in their formulation and application, they were also extremely wasteful. This woman's personality problems were not really being addressed in any useful way, at the same time as massive National Health Service resources were being wasted on her.

The careful assessment of many patients/clients using a psychodynamic framework, alongside their medical and social history, would be the most helpful and economic response in many more instances than are tried. This would need a managerial commitment and access to ongoing training and supervision so that the approach could be flexible and appropriately offered.

It is a telling comment about current attitudes towards psychiatric casework that such a lesson needs to be recalled. The idea of applying the casework relationship to individuals with personality disorder is hardly a novel one. The move away from applying psychoanalytic theory exclusively to 'neurotic' symptoms towards persons with pre-oedipal levels of personality development and requiring very 'primary' corrective emotional experiences was already well in progress by the middle of the 1950s and the literature on the subject is, of course, fairly well-developed. (For a useful review see Brown,

1971.) The experience of this case, however, suggests that it is a point worth reinforcing at least in the minds of colleagues from other disciplines who should welcome the availability of professionals whose established practice makes them suitable to take on such difficult cases.

Women and mental health

This case seems an extreme, though much repeated example, of how psychiatry (or for that matter psychotherapy or social work) may unintentionally oppress women. The well-recognised developments of theoreticians and practitioners were obviously unknown to those clinicians who wrote the extracts used in this description. Women still form the main body of adult psychiatric patients and men the main body of those, the psychiatrists, who decide on their treatment. As Brodsky and Holroyd (1981) have pointed out, therapists are often 'ignorant of important aspects of female psychology' (p. 102). Their research has shed valuable light on the phenomenon of sexism in therapy by investigating the experiences of 320 female American clinical psychologists during their own period as clients in therapy. In their research, as with Sue, it was not unheard of, sadly, for the therapist to defer 'to the husband's needs in the conduct of the wife's treatment' (p. 104).

Understanding the significance of self-esteem in psychological ill-health should mean a major rethink of responses to clients, and to women in particular. One would say women in particular because low self-esteem is such a common theme in many of the areas of difficulty that bring women along the psychiatric route with the labels of 'self-abuse', 'depression', 'phobias', and 'anxiety', 'substance abuse' and 'sexual difficulties'. In the UK, as in the USA, there is probably a need for us to re-examine continually the values and attitudes that underlie our practice, sexism being but one area requiring attention.

20 Peter:

encopresis and child protection

CASE HISTORY

As a social worker in a child psychiatry setting, I was first asked to become involved with Peter when a registrar in child psychiatry (Dr Jones) came to me and asked if we could both visit Peter as a matter of urgency, as she feared he might be in considerable physical danger. The reason for her fears was that two days previously she had come into the Child Psychiatry Out-Patient Clinic, and 'bumped into' Peter's mother (Mrs Smith), who had brought Peter for a session of individual therapy with the nurse/therapist. Peter's mother had told her, as she passed, that his 'father [had] tried to strangle him at the weekend'. The registrar had not been sure how seriously to take this; and so she had asked Mrs Smith to bring Peter the next day to the unit. A consistent story had then emerged from both of them independently, that, following a temper tantrum on the previous Sunday morning, Mrs Smith had left Peter with his father, instead of taking him with her and her older son, James, to church. However, she had only walked down the street when she realised she had left her purse behind, and returned to find Peter gasping for breath, shaking, crying and accusing his father of having attempted to strangle him. Peter showed the registrar how his father had shaken him and then put his hands around his neck and squeezed. On physical examination, Peter had a red mark on the front of his neck, which the registrar thought to be consistent with a thumb impression. There was no other bruising. The child had not seen a medical specialist in non-accidental injury before being allowed to reurn home. (In both these respects common child abuse 'procedures' were neglected, causing, to my mind, further risk to the boy and making his eventual removal from home all the more painful. It also left the various professionals involved open to the charge that we had not obtained the most thorough medical evidence available at the time we were alerted to the possible abuse.)

Dr Jones had then discussed the case with her consultant psychiatrist who had recommended immediate referral to a social worker. Dr Jones saw me the following day. I read through the psychiatric notes on Peter and also on his brother along with the social work notes on the family, and we agreed to visit later that afternoon.

Peter, his mother and James were at home and they told me the same story they had previously told Dr Jones. However, when I suggested that if what they said was true, Peter was not at all safe in the home, Mrs Smith strongly disagreed. In front of Peter, she kept saying how upset he would be to have to leave, even for a few days. As a result, Peter became quite distressed. Mrs Smith refused to agree to my request that Peter leave the room and went on to accuse Dr Jones and me of making Peter upset. At this point Mr Smith arrived and asked why we were present. On being told the reason, he denied the whole story. Mrs Smith then agreed with her husband and said that there was no truth in what she and her son had told Dr Jones and me. I had to say that all of this was very suspicious, that we were still extremely worried about Peter, and that I felt he would only be safe outside the home until we had a satisfactory explanation of what had occurred. I told the Smiths that if they were unwilling for Peter to be admitted to the care of the local authority voluntarily, I would have to seek legal empowerment for his removal. They refused and, after conferring with my supervisor, I petitioned the court for a Place of Safety Order (Children's and Young Person's Act for England and Wales 1969) which was granted and which I served that evening.

Dr Jones and her predecessor had been treating Peter for problems of soiling and school reluctance/refusal for about a year. It emerged that her predecessor (Dr White) had suggested that a social worker from the psychiatric team become involved but the parents had refused. Mrs Smith had been given clothes and emotional support by the local Social Services department area team. In addition, James had been referred to the child psychiatry team ten years previously because of problems of extreme anxiety and school reluctance. A social assessment, at that time, had been made and both social work and psychiatric support offered but was not accepted. On the other hand, James had been moved to a special school for children with emotional problems and chronic physical illnesses. This appeared to have helped him to overcome his school reluctance, although James blamed the special school for his poor academic attainments, especially in maths. The educational psychologist involved with Peter felt that James was not altogether fair, since it was clear that James had never learned the fundamentals of arithmetic, due, perhaps, to a mixture of poor school attendance and emotional disturbance.

Peter was a precise, socially aloof child with no friends, and no capacity for play with others, including a complete unwillingness to participate in any sport. He seemed quite unable to let himself go. He had been admitted to hospital for a month almost six months prior to the case being referred to us. During his admission Peter achieved bowel control, only to relapse again six weeks after discharge. The parents had been asked to allow him to remain in hospital until his bowel control was a little more secure, but had refused.

There had been severe marital tensions within this family for several years, leading to Mrs Smith being treated for reactive depression. The psychiatrist treating her had attempted marital therapy, and the couple had also attended for marriage guidance counselling, but there was said to have been no improvement in their relationship. Family therapy had been tried, apparently unsuccessfully, by the registrars who were treating Peter. The chronic state of problems was given added confirmation by the fact that the social assessment made when Peter's elder brother James had been referred to the child psychiatrist had drawn attention to the severity of these problems. It had suggested that the elder brother's problems appeared to be a reaction to marital tensions and Mrs Smith's consequent overprotection of him, leading to frequent school non-attendance. However, there had also been suspicions that an injury to the head sustained by James at the age of two, and which had led to convulsions, might not have been accidental.

Mrs Smith appeared to be a well-meaning, but pathologically anxious woman, who was grossly over-involved with her two sons and at loggerheads with her husband. Mr Smith presented as a dour and unhappy man who was excluded from most of the family functioning. In fact, Peter called his elder brother 'Dad' and Mrs Smith consulted with James on family matters rather than with her husband . The family structure was a classic form of inappropriate generation boundaries and alliances (Minuchin, 1974). Mr Smith was in regular employment and was a devout Anglican. He claimed to be a loving father and seemed, in a strange way, devoted to his wife. She had, herself, recently joined an extreme religious sect and taken her children with her, thus increasing the family split. The sect's frequent religious meetings had provided her with the social life she had previously missed. On the other hand, it had deprived Peter of Christmases and birthdays since the sect did not allow these to be celebrated. Mrs Smith had alleged for many years (to health visitors, social workers and teachers) that her husband kept her very short of money (which he was said to have in the bank), so much so that she had to 'beg' for clothes for herself and the children and even, occasionally, for food. The two parents seemed diametrically contrasting in temperament, with Mr Smith appearing very taciturn and intraverted and his wife extraverted, even slightly histrionic.

When I had obtained the Place of Safety Order to remove Peter from home, I took Mrs Smith and James with Peter to visit the foster mother. This was to enable Mrs Smith at least to be able to picture where he was and to let the foster parents seen the natural parents. It was also essential that 'rules' about visiting might be clarified. The foster parents lived nearly three miles from the natural parents but on a direct bus route. I also wanted to allow Mrs Smith to tell the foster parents about any fads or idiosyncracies peculiar to Peter. It was revealing that, on entering the house, Mrs Smith said that Peter could not stay there since we were met by a large friendly dog and she told me that Peter was allergic to dogs. As soon as we got into the living room, Mrs Smith said that Peter could not stay in the living room as he was allergic to budgies and there was a budgie in a cage in the corner. Since it was now late on a Friday night and Mr and Mrs David seemed by far the best of the foster parents available, I had to say that I would discuss his allergies as soon as possible with his consultant paediatrician, but that I could not arrange another placement. I was also rapidly forming an impression of a mother who saw her child as much sicker and more fragile than he probably was. Arrangements were made for Mrs Smith to visit in mid-week and to take Peter to church on Sunday and then return him to his foster home. Since the foster parents were clearly taking on a difficult case, I arranged to meet them the following day (Saturday) to discuss Peter.

Once we had left Peter at the foster parents, I was immediately asked by Mrs Smith and James as to how they could best increase their chances of having him home again. I had already explained that Peter's removal was, in my eyes, temporary, but that return home would depend upon (a) decisions of a case conference I would have to call, (b) the magistrates and, above all else, (c) whether a satisfactory explanation could be given of the allegations about the attempted strangulation. Also, I had already strongly advised them that they obtain the services of a local solicitor and had suggested how they might go about doing this. They then explained to me that all of the problems in the family were due to the tensions each of them experienced with Mr Smith. I said that I knew there had been these difficulties for a long time and that I would be prepared to see the mother and father together, or separately, but that I was not very optimistic about change in the short term and that the immediate problem was to protect Peter. Mrs Smith's solution was that her husband should leave and she told me that neither she nor the boys could stand him. James agreed, describing a history of rather cruel attacks on him by his father. When I asked Mrs Smith why she had not prevented these, she replied that they had always taken place when she was out of the room. She said she would often come into the room to find Mr Smith and James apparently wrestling on the floor and James upset. His father would claim that they had only been having a 'pretend' fight and that James could not take it in the right spirit.

I made it clear that Mrs Smith would have to take the decision herself about leaving her husband. She replied that she would have left him years ago but was prevented from walking out by religious beliefs. She asked if Peter would be allowed home if her husband was no longer there and I had to say again that I could not tell her to ask her husband to leave, but that if it were clear that Mr Smith had left the family for good, the Social Services department would have much less anxiety about Peter visiting home and possibly, eventually, returning.

My own position, which I made clear to Mrs Smith, was that we had removed Peter from home because it did not seem safe to let him stay there. If we could be reasonably sure that there was no further danger of physical harm to him at home then, I told Mrs Smith, I would argue that he be allowed to reurn. However, if, as seemed likely, my department applied to the court for a Care Order, it was probable that the court would make an Interim Care Order at the first hearing and that it might go on making Interim Orders for a further two or three months. In view of the magistrates' reluctance to separate family members for long periods without a proper hearing, they would try to prevent this state of affairs continuing for several months.

As it turned out, I was wrong on both counts. Further evidence emerged which suggested that there were grounds for anxiety about the level of Peter's physical care at home, quite apart from the allegations of attempted strangulation, and several professional people (including myself) had considerable concern about the emotional atmosphere in which Peter was growing up. Although teachers, educational psychologists and psychiatrists had had these anxieties for some time, they had not shared them together and nobody had tried to involve Social Services in intervening on Peter's behalf. The psychiatrists had made it clear they had wanted social work involvement, but had deferred to the wishes of the parents; especially since they did not see any grounds for statutory action.

Also, events proved me slightly over-optimistic about the length of time it would take to get a full hearing. The court ran into delays in finding a suitable 'guardian *ad litem*', so that it was over four months before the case was fully heard. The fact that, in view of further evidence, I had to change my mind regarding Peter's return home, coupled with the extra delays in getting a full court hearing, gave the parents added reasons for feeling that I was not trustworthy.

The first case conference was held on Peter just over a week after the making of the Place of Safety Order. It was well attended by members of the Social Services and Education departments, by psychiatric and nursing staff and the family's health visitor. The conference did not reveal any previous suspicions of physical abuse to Peter. However, considerable concerns were voiced about previous neglect, Peter's school non-attendance, his strange social and emotional development and his mother's belief that he was a sickly child.

The most surprising new evidence to emerge was from the teacher in charge of the special unit to which Peter had been moved eight months previously. She claimed that for over a period of about a week, he had been repeatedly sent to school with his bottom covered in layers of faeces. Notes had been sent home via the bus driver about this but had not been acknowledged or acted upon. It appeared that after soiling himself, Peter had been permitted simply to cover the faeces with toilet paper and was sent to school with layers of impacted faeces. The teachers had had to shower him each day, but his trousers had not been washed for over a week and the turn-ups were full of dried faeces. At school—which consisted of one small class of children of the same age as Peter—he seemed to be virtually an isolate and had no idea of how to participate in a game, e.g. rounders or football. His isolation had been intensified by the rules of his mother's new religion and he had missed almost a half of his schooling in the year prior to admission to the special unit.

The case conference resolved to apply for a Care Order and agreed to place his name on the Register of Abused Children on the grounds that he had probably been physically abused and was in danger of further physical abuse. The conference also noted the history of possible neglect, and the chairman commented on the fact that the education and health services had been slow in calling on social services to protect Peter.

When I next visited the Smiths, I found Mr Smith packing his belongings. He still denied doing any more on the Sunday morning when Peter alleged he had tried to strangle him, than slapping Peter's arm. He protested very much about leaving and said that he had been a good provider and wanted to remain a husband and father. He blamed me for 'having to leave'. On my second follow-up visit I was asked by Mrs Smith if, now that her husband was gone, she could bring Peter home for lunch on Sunday before returning him to his foster parents. I said that this seemed a fair request and that I would put it to my colleagues as soon as the court made an Interim Care Order. I made it clear that it would not be right if Mr Smith were present at these times. Mrs Smith said that she had decided to part with her husband for good and wanted my advice as to how to go about it. I said that we could do that in future, but at the moment I still had matters pertaining to Peter which needed to be resolved. I then raised the matter of Peter having been sent repeatedly into school caked in faeces. She became extremely angry at this point and denied all that the teacher had said, claiming that the other woman had always been prejudiced against her because of her own Anglican beliefs. I said that I found it difficult to believe that the teacher, Mrs Foster, would make up the whole story. I subsequently had to admit to myself that Mrs Smith's denial was extremely heart-rending and believable, and I wondered to what degree her plausible manner had influenced professional descisions previously.

A second case conference was needed to confirm our resolve to apply for a Care Order and to make provisional plans for Peter if a Care Order were made. There was no point in seeking a Care Order unless it was necessary for the purpose of protecting Peter and aiding his development. Packman *et al.* (1986) comment on the fact that social workers did not appear to use the control given them by Care Orders to make more achievable plans and that the use of the courts often antagonised parents. I had to ask myself and my team leader if, supposing Peter's parents were to accept residential schooling, and supposing it were certain they were living apart, would this not be sufficient to protect Peter from harm and provide an environment which would be most likely to allow his personality and relationships to develop normally. There were also worries about whether we were likely to be given a Care Order, especially since a great deal would hang on the evidence of Peter's teacher. On the other hand there did seem an unacceptable level of violence in the family, and not to seek the legal means of protecting Peter seemed to imply a readiness to collude with Mrs Smith's toleration of abuse.

The second case conference resolved that we should continue with our application for care proceedings and that if granted a Care Order, Peter should first be admitted to a child psychiatry ward and then sent on to a boarding school which treated children with emotional disorders, assuming that the education and Social Services departments would finally commit themselves to this plan.

The care proceedings lasted a full four days and ended with the making of a Care Order. The magistrates seemed to be particularly influenced by (1) the evidence from Peter's teacher, (2) by the 'guardian *ad litem's*' report which stressed the distortions in the family and Mrs Smith's inability to separate Peter's needs from her own, (3) by the consistent views of all the expert witnesses about Peter's worrying social and emotional development (4) by Mr Smith's admission of serious marital difficulties (although these were denied by Mrs Smith!), and (5) by James' admissions (under cross examination) of frequent fights between his father and himself, not only in the distant past, but right up to the time his father had left home.

Peter was readmitted to hospital for eight weeks where he became clean. He has remained clean since then, that is to say for a period of about eight months. A third case conference had to be held at which it was eventually agreed to go ahead with our plans for a residential school and that Social Services would pay the residential fees and the Education Department the costs of teaching. The court case also brought the parents closer together. Mr Smith had been able to give some support to his wife during the care proceedings and began to woo her again—something she greatly appreciated. In view of the uncertainty about the alleged strangulation, Social Services agreed that it would be wrong to prevent Peter from going home for weekends and holidays even if Mr Smith were there.

COMMENT

Mental Health Aspects

Peter's social and emotional development had gone seriously astray. He was not only soiling but showed marked school reluctance and was unable to play or make friends with other children. Peter's soiling was a somatic expression of his maladjustment. It was of the form described as retention overflow, characterised by constipation, frequent leakage and occasional dramatic evacuations of his bowels. His school reluctance was an aspect of his anxious attachment to his mother, and his 'frozen' inability to play or make friends, a reflection of similar difficulties in his mother which she saw as being the result of her own severe emotional deprivation in childhood.

Casework Aspects

What are the lessons to learn from this case? There seem to be several of which I should like to highlight only a few.

As the social worker in the case I felt that I benefited from case management from my team leader because of the powerful feelings of pity and 'awfulness' that Mrs Smith aroused in me. I suspect that social workers sometimes make mistakes in child abuse cases because the evidence of abuse, at first, is not very strong and the parents seem to require support and validation as parents rather than invalidation and loss of their children. Mrs Smith seemed to be saying 'Help me. I'm another victim in all of this. I'm not responsible for the abuse—if it happened.' A number of my colleagues responded by championing her rights. Assumptions about not intervening in other people's private lives and beliefs in the 'rule of optimism' (i.e. that Mrs Smith really would turn out to be an adequate mother and that Peter would grow out of his social withdrawal) were quite rife. In matters of emotional abuse and maternal over-involvement, I suspect professionals are less ready to act, not only because of lack of hard evidence, but also out of an anxiety that admission to care, even if it could be achieved, would probably do more harm than good. It is also very diffiicult not to feel sorry for a mother, who, because of her own needs, and the lack of a good, confiding relationship with her husband, became grossly over-involved with a child.

In this case, line management supported the social worker, but it would not be difficult to imagine a situation in which the team leader or the local authority solicitor had felt that there was not enough evidence for care proceedings, or Social Services or the Education Department had argued that it could not be demonstrated that special residential schooling would benefit this boy. In that case, Peter would have returned to the same situation at home.

In all of these considerations, I needed managerial support in at least four respects: (1) in coping with my own inner debate as to what was best for Peter; (2) in dealing with Mrs Smith's more and more desperate pleas to have her child returned, which were followed by extreme anger when I refused. She was unable to see that Peter needed very special help, although she came round to agreeing that another spell in hospital was necessary for him to overcome his soiling disorder. When I said he needed space in which to grow up, she would counter that she knew Peter best, and knew he would be very unhappy in a boarding school. Pointing out that the very wealthy would often pay the earth for such opportunities made very little impression—at this stage. I also needed managerial backing (3) in conflicts with powerful people in other agencies who were supporting Mrs Smith in demanding her child be returned, and (4) in applications for special resources from both the Education Department and Social Services.

A Care Order was eventually made on grounds of neglect, emotional abuse and the parents' refusal to acknowledge that Peter needed special help. These deficiencies in parental care had been there for some time, but it took allegations of cruelty to bring Social Services into the case. From the outcome it appeared that the magistrates were not prepared to allow neglect and emotional abuse to recur, but until the case went to court there seemed to be assumptions around that there were no grounds for statutory action.

It appears that so far the outcome had been beneficial. The parents' relationship seems to have improved in every way, although several previous attempts to work with them on a voluntary basis led nowhere. Peter has an opportunity to become himself and escape from his mother's over-possessive preoccupation with him. Social workers are, perhaps, so used to working on cases where there is a lack of bonding or distorted bonding on the parents part, that it is difficult, sometimes, to see the dangers held by an exclusive over-attachment to a parent for normal social development.

The manner in which cases are referred to social workers often has an influence not only on how the social worker sees the case, but even more on the way families perceive the social worker and his or her intentions. To that extent, the reason for and nature of, the first meeting may well limit the social worker's subsequent freedom of action, and create an emotional climate in which the level of trust necessary for therapy is difficult, perhaps impossible, to achieve. This, in turn, may propel the worker into trying to over-compensate for what may have been a painful and threatening first meeting for both the parents and the child. If the social worker has had to separate children from their parents, he may want to make up for this by conveying to them both that he wishes to reunite them all as soon as possible. As can be seen from the case, I was guilty of this myself, because I knew little of the case and assumed that since the other professional people involved had not previously considered the use of care proceedings, that the main need for separation lay in fears of further physical abuse.

21 Maureen and Wendy:
the behavioural approach

CASE HISTORY

Maureen was twenty-seven years old at the time of her four-year-old daughter Wendy's referral to the child psychiatric service. Wendy was referred to the consultant psychiatrist in child and adolescent psychiatry. According to the general practitioner's letter, Wendy had been soiling for some time, refusing her food, cursing and being disobedient. The family was well-known to the local Social Services department, who had been 'involved' with them for several years. By the time of the referral, community-based social workers and the general practitioner had both made attempts to improve the home situation and clear up the child's symptoms, but had failed miserably. In what amounted to a final act of desperation, Social Services particularly had requested that the general practitioner make the referral, with an eye to the fact that the child was soon to begin school.

Maureen came from a local family, her father a miner and mother a housewife. She was the youngest of six children. She had led what she described as an uneventful childhood with the exception that she had been a small baby herself and was barely five feet tall as an adult. She attended a secondary modern school and achieved four CSE passes. Later investigation showed that her own parents had rowed a lot throughout her childhood. While both her mother and father had been very 'strict' with all of the children, she, in particular, had been treated very much as an infant, even into her adolescence. Hence, it had come as a great shock when at the age of sixteen she fell pregnant with John, her other child, now aged ten. The child's father was unknown, but believed to have been a boy she met at a disco. This led to a great family upheaval and she left home. In spite of the rupture in her relationship with her family that this had caused, she still remained in contact with them and spent a lot of her time visiting her mother and her father, who was now retired due to disability. Her mother was a particularly strong influence in her life and gave Maureen frequent, but ineffective, instructions on how to deal with Wendy's behavioural problems which she followed dutifully.

Upon leaving home, Maureen had tried to establish an independent life and at the time of referral had been working for several years, part-time, as a receptionist at a local bingo hall. Her income had been supplemented by state benefits. At age twenty-two she had been 'caught out again', and again the father appears to have been unknown. This time she believed that it had been a man she had met through work but was not certain of his name and could not trace him. She lived alone with her children in a moderately well-furnished and maintained council flat. Maureen was a lively, petite and attractive, if somewhat shy, person with a high-pitched voice and a strong regional accent. She had high standards of dress and cleanliness, and both she and her children were always turned out immaculately.

Wendy had been difficult almost from the beginning. Not only had Maureen been upset at the idea of a second illegitimate child, she had experienced a lot of sickness during pregnancy and, in the end, the child was born prematurely, by Caesarian section. Maureen provided insufficient milk for the child who, at any rate, appears to have 'rejected her feeds'. This led to a very prolonged early separation where the child was retained in hospital after the mother was discharged and the two did not finally live together until Wendy was six months old. It was during this early period of separation that Social Services had become involved, fearing that the mother would not accept the child. There had always been some conflict over eating and the mother was very anxious over the child's inability to 'eat properly'. When it came time for the child to become potty trained, there was more conflict, and Maureen never actually succeeded in getting the child fully clean and using the toilet appropriately.

At the time that the child was referred to the out-patient service, the Social Services department was considering applying for a Care Order (*Children's and Young Person's Act 1968*) in respect of Wendy on the grounds that she was 'beyond parental control'. Wendy and Maureen were seen by the consultant psychiatrist who attempted, unsuccessfully, to treat Wendy as an out-patient. At this point the psychiatric social worker was asked to visit and make a social assessment prior to Wendy's hospital admission.

It was the practice of the regional in-patient child psychiatric unit that only 'failed' out-patients be admitted except in emergency, and that all patients and their families be visited by staff members prior to admission to make arrangements and to gather a full social history and make a full assesment. What emerged was that Maureen was nearing the end of her ability to cope. The structured personality assessment, the Eysenck Personality Inventory, showed her to be exceedingly neurotic and introverted (Eysenck and Eysenck, 1974). Also, her current mood, as measured by the IDA Scale (Snaith *et al.*, 1978), contained a highly elevated level of anxiety and slightly elevated levels of depression and outwardly directed irritability. Wendy's problems were so severe that no treatment or assessment was likely to be successful in the home setting. The child's clinical state and home situation were both either stable at a poor level or deteriorating rapidly. As this state had prevailed for a considerable period of time, spontaneous remission of her problems was not considered to be a possiblility. Consequently, the child was offered a place as an in-patient and was admitted soon afterwards.

The unit was an eleven-bed facility, located in a large detatched house within the grounds of a rural psychiatric hospital. It was staffed by a large interdisciplinary team, of which the consultant was the team leader. Upon being admitted to the unit, Wendy was treated by the staff as was any other child. She was assigned a personal 'nurse therapist' whose task it was to form a relationship with her which would serve both as a means of engaging her in whatever treatment the team felt appropriate, and act as a prophylactic against the possible negative short-term and long-term effects of separation and hospital admission. In addition, she attended the unit's own school, staffed by specially trained teachers to prepare her for beginning normal schooling upon discharge. Medical examination and psychological testing revealed that the child had a full scale IQ of 97 with no indications of organic disorder. Also, as with all children resident in the unit, Wendy returned to her own home and family at the weekend.

The treatment regime of the unit tended to be loosely structured milieu therapy coupled with behaviour modification programmes instituted as needed for specific behaviour problems. At first, some aspects of Wendy's behaviour did respond readily to this treatment. A behaviour modification programme based on frequent toileting and systematic reward for performance began to make an improvement in her encopresis. At staff meetings, her progress in the unit was described as 'slow but satisfactory'. However, when she had returned from weekend home visits, it always seemed that her behaviour had regressed to 'square one' again, a phenomenon which the unit staff found most disheartening.

A close investigation of this deterioration revealed that Maureen simply lacked the parenting skills adequate to the task of carrying on the progress being made by the professional staff. Her own parents, particularly her mother, had not provided her with sound role models when she was young and their advice, now that she was older, was unhelpful. She had few opportunities for learning as she had few friends and no support from her siblings. Attempts to improve Maureen's parenting skills through frequent home visiting and instruction failed. After approximately four months, it was decided to offer Maureen a place in the unit for a limited period, during which time she could be with Wendy and could actually be taught how to handle her. This was fully discussed with Maureen by the social worker and she accepted. A room was made available for the two.

When Maureen came into the unit she was given the opportunity to have special help with the task of child management. To do this a thorough behavioural assessment was made of how she interacted with Wendy. This was done by the unit social worker and clinical psychologist observing Maureen interacting with Wendy in a number of structured and unstructured situations through a one-way mirror. These situational observations centred on such activities as play with lego, wooden blocks, doll play and other games, some of which were competitive in nature and others which demanded co-operation. Few instructions were normally given, although there was a uniform fifteen-minute time limit. No training programme was in operation at this time, but the opportunity was used to evaluate Maureen's established pattern of control and management and Wendy's behaviour in response to this.

At the end of one week, a rough behavioural check-list was compiled. Its elements were drawn from the first week's observed interactions. This check-list was used for a further period to identify the frequency of certain of Maureen's behaviours. Occasionally inter-rater checks were done to establish the level of reliability. The initially low correlations of observations led to the the check-list being redesigned using less ambiguous terms and including Wendy's behaviours as well. In the end it contained such items as praise-giving, encouragement, criticism, eye contact, physical contact, facial expression and conversational elements such as questions, answers, advice, suggestions, commands and corrections.

Each observation session was followed by some period of 'sharing' or general information-giving with Maureen. She was well aware of the fact that she was being observed, though the child, obviously, was not. Maureen claimed to feel self-conscious at first, but soon accommodated herself to the setting. One of the problems identified during early sessions of observation had to do with the way in which Maureen gave the child attention. It appeared that she tended to avert her gaze from Wendy unless actually forced to look at the child. Maureen's posture was always rigid when in Wendy's presence and she seldom smiled at the child. This meant that Wendy could not get her mother's attention unless she made a considerable disturbance. Sadly, this also meant that Maureen was inevitably quite angry by that time and when she gave attention to Wendy, it was usually only to scold the child. Maureen did not differentiate in her response between times when Wendy sought attention for something constructive or for something anti-social which might justly require her to exercise authority. When she did respond, sometimes making threats, she seldom followed them up by exerting any control, apparently unsure of what to do. Instead, she simply complied with the child's demand, irrespective of how unreasonable it might have been. This really promoted a vicious circle of attention-seeking behaviour by Wendy, leading to recriminations by Maureen, further anger and avoidance by Maureen, and further misbehaviour by Wendy.

To overcome this problem a behavioural approach was employed. It was pointed out to Maureen that she had particular difficulties in the area of eye contact, praise, encouragement, physical contact with Wendy and appropriate direction-giving to the child. Her interactions were recorded on video and then fed back to her. As problems began to emerge these were discussed and she was given plenty of opportunity to try again and again. The overall approach was positive; to look at the acquisition of new skills rather than dwelling on the extinction of her old, inappropriate patterns; giving praise for her successes and commenting neutrally on, or ignoring, her failures. Also, the particular nurse therapist who had been dealing with Wendy on the unit was available. This woman had many years experience in dealing with highly disturbed children. She was able to serve as a model for Maureen who was able to observe the nurse-therapist at work. The results of the first thirty-eight days of parental training in three sets of skills are shown below in Figures 1a, 1b and 1c.

Figure 1a Frequency of praise and encouragement-giving by Maureen

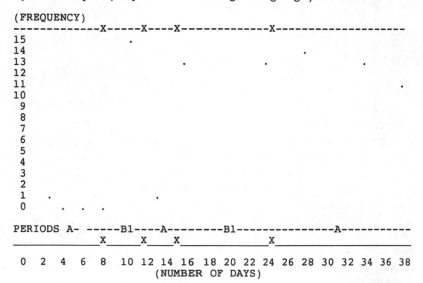

Figure 1b Frequency of smiling by Maureen

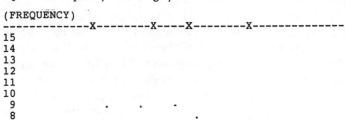

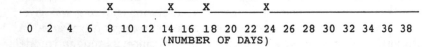

Figure 1c   Frequency of eye contact by Maureen

```
(FREQUENCY)
-------------X------X----X-------------X----------------------
15                     .
14
13                            .
12                          . .
11
10
 9
 8                                                          .
 7
 6                                                              .
 5
 4
 3
 2
 1        .   . . .
 0     .

PERIODS  A-------B1----A-------B1----------------A------------
                 X     X    X                    X
_____
 0   2   4   6   8  10  12  14  16  18  20  22  24  26  28  30  32  34  36  38
                            (NUMBER OF DAYS)
```

As can be seen in Figures 1a, 1b and 1c, by the end of the fifth week, work with the mother had begun to show durable improvement. Maureen was able to initiate eye contact and smile at the child for appropriate behaviour. She had succeeded in increasing her praise-giving and had decreased her frequency of punishment.

In all instances, the first eight days consisted of a non-treatment, baseline period (Period A). During this time behaviours were observed and recorded, but no specific treatment was offered. The frequency of adaptive responses tended to be very low, smiling, eye contact and praise and encouragement giving occurring on average less than once per session. Following these baseline periods were the first treatment periods (Period B1). Here, some form of behaviour modification was used to increase the desired behaviour. This was generally instruction or guided practice, rehearsal, performance and feedback followed by praise and encouragement. The results show a substantial improvement in terms of frequency of behaviour (the dependent variable) during the experimental period.

After the experimental period, Maureen was allowed to carry on as she chose, amounting, in effect, to a return to non-treatment conditions (Period A). This showed the strong amount of stimulus control which the treatment techniques exercised over Maureen's behaviour. The trend was uniformly towards decreased baseline levels of performance. Before the newly acquired behaviours were extinguished, however, additional training was given. In some instances, it was more of the same type given previously (Period B1). In the instance of smiling behaviour, additional relaxation training and modelling by unit staff were added to the treatment, making it substantially different (Period B2). For all behaviours, the second treatment period again caused the predicted increase in frequency of behaviour performance. This additional training was discontinued as Maureen became better able to monitor her own performance. During these following non-treatment periods (Period A), the gains were maintained much better than previously though the graphs show a slow decline. In fact the behaviours were all subjected to further treatment periods and, in the end, stabilised at appropriately high levels. The entire process took more than sixty days, with the length of time varying between sessions, but the sessions becoming less frequent as time went on. At the end Maureen had acquired a repertoire of appropriate behavioural cues and responses which she could use effectively in her interactions with her child under controlled play-room conditions.

As well, one could say that mother began to achieve 'insight' in so far as she began to be able to link up problems of management with her daughter in the 'here and now' with her own previous and current relationship with her own family. The focus of the work was still on non-threatening situations in which there was a minimum of anxiety for Maureen. This seemed to enhance her capacity to learn new child management techniques, to incease her actual rewards gained from participation with her child, and to increase Wendy's ability to get positive responses from Maureen for 'good' behaviour. This latter interactive effect was found to be increasingly true as eye contact increased. The possibilities for mutual behavioural regulation strengthened and some change began to generalise. It was noted, for example, that when they returned to the unit, after a weekend at home, there was increasingly less deterioration. Also, Maureen became bolder and more confident within the unit and more directly challenging of her own mother's judgement.

Finally, the problematic behaviour of Wendy was tackled. Wendy tended to refuse food when it was offered by her mother. She would often throw food about and smear it on the table, as part of her general pattern of misbehaviour. Although the procedure and results for this training were far too lengthy to be reported completely here, the first stage which worked on Wendy's poor eating habits and anti-social behaviour are worthwhile discussing in order to gather a flavour of how the treatment was organised and conducted.

The social worker sat in the unit dining room during mealtime and observed Maureen and Wendy eating. At a purely descriptive level it was noted that Maureen appeared anxious about Wendy's lack of appetite. To this she was regularly punative and critical of the child's lack of appetite, and spent a lot of time standing over Wendy, policing her behaviour. Maureen's posture at such times was rigid, and her facial expression consisted exclusively of frowns and scowls. Maureen placed far too much food on Wendy's plate and was upset when the child failed to finish every course. Maureen was also very 'picky' about various table rules such as placing elbows on the table, and never praised Wendy for having made an acceptable effort. The result was that when they ate together Wendy seldom ate well.

A structured programme of behaviour modification, including a star chart and systematic rewards for success by Wendy, was initiated. A mealtime modelling session with the therapist was arranged to help Maureen to learn appropriate management techniques. The therapist first rehearsed how to sit opposite Wendy with a relaxed posture and a reassuring tone of voice. She was not punitive for non-eating and did not criticise the child for table manners. She did not give any commands on how to eat, and gave the child small amounts of food that Wendy could eat. She gave the child intensified praise for small successes. If the child began to throw her food about, it was simply taken away, the child dismissed from the table and cleaned up. Wendy was not fed except at mealtime. There was an emphasis on firm, consistent but affectionate handling of Wendy. Demonstrations were given to Maureen for a period of a week at lunch. In the evenings she attempted to duplicate the behaviour of the therapist and was observed in this by the social worker. The results for behavioural treatment of the child's eating problems are shown in Figures 2a, 2b and 2c. They are given in conjunction with treatment measures for two

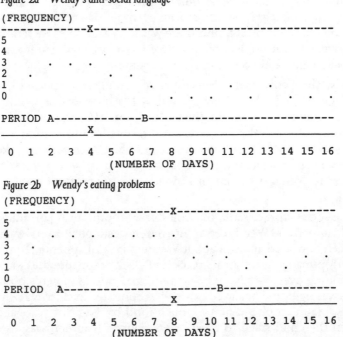

Multiple baseline across three anti-social behaviours: daily frequency of misbehaviour in language, eating (per meal) and hitting

Figure 2a   Wendy's anti-social language

Figure 2b   Wendy's eating problems

Figure 2c   *Wendy's aggression towards other children*

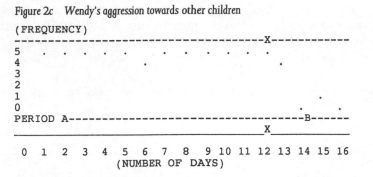

other behaviour problems, the use of bad language and striking other children, in the actual order in which they were treated.

As can be seen in Figures 2a, 2b and 2c, Maureen was successful in modifying her own child's troublesome behaviour with support and active guidance from the unit staff. All three target behaviours (i.e. abusive language, eating problems and striking other children) were dealt with systematically. All were monitored for an initial non-treatment period (Period A), although this varied in length from four days for abusive language to twelve days for hitting. Each behaviour was treated as functionally independent of other behaviours, and was attacked separately with a different behavioural regime. Eating problems were given as an example. It can also be seen that in all three instances improvement took place only after the the treatment phase (Period B) had begun. Treatment gains were always maintained once established, but there were no changes in untreated conditions. There is good probable evidence that the effectiveness of treatment is a consequence of the imposed behavioural regimes.

As part of the pre-admission assessment for the unit, a number of measures were routinely taken to determine the levels of psycho-social functioning of the child and his/her family, especially mother. The results of these structured observations were used as baseline measures against which the effects of subsequent treatment could be judged. Each child admitted, in that sense, served as their own control, against which levels of psychopathology at discharge and one-year follow-up could be compared.

In every case admitted, a behaviour rating scale (Rutter A [2]) developed elsewhere (Rutter et al., 1970), standardised on a British population and found to be a useful indicator of levels of behavioural disturbance in children was employed. This behaviour screening instrument has a range of scores between 0 and 64 and a cut-off point of 13, at or above which a child is likely to have a pathological behaviour disturbance, and is completed by the parent or caretaker. In addition, at discharge and follow-up, Maureen had been asked to comment on her daughter's progress in respect of the specific symptom(s) for which Wendy was admitted. This Likert scale measure was a more sensitive measure of behavioural improvement. It rated the child's condition against admission as 'greatly improved' (5) to 'greatly deteriorated' (0). The results of repeated measures utilising these two instruments for the case of Wendy are reported in Table 1 below.

Table 1   Rutter A(2) total and anti-social/neurotic subscale scores and likert scale scores for Wendy

Time	Rutter	Likert
Admission	18	X
Discharge	8	5
Follow-up	11	5

When Wendy was admitted to the unit, her general behaviour was far more disturbed than an average child of her own age, who would probably have achieved a total score of about 4 on the same scale (Rutter *et al.*, 1970). At discharge she had improved substantially and her behaviour was within normal limits. Although there was a slight deterioration, she remained very much improved at follow-up and it is important to keep in mind that there will always be a small amount of test-re-test score variation due to the inaccuracy of the testing technique. Finally, her specific symptoms were also measured. The Likert scale results reveal that she was greatly improved at discharge and that she was still greatly improved at follow-up compared with admission.

It was the opinion of unit staff that when Wendy was discharged she was clear of her major problems, including her encopresis. She returned to her own home with Maureen who had done a lot of work on weekends redecorating it in anticipation of their return. Wendy attended a normal school and at follow-up was maintaining behaviour which was within normal limits both at home and at school. The Social Services department had set aside their intentions to pursue care proceedings.

COMMENT

Mental Health Aspects

Wendy was disgnosed as having a conduct disorder. This condition included anti-social behaviours such as using abusive language, hitting other children, and eating difficulties, comprised both of food refusal and general misbehaviour at table. Also, she displayed a developmental delay (i.e. continuous encopresis) in that she had never achieved successful toilet training at an age when it would have normally been expected in the absence of an organic cause. In practice, these symptoms and others similar to them are often found together in pre-school clinic attenders, the general picture being typified by disobedience and non-compliance.

There are many different ways of construing such problems in children. Certainly, there was much evidence in the psychosocial histories of both Maureen and Wendy to support psychodynamic investigations. Experience has shown, however, that while such explanations are more satisfying to the clinical mind, they are often of limited use for the purposes of planning, implementing and evaluating treatment. Indeed, Wolff (1977, p. 505) says that 'there is no evidence for the successful treatment of antisocial children with psychotherapeutic or social case-work techniques ...'.

The weight of current opinion favours seeking answers to such cases is in the field of applied behaviour analysis, which concentrates less on the developmental history of a disorder and more on the degree to which it is either the end product of or otherwise associated with faulty learning. In this case treatment included a not uncommon combination of milieu therapy and behaviour therapy.

The advantages of involving the parent in such treatment are quite clear. First, the personality and the mood of the caretaker have been found to be important in the genesis of such conditions, particularly depression, anxiety and irritability, all of which Maureen displayed at excessive levels. Second, parent-child interaction is a crucial factor in the maintenance of these problems. Here Maureen's rejection of Wendy, typified by her rigid, punitive, harsh and inconsistent behaviour towards the child, produced a powerful set of behavioural contingencies which maintained, if not strengthened, Wendy's misbehaviour. (See Quay and Werry, 1986 for a good review of this area.)

This case also typifies, in several respects, the process by which most children come to be in-patients in child psychiatric units. In particular, this case illustrates three of the conditions under which in-patient hospital care is generally regarded as the treatment of choice: 'Where socially unacceptable behaviour arises from a degree of psychiatric disorder which is unaffected by ordinary social measures or outpatient treatment'; 'where a complex psychiatric problem requires skilled observation, assessment and treatment which must be continuous and of an intensity not possible on an outpatient basis'; and 'where the family interaction is so distorted that life at home leads to a continuing or progressive interference with the child's development and progress. In this situation the child may need a controlled therapeutic environment to provide healthier life experiences and relationships.' (Hersov and Bentovim, 1977, p. 883).

Casework Aspects

The importance of the integration of experimental methodologies into conventional social casework practice cannot be over-emphasised. The days in which the enterprise was valued for its own sake appear, perhaps sadly, to be over. More and more, people from within and outside the profession are demanding to see evidence that what social workers do really works. This is a challenge which, in order to progress, social casework must address directly. In particular, we need to think closely about determining in precisely which sets of circumstances casework is likely to be effective and in which it is not. As well as this, there will be areas in which one particular style of casework (e.g. the behavioural approach) has the best record of outcomes and is, thus, the 'treatment of choice' over its rivals.

To determine such things there is a certain necessity for continuing research into casework at all levels. While there will always be a need for large-scale research to investigate casework outcomes with confidence, there remains a need to explore this broad field in a detail to which large sample studies could never realistically be applied. It is in this area that we need to move beyond the naturalistic methods by which we regularly report cases, and to enhance our observations by applying the more rigorous canons of science.

As Sheldon (1982, p. 137) states, 'these designs hold out the possibility that in certain areas of social work we could see the emergence of the practitoner-researcher, someone who contributes to the literature specific information and potentially replicable results drawn from his own caseload; someone who is more than a passive consumer of other people's theories'.

Along these lines, this case illustrates three different approaches to evaluation, all of which are based on the systematic examination of the single case. In particular, it applies scientific experimental methodology to a single case (i.e. conditions of N=1). This offers the posssibility of testing hypotheses and ultimately drawing causal inferences from the results (Hersen and Barlow, 1976). This approach has been employed widely in the field of behavioural therapy, chiefly by psychologists and psychiatrists, but has yet to become common practice in the evaluation of social casework (Sheldon, 1982; Hudson, 1986).

The first example is the full reversal design. This was employed to assess the impact of different forms of training on Maureen's mothering behaviour (Figures 1a, 1b and 1c). There are many different reversal designs, two variants of the A-B-A-B-A design being given here. This is the most powerful reversal design as it demonstrates unequivocally the control of the independent variable (i.e. the conditioning programme) over the dependent variable (i.e. Maureen's measured responses). The likelihood of the changes having occurred as they did due to random circumstances is very remote. Such designs can be used where there is no strong ethical objection to the behavioural condition reverting to pre-treatment conditions as in the instance of smiling, eye contact or praise-giving and encouragement behaviours. Also they can be employed where the target behaviours are not likely to become so fixed after a single trial or exposure that they are maintained indefinitely. This was the case with Maureen's learning of appropriate interpersonal skills which required really sustained operant conditioning to produce enduring change.

The overall programme evaluation was another variant of the reversal design. Here an extended A-B design or 'quasi-experimental design with follow-up' formed the basis of overall individual case evaluation. This simple design is not as manifestly powerful as the design cited above as the control is less evident. Nevertheless, the follow-up does add considerable strength to its explanatory power. Instead, its power lies in its utility, where a complete reversal to a baseline level is either impossible or manifestly unethical. It also allows for many cases to be aggregated and for overall conclusions to be drawn about the general performance of such a unit. The child's overall behaviour was first measured during a non-treatment period (i.e. the pre-admission phase). This determined that Wendy was at a high level of pathology before the commencement of treatment (i.e. admission). A second measure, using the same instrument, was taken just prior to discharge. This gave an indication of the level of disorder at the end of the treatment period. There was a final measure after a period of non-treatment (post discharge). It was predicted that her condition would change during the treatment period. It did this. It was also predicted that the change would be in the desired direction (i.e. improvement). It did this as well. Finally, it was predicted that there would be little, if any change during the post-discharge period, and this was the case. One of the strongest arguments for the effectiveness of a scientific procedure is that such a procedure is predictive. The predictive value of treatment within this design was strong. Useful treatment evaluation can be based on the aggregation of such cases, looking at consecutive or random samples of admissions in such a fashion. The frequent repetition of the same pattern of predicted success in several cases is similar to the replication of experiments with group designs. Each direct replication of patterns of case outcome improvement lends weight to the argument of causality and treatment effectiveness.

Finally, there are instances where it is impractical or unethical to employ a reversal design. An alternative is the multiple baseline design. In the instance of Wendy's conduct problems, it would not have been desirable to make them worse intentionally or to allow progress to deteriorate by withdrawing contingencies which were effective simply to demonstrate effectiveness. Instead, a systematic comparison was made between treated and untreated problems (controls) across a period of time. This systematic introduction of treatment and the observation of comparative patterns of change, gives strong evidence to support the effectiveness of such conditioning techniques.

22 Julie:

a case of chronic pain

CASE HISTORY

Julie, a seventeen-year-old girl, was referred to a psychiatric out-patient clinic by an orthopaedic surgeon. One year previously, while working as a care assistant in a residential home, she had fallen, striking her elbow against a wall. She was in great pain and was taken immediately to the nearest casualty department. The medical examination did not reveal any significant damage. Julie continued to complain of pain in her elbow and lower arm; the pain persisted and she did not return to work. Her complaints mystified the surgeon particularly as her injuries showed marked improvement. Power and movement returned to her arm, but she continued to complain of pain.

After many relevant tests proved negative, the surgeon wondered whether Julie's pain might be associated with her claim for compensation from her employer and decided to investigate psychological aspects of the pain. He referred her for assessment to the consultant psychiatrist. Julie and her parents furiously denied that there was any psychological component, but they agreed to a psychiatric assessment. They thought the psychiatrist would eliminate psychological factors and then the surgeon would continue his physical investigations. Although both parents were invited to the initial psychiatric out-patients appointment, the father did not attend. All subsequent efforts to involve him failed.

Julie and her mother attended the first appointment. Julie was a rather plain, overweight, diffident girl. Her mother was also rather plump, but had a more forceful personality. Julie was seen by the psychiatrist and her mother by me. In the interview with me mother was openly hostile. Both gave a similar history of events; the accident occurred just before two stressful family events. The first was Julie's younger sister Jane's departure from home. She went to live with her boyfriend (by whom she was pregnant) and several other young people in a communal house. Julie had been taken by surprise and was quite shocked by this news, and had refused to talk to her sister. Julie's parents were stunned and had broken off contact with Jane. The second event was the sudden unexpected death of the paternal grandfather. Both Julie and her mother became tearful in the interview when reporting his death, but both denied that Jane's exit was an 'upsetting' experience.

The current family situation was unsettled because they had no permanent accommodation. They regarded their paternal grandfather's home as their base; Julie's parents had had temporary employment in different places and they had never settled anywhere for long. Julie's mother was rather guarded about their prospects of finding more permanent employment; they seemed resigned to the idea of living with these uncertainties.

Julie and her mother independently described their relationship as 'more like sisters'. Since her accident Julie had stopped mixing or going out with her peers. By the time of the first psychiatric appointment the Department of Health and Social Security (DHSS) saw Julie as a permanently disabled person. She was in receipt of a disability allowance; her total income was about £60 per week. Her status was regularly reviewed by the DHSS and these reviews were later to cause problems.

At the assessment interview there seemed to be enough evidence of underlying personal and family problems to warrant further exploratory work with Julie and her mother. The team decided that initially mother and Julie would be offered individual appointments and that joint sessions would be the ultimate objective. The aim would be to explore their relationship and help both to express feelings about the grandfather's death and Jane's departure. A primary aim which was discussed with the family, was the encouragement and facilitation of a greater degree of independence and physical activity for Julie.

In the first interview Julie's mother expressed some of her anger about the referral and some of the grief she felt about the death of the grandfather. It became clear during this and subsequent interviews that (a) mother's grief was about grandfather but also about 'losing' Jane from the family; (b) she preferred not to talk about her husband. There was always a degree of vagueness and reluctance about her responses whenever I mentioned him; (c) Julie was her main confidante and companion and that mother's view of Julie was 'idealised'; (d) she showed a marked lack of concern about the fact that Julie might be 'socially disabled' for a long time or that she was becoming completely cut off from her peers; and (e) her view of the disorder as entirely physical in origin was firmly held in the absence of any medical evidence.

Julie had a series of open and useful sessions with the doctor before the joint sessions began. In her mother's presence she was still rather subdued. She had taken some steps towards greater activity—she had taken on some babysitting and started to do her own washing and ironing.

Three events of importance occurred while the joint sesions were in progress. First, Jane made an approach to be 'accepted' by the family. Second, relations between the family and the grandmother deteriorated and the family approached the housing department. Third, the DHSS doctor questioned the nature and extent of Julie's handicap and asked for a report from the psychiatrist. All these issues were discussed in the joint sessions.

It emerged that Julie had been jealous of Jane and still felt jealous to some extent. Jane's acceptance into the family was on balance a positive event, especially for mother who became visibly less drawn, less hostile and more relaxed. She was then able to talk about how hurt she had felt when Jane left home. Julie began to visit her sister and to help with the baby from time to time.

Negative feelings about Julie's father began to be expressed in the joint meetings. The mother was particularly critical of his attachment to the grandmother. Further attempts at this point to re-engage the father were sabotaged by Julie and mother.

Julie and her mother were able to talk about their own relationship when these negative aspects of father had been discussed. While the mother continued to present their relationship in positive tones Julie began to demur. She managed to tell her mother that she found it a burden to be the one who received all the confidences. For instance, instead of telling her husband that she had a lump in her breast she had told Julie who had felt terrified. (The lump was benign.) Gradually Julie faced her mother with her feeling of being responsible for her. The question of whether Julie really wanted independence was tested out in the matter of rehousing. Here was the opportunity to find her own accommodation. In addition, she was going to start a full-time course at a college of further education.

Her painful arm intervened. Under this pressure to take steps towards independence her arm got worse, and it became even worse the more the medical officer from the DHSS asked questions about it.

Julie and her mother did not take up the offer of further joint sessions. We concluded that the goal of independence (for them both) was unacceptable at that time. Neither was able to be independent of the other.

COMMENT

Mental Health Aspects

The adoption of certain behaviours appropriate to being a patient and a carer are usual in times of illness. These behaviours tend to vary in accordance with family culture and probably arise from early modelling. Families have different thresholds of tolerance for illness, as general practitioners will testify.

Illness behaviour becomes abnormal when the need to communicate through symptoms of illness outlasts any real physical pathology (except for that brought about by the disuse of limbs). The stances adopted by the 'invalid' and the 'carer' are perpetuated for reasons which fulfil needs on both sides. Since there has usually been a physical event, the reason for a failure to recover is pursued in physical terms. Family and psychological problems are strenuously denied, and in many instances family relationships are 'idealised'. Some patients consult many specialists and may spend a great deal on adaptations and equipment. Few physical diagnoses are in fact ever made as a result of further medical investigations more than six months after the initial consultation for a problem (Goldberg *et al.*, 1987).

Specific causes of this sort of illness often take a long time to emerge; the patient's view of the disorder as entirely somatic in origin makes the assessment of possible factors influencing the patient's behaviour a more difficult and time-consuming, albeit essential, exercise. If the problem fails to improve during the first year or two a chronic course is quite likely.

Casework Aspects

Research into family perspectives has shown that family attitudes are crucial in the aetiology and maintenance of illness behaviour (Swanson and Maruta, 1980). Guilt about resentment felt towards a breadwinner who has ceased to function as such can be turned into over-solicitousness. Patient illness behaviour can be rewarded as a result.

Because of the complexity of the family dynamics involved a patient cannot be treated in isolation and working with the family involves attempting to alter family attitudes (Hudgens, 1979). One priority is to encourage the patient to be more active in spite of the pain involved—in some cases this can be achieved only by removing the patient from the family environment for a time. Resistance and disbelief are common at this stage and the helping process may have several 'starts'.

If the patient does become more active, this is the time to involve the patient and family members in joint sessions. It is best to try to arrange for all parties to agree on the strategy for rehabilitation. Where appropriate, work can continue on the exploration of the development of the behaviour and the possible reasons for its maintenance. Parent-child relationship problems, or sexual or marital problems may exist. In spite of genuine attempts to 'get better' many patients relapse during the course of treatment. As in Julie's case, it is sometimes impossible to do other than point out possible problems. People may choose the status quo rather than looking at the other problems. They would rather not make changes to a stable situation which, for the moment, is meeting the needs of the participants.

23 Tim:
death in the family

CASE HISTORY

Tim, aged ten years, was referred to a department of Child and Family Psychiatry because of his refusal to go to school. The problem had been present for two months and was becoming serious. An assessment visit to the family home revealed a complex picture of stressful life events which were clearly important to an understanding of Tim's difficulties. In a long interview, punctuated by many episodes of weeping, the mother revealed what she saw as the 'wreckage' of her life. The current family structure was that she and Tim lived together, the father having died a year previously and Tim's only brother (Robert) having recently left home to join the army. From the family history it seemed that the most significant experiences for the mother and Tim had been the events surrounding the father's death, and the aftermath of this.

The father's medical history had been quite unremarkable, and his sudden death from a massive heart attack came as a complete shock to the family. On the evening of his death, the mother had gone out on the pretext of visiting a friend, but, in fact, had gone to a bingo hall with a group of her workmates. Her husband, a man of rigid views, disapproved of any form of gambling, and had forbidden his wife ever to visit a bingo hall. Persuaded by her friends, however, she had now practised this deception on a number of occasions, without discovery. It was during her absence that the father succumbed to a heart attack which was to prove fatal. Tim was the only other person in the house at the time and had to help his father. Realising that there was something very wrong with him, the boy had run up and down the street trying to summon help from neighbours. Tim eventually managed to get a neighbour to accompany him home and contact the emergency services. His mother's friend was also contacted only to reveal that she had not been seen by her all evening. Tim stayed with a neighbour until his mother returned finally. Unfortunately, his father was dead on arrival at the hospital.

On assessment, mother described herself as having been 'in a state of shock' ever since then. She had been 'wracked with guilt' for having deceived her husband by visiting the bingo hall against his wishes, and regarded his sudden death as a 'judgement from Heaven' upon herself. Her guilt was made even worse when, some months later, she obtained employment as a nursing auxiliary and was sent to help out in the coronary care unit. Here she saw daily evidence of how, if dealt with in time, may patients survived quite serious heart attacks and were still able to lead reasonably rewarding lives. She began to regard her work on the coronary care unit as almost a penance, and as a constant reminder of how she had failed her husband and family.

Social work assessment indicated that there were three major problem areas to be addressed within this family: first, the mother's unresolved grief and the many conflicts that stemmed from it and maintained it; second, Tim's delayed grief reaction; and third, Tim's recent school attendance problems. These three issues were inextricably linked and could not, therefore, be considered in isolation. Each had a profound bearing upon the other, and it seemed likely, therefore, that therapeutic improvement in one would lead to improvements in the others.

Mother's unresolved grief

Although her husband's death had occurred a year earlier, the mother was still in a state of profound grief and had been unable to complete her mourning. Individual casework intervention with her was aimed at helping her to 'move on' through the grieving process so that resolution of her mourning could be achieved. It was hoped that this would then create space and opportunity for Tim to mourn his father too.

The key to helping the mother forward lay in considering and re-evaluating with her (a) her relationship with her late husband, and (b) the circumstances surrounding his death. She maintained that she and her husband had always had a close and warm relationship, but it became clear from discussions with her that this had been somewhat one-sided. Descriptions of the father indicated that he had been a rigid, fussy and irritable man, who clearly liked to have his own way in most things, and seemed used to getting it. He had strict views on most things, commanded obedience to his authority as head of the household, and this created a number of family difficulties. The most obvious was that their eldest son, Robert, began to challenge his father's authority, and this produced friction in the home. For her part, the mother was used to conceding to her husband's views and to taking the course of action which would lead to the quietest and least disruptive way out of a difficulty. She had never really challenged her husband's opinions or actions, and had counselled her sons to do likewise. Robert, however, was made of very different metal, and found his father's behaviour provocative and productive of dissent. The continuing friction between father and son led Robert to think about joining the army as a way of getting away from the oppressive home atmosphere. Discussion helped the mother to see how her own strong dependency needs towards her husband had made her over-compliant and uncritical of him as a partner. In addition, his death and the guilt that this had produced, had led her to idealise him, so that it was not easy for her to admit to any negative feelings towards him.

A reconsideration of the circumstances surrounding his death was difficult and painful for both the mother and the worker. His death, occurring as it did, had left her with profound guilt feelings. She had lied to him before leaving the house and had, she thought, invited the disaster of his death upon herself. She had made herself a widow and her children fatherless! She had convinced herself that, had she been at home, his life would have been saved. Tellingly, since his death she had been unable to talk to anyone about it. Currently, she refused to leave the house in the evenings and denied herself any social life. Mother thought that punishing herself in this way would make the grief easier to bear, but found that her self-imposed social isolation only made it harder. One of the few positive things in her life was her work, but this also was a reminder of her sad loss. The generally heavy emotional atmosphere at home was also taking its toll of the two boys. Following the death, Robert initially thought that his plans for leaving home had been thwarted and viewed his grieving mother as an unwelcome responsibility that he might be expected to shoulder. For young Tim, his main concern was that his mother was making herself ill, and he found himself worrying about her while he was in school. The mother's grief seemed to permeate all spheres of their daily lives and, though some contact from relatives offered a brief respite, Robert found the situation too difficult to live with. He had, therefore, taken the decision to join the army and left home.

By patiently guiding the mother through the events surrounding her husband's death, the caseworker was able to gain access to her feelings and to help her explore these more productively. Her exaggerated sense of guilt was looked at in more realistic terms, and she was encouraged to express the more suppressed emotions of anger and hatred. Her feelings of abandonment had been exacerbated by the departure of her son Robert, but she had never been able to express these before. She had, instead, withdrawn into depression.

Tim's delayed grief reaction
Tim had been shocked and bewildered by the trauma of his father's death and its aftermath. He felt overwhelmed by his mother's sadness, and unable to relate to this in a way which was helpful to himself. Since he had been a first-hand witness to the traumatic event, he was regarded by the adults as needing shielding from further trauma. As a result, he had not been included in the plans for the funeral and was sent to stay with an aunt in the country following the funeral.

When he returned, he found little remaining evidence of his father ever having been part of their lives. Many of his father's possessions had been tidied away, the furniture had been moved about so that their living environment looked and felt quite strange to him, and a previously prominent photograph of his parents had been removed. In individual sessions, Tim said that he felt the subject of his father's death had become taboo, and that discussion of it felt prohibited. It seemed that Tim had surrendered his own feelings of grief, and his need to mourn, in order to help and support his mother. During sessions with the caseworker, he expressed a lot of anxiety about his mother's health, and his fears that she too might die, and he would be left alone. The caseworker was able to reassure him about his mother's health, and about the slow but sure progress she was making.

As work with the mother progressed, she was encouraged to replace some of her husbnd's belongings around the house. This meant that she and Tim could begin to share the feelings that these mementoes evoked in them. This therapeutic procedure was conducted very gradually over a period of several weeks, and was carefully paced so that if did not make unacceptable demands on either mother or son.

Tim's school attendance problem

Tim's recent reluctance to attend school seemed directly related to his anxiety about his mother's well-being. Her bouts of sadness and weeping, her withdrawal from normal social activities, and her increasing social isolation were features that caused him growing concern. When relatives visited, mother would put on a brave face and Tim was not in a position to contradict her in their presence. He began to feel that he needed to keep her under surveillance and at first he began to run home from school in his lunch hour. This gradually escalated to regular non-attendance. He produced assorted ailments in order to explain his non-attendance to his mother. After a few weeks, mother began to worry about his school refusal and started to pressure him to return to school. This placed Tim in a conflict, since his presence at home reduced his anxiety about his mother but, at the same time, it increased his mother's anxiety, about which (along with her depression) he was anxious in the first place!

Once the casework was under way with mother and Tim, a gradual reintroduction to school was started. This had been carefully negotiated beforehand with school staff, and was structured so that any temporary set-backs could be accommodated without difficulty. His mother played an important part in this phased reintroduction by initially accompanying Tim to school and spending some time there with him and his teacher.

COMMENT

Mental Health Aspects

The extensive literature on death and bereavement illustrates many of the features presented in this case. Guilt is always a part of the bereavement process and, as in this case, may become an exaggerated feature. Studies of widows and their families (e.g. Marris, 1959) have concluded that in many of the families seen it was the mother's grief that permeated the household, and that this often impeded the grieving process for the children in the family.

In this case, ambivalence and unacknowledged conflicts within the marriage led to a degree of falseness within the relationship, and this had also promoted minor deception on the part of the wife. It was not unexpected, therefore, that following the husband's death the mother should resolve her ambivalence by idealising her relationship with him. Sudden death had absolved him of all his faults, rather in the same way that historically martyrdom conferred blamelessness and sanctity upon the victim.

We know from studies in child psychiatry that children who present with school refusal may be suffering from varying degrees of separation anxiety from a parent figure. Tim's case illustrates very clearly how this phenomenon can develop, and how the continuing conflict around it can render a solution difficult to achieve. Of course, in most instances individuals manage to adjust to such losses. It is where the natural process is impeded, by circumstances such as seen here, that we find people eventually becoming clinical cases.

Casework Aspects

In this case, individual casework was undertaken with mother and son, the therapist later moving into joint work, and the use of behavioural techniques. Where there is a failed or unresolved bereavement, the 'guided mourning' technique can help the individual to recognise those feelings which the bereaved often reject as being too awful to think about. These feelings, such as anger and hatred towards the dead, are important features of mourning within most societies and cultures. Failure to recognise and accept such feelings, however, will often produce blocks in the bereavement process. The grieving individual becomes stuck and cannot move forward unaided. In this case, the mother dealt with her guilt by idealising the memory of her dead husband. She could not begin to resolve her grief until she was helped to take a more realistic view of her husband and to recognise and acknowledge some of his less virtuous qualities. Mourning is helped by having the impedimenta of mourning available—photographs of the dead person, small keepsakes, mementoes, etc.—all serve to remind the living of their loss, and give the opportunity for releasing emotion. It was important to complete some of this work with the mother before involving Tim in his mourning, since he would need to feel that his mother had regained some strength in order that he could begin to rely upon her to help him.

Several practical suggestions were made to mother, in addition to the more psychotherapeutic aspects of the work. She was encouraged to apply for a transfer to another part of the hospital, so that she was not constantly reminding herself of the trauma of her husband's death. In addition, suggestions were made to encourage her to develop a social life for herself. This began with fairly modest suggestions such as visiting a neighbour for a coffee. She was encouraged to undertake some shopping for an elderly housebound neighbour while she was doing her own . This served the dual purpose of extending the range of mother's social contacts, but of also making her feel that she was important in the eyes of others. As Tim began to grow in confidence, he spontaneously began to re-establish some of his friendships and to spend less time with his mother. This was a very healthy and positive development for Tim, since studies have shown that following the death of the father, the son can develop an exaggerated sense of responsibility and protectiveness towards the mother. This kind of development can often impede maturity in boys, particularly during adolescence, so that they remain tied to the home in the pseudo-role of husband/father. This has often been noted to have a disturbing effect upon their capacity to cope with heterosexual relationships in adult life. It may have been an anticipation of these kinds of difficulty that prompted Robert to follow his original plan to leave home and join the army.

Finally, it seemed important that Tim and his mother should, at some point, make contact with Robert and encourage him to visit home during his leave periods. This would help Tim feel that he had some semblance of family, still intact, and might give Robert an opportunity to make sense of some of his own conflicting feelings (see Black, 1978; Speece and Brent, 1984).

24 Yvonne:

casework with an adolescent with hysteria

CASE HISTORY

According to the medical record, Yvonne was admitted to hospital for the first time in October, aged sixteen, with a major attack of hysteria following a severe family disturbance. Her father was an alcoholic who had been repeatedly separated from her mother, and the patient had a history of conflict with the family. In January, when the situation had become intolerable and the patient had run away from home, she was placed in a foster home where her adjustment was described as precarious. This was unlike her elder sister, Jean, who remained living at home. Yvonne seemed resentful of authority and was frequently seclusive and withdrawn.

It was on a visit to her family, at the invitation of her mother, that this hysterical attack had apparently been precipitated. Her father, of whom the patient was very fond, had been highly intoxicated and had awakened from a nap to hear the voice of a male relative who had come into the house. A violent scene ensued, during which the relative was physically assaulted by Yvonne's father. Her mother had become 'very hysterical', lost consciousness and a doctor had been called to assist. The doctor was also attacked and beaten by the father, who was only subdued when the police finally arrived. It was in the midst of this scene that the time came for the patient to be returned to the foster home. After arriving there, Yvonne collapsed and was admitted subsequently to a casualty ward in a general hospital, from which she was transferred to an adolescent psychiatric ward. While there she had daily interviews with the psychiatrist. The hospital-based psychiatric social worker became involved after the patient's fifth week of hospitalisation to work with Yvonne on her discharge and follow-up plans. After liaison with the local Social Services department social worker, Miss W. who had been supervising the girl in her foster home, the psychiatric social worker agreed to try and work with the patient.

The worker first visited Yvonne on her ward during November to discuss her plans following discharge. Yvonne was an attractive, rather stout girl, with lovely teeth and an engaging smile, although during the interview she smiled very little. As the social worker greeted her, the nurse prepared to unlock an interviewing room, but Yvonne said that she did not want to go in as there was no window. The worker remarked that they did not have to go there and asked where she would prefer. She did not care and wanted the worker to decide. The worker asked her if she thought the settee in the day room would be all right and she agreed. As soon as they had reached it, Yvonne sat down solemnly, immediately lit a cigarette and continued to smoke constantly throughout the interview.

The social worker said to Yvonne, 'The reason that I have come is to see if I could be of help with plans.' The worker wondered if Yvonne had been able to think much about what she would like to do. Yvonne asked what difference it would make as she was not old enough to decide what she would do anyway. The social worker said that, however true that was, Yvonne was certainly old enough to have some feelings and to know what she would like most ... and that was what really mattered at present. After this the patient spoke more readily, telling the worker about home, school, jobs, her foster home and the doctor.

She said that the only thing that she really wanted was to return home. She did not wish to return to school as she had never liked it, although she could not say exactly why this was so. When asked if she thought that she would like to work she replied affirmatively. She recalled how her one experience of work had been during the previous summer when she had cared for two small children and had loved it. She and the social worker talked about the foster home, and the social worker wondered if it had been the only one in which the patient had lived. Yvonne said that she had been in two temporary homes first. She had not liked the girls in these homes at all ... they were 'too tough'. When asked what her foster parents were like, she replied immediately that they were much too old to have foster children in their home. Mrs Cochran, the foster mother, was always finding fault with Yvonne's ideas and getting shocked at things. She reiterated her desire to return home but added that as far as her mother was concerned 'it wouldn't matter if I never came back'. Here she grew morose and did not say anything for several minutes. The social worker asked how she liked the ward and whether she had any special friends there, and was told of two girls whith whom she got along best. One was a 'mama's girl' and was always shocked at everything, especially the language that the other patients used. Yvonne said that this did not bother her though. Again, the patient said that she did not know what she should do; 'Maybe I should stay here for good.'

The social worker asked Yvonne, 'Do you feel any better since coming on to the ward?' and was surprised by the answer. 'If I am better it isn't because of that Dr C.! I don't care. He never tells me when he is coming anyway. As far as I'm concerned he is just unpredictable.' 'It must be an uncomfortable feeling, not knowing what time to plan on his visit', replied the worker and Yvonne agreed. (It later transpired that one of the patient's chief complaints about her father, which she voiced often, was that he was so undependable about time and would rarely come home when he was expected.)

Near the end of the interview the worker remarked, 'It is not necessary for us to settle now what you would like to do when ready to leave ... We have time to think it over. How would it be if I came back again?' Yvonne said that this would be fine and the worker arranged to return in two days. Yvonne said, 'I hope that you won't be angry if I don't talk then though.' 'I suppose all of us feel at times that we would rather not talk. Maybe when I see you again some new ideas will have occurred to us', the worker replied. Yvonne smiled and said, 'At least I can tell you if I like your ideas or not.'

When the worker visited two days later, Yvonne was dressed in her pyjamas and robe. When the worker suggested that they talk there in Yvonne's room, the patient climbed into bed where she remained. She said that she was beginning to feel annoyed at the ward. People had to be watching the patients all of the time and this seemed, to her, a sneaky thing to do.

The patient said that she was sure that to go home for a trial was the best plan for her, but that it was very important that everything go well. She knew that a social worker would see her mother about her plans for going home, and talked a bit about how difficult it was getting along with her mother. She complained that she wished that she were just six years older and then maybe understanding her mother would be easier!

The patient was seen again a week later and again she was wearing a housecoat and pyjamas. She was more active than usual, walking restlessly around the room. After the social worker and she had talked about how it would feel to leave the ward, they discussed the things to which it would be good for Yvonne to return. 'We [i.e. the doctor and I] will both be interested in how the home visit goes', said the social worker.

At this point Yvonne spoke of how troubled she was about the doctor and the social worker talking together about her. The social worker encouraged Yvonne to say what things she thought that the two might be sharing concerning her. She readily told the worker that she had been shocked to discover that they had discussed her at all ... it was not so much a matter of what they said but that they said anything! The worker said that most patients would be bound to feel anxious about this and told Yvonne that they should have discussed it with her rather than assuming that she knew what use was to be made of the material she presented. The worker explained carefully saying that 'Dr C. and I are working together to help you get well so we exchange information which we think will be helpful to accomplish this.' The patient kept returning to this during the interview and she pointed out that she guessed that she had never learned to trust people. Maybe that was why she got so concerned about the doctor and the social worker talking over her situation.

The patient told the social worker that she hated Miss W. who was her social worker in the Social Services department. The reason was that she did not treat any of the girls as individuals but tried 'to make them grow into whatever she wanted to be when she was little. She tells the foster children what to do every minute.' The psychiatric social worker said that even when girls were learning to make decisions for themselves, it would be natural for them to need help with these sometimes. Yvonne could see this, but said that she did get angry with Miss W. When it was suggested that the time might come when the patient might get angry with the psychiatric social worker, Yvonne denied this vigorously. Nevertheless, the social worker said that it would be all right if Yvonne did get angry as people do not always agree on everything.

As the interview proceeded, Yvonne told the worker about a great many things which revealed her hostile feelings towards her mother. It was difficult to find anything positive in their relationship. Finally, after extricating a promise that the worker would not smile or think it was foolish, she asked how long a girl had to wait to get married. The worker said that most girls of fifteen or sixteen liked to wait a while, to know what things they wanted 'for keeps' before deciding about marriage. Yvonne talked about her boyfriend Jerry, whom she had known for three years. They found waiting very hard. Both families objected to their seeing each other, as Jerry was a Roman Catholic and the patient was not. The patient's concern was whether she should sneak out to see Jerry while she was home. Did the worker think that she should? The social worker did not think, as apparently Yvonne did not, that sneaking about was a very happy way to see him. The worker wondered how else Yvonne might arrange to see him, perhaps letting him know that she was to be home for the day. Yvonne replied that she might not see him tomorrow anyway. To this the social worker replied simply, 'Have a pleasant visit. I look forward to seeing you when you return.'

After the home visit the patient told the worker slowly about her trip. She had never been so scared in her life, she said. She thought it was nice having someone to talk to about it. She was still sure that she wanted to go home to live. However, she would want to work and that was something she had to be thinking about. The social worker encouraged her in this. Yvonne said that she would like to take some aptitude tests if possible. She thought that if she could have some vocational test, she would be in a much better position to decide what course of action to take. The social worker agreed to follow this up on Yvonne's behalf and report back. Once she started talking about her experiences, the patient seemed in good spirits and as the social worker walked away nurses were heard commenting upon how happy Yvonne seemed to be.

It was a week later when the patient was next seen. The worker had arranged for a psychologist to come and give the tests as soon as possible. In the meantime, the social worker suggested that they might work on some other things about going out of hospital. Yvonne agreed, but said that from her trip home she knew that she was not yet ready to leave the ward. She just hated to think of going home already. The social worker said, 'You must hate to see me coming, then, as we talk about home.' The patient denied this. 'No. When we talk about it it is as if it were "some day".' 'One of these days the time will be closer. If you do get feeling shaky about leaving, I wouldn't blame you for that. I think that all patients find it hard to leave the ward.'

The question came up again of what Dr C. and the social worker talked about when discussing the patient. It developed that what really bothered Yvonne was whether the social worker had told the doctor about what Yvonne had said about Jerry. She, at last, revealed that she had wanted the social worker to tell him. 'I couldn't', said Yvonne, 'bring myself to talk about my feelings for Jerry to Doctor C.' 'I think that all of us find it easier to talk to women about some things and to men about others', said the social worker. Yvonne asked again how much longer she would have to wait to know if the feelings which she had for Jerry were right. They talked about what it felt like to be sixteen and how different she felt now than from when she had been thirteen. The social worker still felt that for Yvonne there was going to be a lot of growing up in the next four or five years and said so.

When they met two days later the patient seemed quite unsettled and her mood swung from near hilarity to moroseness. She was much preoccupied with Dr C., about whom she talked a great deal. First she said that he was strange. Next she showed intense interest in everything about the doctor's appearance, commenting upon his eyes, the colour of his hair, and whether or not he had freckles. She revealed that she was both afraid of the doctor and angry at him ... she thought it was because he knew so much about her. She was somewhat anxious about what the doctor would do with all these things he knew about her. The social worker spoke of the naturalness of such concern.

Yvonne also told the worker that she did not know what people would do if she got angry at them, and this was a problem. If they got angry back she guessed she would feel better. She said she bet that the worker never got angry. The worker told her that she guessed that all of us had angry feelings at one time or another, and that she thought these were all right. She suggested to Yvonne that these were the kind of things the doctor could help her with. Yvonne expressed a fear that he did not really care about her and her might walk out and leave her. Yvonne suddenly said that she wished she were a boy. Boys had much more freedom and could do so many more things than girls without having to be looked after. They talked about what it meant to be a girl and the social worker told her that she could scarcely be so pretty if she were a boy instead. The patient looked shy, then burst forth telling the worker that she had handed her a 'line long enough to hang clothes on!' 'I look just like Frankenstein, and you know it', she said. The worker assured her that she did not know any such thing.

Yvonne mentioned Miss W. again and said that she hoped that she would never have to see her again. The social worker told her that this was not something that she could promise her. She asked Yvonne for her recent thoughts about a job and she replied that she wanted work that was exciting; by exciting she meant a job that was not always the same, but something different happening all the time. The patient said that she was not ready to go home and the social worker told her that the doctor just felt that she was ready to think about it.

When they met a week later the patient was greatly elated, as her visit home and her discharge date were both coming closer. The worker attempted to talk with her realistically about her plans, but the patient said only that everything was going to be fine. The worker asked her about her heavy smoking, of which she had said her mother strongly disapproved. After several minutes of reflection, the patient said that her mother would 'just have to get used to it, that's all!'

The patient pointed out that the doctor had accidentally called the social worker by her first name to her. When the social worker asked her what this meant, Yvonne replied that this meant that not only did the two work together, but that they were also good friends. She asked the social worker the doctor's first name but the social worker said that she didn't believe she even knew what it was.

When next seen four days later, Yvonne was less jubilant. She had her hair curled nicely and the social worker commented on this. Yvonne asked the social worker not to tell the doctor. He would probably make something of it, as he had one day when he noticed that she wore lipstick. Yvonne said that she did not know why she wore it. The worker wondered if perhaps she just wanted to look more attractive. The patient did not answer and the social worker said it was quite understandable to want to look as nice as possible. Yvonne laughed at this and said that she was never going to wear lipstick again!

During January and February the social worker continued to see Yvonne regularly. Although anxious, Yvonne did well on the aptitude tests, particularly on intelligence, judgement and interest. She made her weekend visit home which was not happy, and for which she was totally amnesic afterward. She decided that she did not want to go home to live and her discharge date was again postponed. School was considered by the patient but abandoned immediately. In January she began to wear make-up and went on a weight-reducing diet which had the effect of improving her appearance considerably. After long consideration, the patient said that she would go to a foster home, but at the last minute refused. She asked to be allowed to go to her own home. She remained at home for one week during which time she was seen in the out-patient clinic by both the doctor and the social worker. At the end of that week she was brought back in a state of collapse. Her period of ward-based treatment was extended indefinitely and the worker sought to maintain the relationship which had been begun, until further treatment rendered her able to begin making new plans.

This proved to be a very arduous time for both the worker and the client. The worker had to devote more time to another case which had erupted and, upon returning to the ward one day, having been out with that patient, she was greeted by Yvonne looking very distressed. It seems that she had been vomiting ever since the social worker had left and was still very ill. In the subsequent week, when the worker was again called out of hospital for work on another case, Yvonne collapsed again into a comatose state and was removed to a medical ward for closer investigations. As before, these proved negative. When the social worker had gone to visit Yvonne on the medical ward, the patient had been in bed looking unkempt and dazed. At first she would neither look at the social worker nor speak, but gradually focused her eyes and spoke in whispers. As the worker left, she smiled weakly and seemed aware of who had been visiting her and that she would be returning.

When next seen the patient seemed depressed and out of sorts, saying that she thought that she 'must be jealous or something'—perhaps wanting some attention and sympathy. The social worker allowed Yvonne to express her irritation at her and the doctor for not making her feel better, and urged her to talk to the doctor about the things which bothered her about treatment. Yvonne said that she was beginning to agree with her mother that even being in hospital was all foolishness.

Another two months elapsed, during which time the patient's progress appeared quite static. She was emotionally insecure and required constant reassurance of the worker's continuing interest. Sometimes she reiterated how her opinion did not count as the doctor and the social worker made the decisions without her. She was fed up with making plans but never carrying them out and would not talk about her future. She was angry that the worker had not found her a job, but was partially forgiving as she felt that the social worker must be very busy. She then thought this over and concluded that the worker had been busy with other patients and refused to speak to her any more.

One day the social worker sat down with Yvonne. The patient was silent. The worker said how it must seem that her being busy with things for other patients prevented her from having time to help Yvonne. She remained silent. The worker suggested that for anyone the business of learning to share was hard, but for Yvonne it seemed especially hard. Yvonne's answer was that she had trouble talking to the social worker but that she didn't think that the other patients or anyone else had anything to do with it. She simply wanted to leave hospital without further discussion. The worker said that she accepted that Yvonne was angry and did not wish to push her.

Nevertheless, the social worker disliked seeing Yvonne so unhappy about things. Yvonne remained very tense and silent and made to leave. The worker asked her to stay a minute longer. 'I would like to tell you what I think the trouble is', said the social worker. 'I believe that this is a repeat of things which have happened to you before. At home. Doesn't it seem that Jean, got everything? You didn't get on with your parents and she did. You left and she stayed. She got everything that you have so badly wanted. If this situation of ours is like another unpleasant one in your life, it will be probably even harder for you to accept than for any other patient. What I hope you understand is that I still very much want to help you.' Yvonne said angrily that the worker had not yet got her that for which she had asked! 'I know that at this moment you do not feel like participating in the planning, but I do not want to plan without you', replied the social worker.

The patient stormed out of the room without saying goodbye and with the social worker following her. In passing Yvonne told the nurse that she never wanted to see the social worker again. Suddenly she turned and cried like a child, begging to be allowed to go home. The worker said that she and the doctor did not feel that she was quite ready to go yet. Yvonne said that nobody was helping her and that the worker was too busy. She screamed that the social worker should go and see the other patient. The worker stayed with her, saying that she had come to see her and to help her if she could. Yvonne cried that the worker did not care at all, that she would never go to any place that the social worker arranged if it was the last place on earth and that she would not let the worker put her anywhere. The worker assured her that it was neither her wish nor intention to do so. Yvonne walked away without another word, still weeping.

Extract from the social worker's file for the following day:
Patient talked to me today. She was strangely mixed, at one time very 'grown up' and at another like a small child. Patient was very interested in what I had been able to find out about employment. We talked a little about how hard it had been for her to see me the last few days. I gave her

as much support and acceptance as I could around her right to be angry with me.

COMMENT

Mental Health Aspects

The case of Yvonne is, in many ways, typical of hysteria which primarily afflicts people at the two ends of the age spectrum. Certainly, it is well described among over-emotional young people, especially young women, and is very strongly associated with psychosexual difficulties and 'matters of the heart (i.e. her boy-friend Jerry). As with Yvonne, stresses encountered in settings such as school or home frequently result in a 'flight into illness' (i.e. hysterical collapse and amnesia) and the adoption of the 'sick role' to avoid responsibilities (i.e. determination to remain a patient).

The diagnosis of hysteria refers to a neurotic condition, psychogenic in origin, in which individuals' symptoms mimic, to varying degrees, a broad range of illnesses (traditionally neurological ones), either physical or mental. Upon investigation, there is often some comprehensible reason for the development of such a condition, normally advantageous to the patient, although the patient remains between totally and partially unaware of this motivation, and the symptoms adopted can have symbolic meaning to the patient. Traditionally, the symptoms displayed by the patient have been related to traumatic past events, and treatment to the abreaction of the emotional forces which have kept symptoms in operation. Basic to conventional notions of hysteria is that the patient has a sense of low self- esteem and consequent inability or unwillingness to face up to unpleasantness in life. Hysteria, then, can be viewed as a psychological strategy for coping with conflict stimulated by fear or anxiety. It is adopted primarily by individuals whose personalities are egocentric, attention seeking, dependent, emotional, shallow, narcissistic, flighty and/or fanciful, and who display a strong sense of the melodramatic in their personal relaionships. As such, it can have a strong characterological flavour as is, to a degree, true of this case. Nevertheless, under conditions of stress, hysterical reactions can occur in people of basically normal personality and strong character.

Casework Aspects

Stages of casework

There are many interesting aspects to this case, including Yvonne's psychodynamics, her family and the part that her relationship with them played in the genesis of her condition, and her relationship (viewed from a distance) with her psychiatrist, to name but a few. But to a social worker, perhaps the most striking thing about this case is the way that Yvonne's total condition was dealt with by the social worker who needed to take into account both the characterological (acting-out) and the neurotic (defensive) dimensions of

Yvonne's presentation. In practice, there was a need to provide, through the medium of casework, a corrective relationship through which the client could gradually develop through introjecting the image of a 'good parent' in order to deal with the characterological element. To deal with the neurotic element, the worker needed to identify the source of Yvonne's conflict with her as residing in her oedipal or 'triangular' family relationships and to 'work through' this. As can be seen, these conflicts were very prominent in this case, with Yvonne's feelings of aggression towards her mother, jealousy towards her sister and affection for her father being readily 'transferred' into her relationships with the worker, other patients and Dr C. The proper casework techniques required to do this are well-known and include environmental manipulation, emotional release, clarification and making selected interpretations (Austin, 1968, pp. 171-5), all of which were employed by Yvonne's social worker. Using them, however, required not only that the worker knew the appropriate techniques, but also the proper time in the treatment process and place in the client's developmental structure for their use.

In their widely read work, Reiner and Kaufmann (1959) deleniated the necessities of treatment for cases such as this. The four-stage casework process they suggested provides a useful basis for analysing the treatment approach employed here. The stages are (a) establishing a therapeutic relationship; (b) identification of the client with the caseworker; (c) psychosexual growth of the client towards establishment of an autonomous, separate identity; (d) helping the client gain self-understanding (see Reiner and Kaufman, 1959, pp. 66-152 for a fuller exposition of the theory from which the following case analysis is derived).

The first stage of psychodynamic casework is relationship building, and this may highlight or reactivate conflicts over authority figures and may require a period of 'testing out' of the worker in order to establish basic trust. This was certainly the case with Yvonne who, for example, was anxious initially to know about the limits of acceptance of the worker in relation to such things as where an interview would take place or what might happen if the patient refused to speak, or if she chose to smoke. Also, in respect of basic trust, Yvonne raised concerns as to the limits of confidentiality for the worker in her own contacts with other professionals. Particularly important were the 'irrational' characteristics of Yvonne's feelings for authority and the need for the worker, during the early stages, to manage the transference of hostile feelings more appropriately placed with parents and other professionals. Through the first three interviews, this case shows several signs of treatment success. Yvonne kept appointments regularly; she showed signs of willingness to accept the worker's explanations; she revealed negative feelings for others, including the other social worker and her mother; she showed a more relaxed attitude towards the treatment; and she showed a genuine interest in what the social worker thought. The worker made an attempt to be accepting, unauthoritative, understanding and open with Yvonne to facilitate the process.

The second stage of casework treatment centres on the identification of the client with the worker. The casework task is to use the opportunity to help to strengthen the client's ego. This stage becomes particularly evident when the client begins to imitate the worker, or display dependency and shows signs of attachment 'bonding' (e.g. distress when separation, rejection or abandonment are threatened). In the case of Yvonne, some indications of the identification process were as follows: after discussion with the worker, the patient decided not to see her boyfriend on a home visit, thus sharing one of the worker's attitudes and corresponding controls; the patient began to voice concerns about leaving the ward; she showed an interest in whether the worker would reject her if she showed anger; and she improved her appearance and made gradual progress away from being confined to bed. The caseworker encouraged her in all of these things and also helped the client 'to deal with misconceptions' which interfered with her ability to perceive reality by, for example, pointing out to Yvonne how very attractive she was, a reality which conflicted with her, own less-flattering self-image.

The aim of the third stage is 'separation-individuation' or the establishment of a separate identity by the client. This is not a simple re-emergence of the previous personality, but of one which has internalised new 'libidinal' objects which will influence both our self-image and our future dealings with others. This stage often entails some expression of negative feelings towards the worker, resembling the adolescent's separation from its parents, and may elicit extremes of emotion. Also, as with any loss, it will be associated with a degree of internal reorganisation and subsequently feelings of depression and hostility. In this case, that proved to be as critical an issue in treatment as it had been in reality, where the patient was striving for independence. During this transitional phase, Yvonne showed signs of emotional regression and deterioration in her condition. Typically, there was a lot of ambivalence shown towards the social worker. Sometimes Yvonne was silent and she suffered a relapse with symptoms of vomiting and emotional collapse associated with feelings related to possible loss of attention from the social worker. This manifestation of conflict through symptoms rather than through acting-out can actually be interpreted as a sign of treatment progress, in the sense that the former requires a more mature level of psychosexual development than the latter. Alternatively, she was sometimes 'depressed and out of sorts' and on one day she had an emotional outburst at the worker. (This case also usefully illustrates the fallacy of expecting therapy to be a story of unbroken progress, 'onwards and upwards' . Usually it is more likely to be a story of 'two steps forward and one backward' where the worker must be prepared for regression as part of treatment.)

In the fourth stage of casework, the patient must have made enough progress towards establishing an individual identity to allow him or her to engage in a relationship at a mature level. Reiner and Kaufman stress the point that it can be observed from the content of the discussions that the patient is, 'able to take independent action and make..... decisions based on realistic factors'...and that, 'requests for help imply that (s)he expects to participate in working on his (her) problems and to take responsibility for finding solutions to them' (pp. 140-1). The worker's final reporting the Yvonne seemed 'grown up' can be taken to indicate considerable progress towards separation. It is very significant that the patient had achieved sufficient control over her internal conflicts to allow her to deal with the task of future employment in a rational, realistic and non-impulsive fashion. It is also a significant mark of progress in the case that eventually the worker was able to use clarification and interpretation with Yvonne and that she, albeit with some difficulty, was able to listen to what was said and to use it to help herself in the task of self-understanding and as a means of changing behaviour.

Of hysteria, psychiatry, psychonalysis and casework

A final point worth considering is the particular relevance of cases of hysteria to social casework. It is important to know that almost from its inception, mental health casework has been strongly influenced by psychiatry and psychoanalysis, and the factors which have influenced their growth. One such factor was the actual description of hysteria and the development of interpersonal methods of treating it which emerged at the end of the nineteenth century. These jointly formed the basis of casework and psychoanalysis, many psychiatrists (e.g. Otto Rank, Alfred Adler) being involved in the evolution of both.

A milestone in this development was the publication of *Studies On Hysteria* by Freud and Breuer in 1895. This series of case studies, derived from the two men's earlier interests in hypnosis and hysteria, made the most significant contribution of this period, the development of free association. This technique actually evolved as a direct consequence of the treatment in the years 1880-82 by Breuer of the first of their reported cases. She was Fraulein Anna O., a twenty-one-year-old woman suffering from, among other things, hysterical anaesthesia, paraphrasia, food refusal, amnesia and hallucinations, and was described by Breuer thus:

> She was markedly intelligent, with an astonishingly quick grasp of things and penetrating intuition. She possessed a powerful intellect which would have been capable of digesting solid mental pabulum and which stood in need of it—though without receiving it after she had left school. She had great poetic and imaginative gifts, which were under the control of a sharp and critical common sense. Owing to this latter quality she was completely unsuggestible; she was only influenced by arguments, never by mere assertions. Her will-power was energetic, tenacious and persistent; sometimes it reached the pitch of an obstinacy which only gave way out of kindness and regard for other people...One of her

essential character traits was sympathetic kindness. (Freud and Breuer, 1974, p. 73)

It was, in fact, the psychiatric patient Anna O. who actually coined the term 'talking cure' for the process by which she, and subsequently others such as Yvonne, was treated by systematically 'talking away' her symptoms (Freud and Breuer, 1974, pp. 83-98). This 'talking cure' was later to be called the 'cathartic method' by Breuer and to become eventually, via Freud's elaboration 'free association', the basis of both psychoanalysis and casework. What is seldom acknowledged about her, however, is that Anna O. 'became the first social worker in Germany, one of the first in the world. She founded a periodical and several institutes where she trained students' (Jones, 1961, p. 204). These students, and those who followed on were taught, used and elaborated on the 'talking cure' in their own way. To some measure this case and this book are some evidence that the elaboration continues.

Tellingly, in a footnote to his biography of Sigmund Freud, Ernest Jones said of the social worker Anna O., 'Since she was the real discoverer of the cathartic method, her name, which was actually Bertha Pappenheim (27 February 1859–28 May 1936), deserves to be commemorated' (Jones, 1961, p. 202). (We rather agree. Eds.)

REFERENCES

Introduction

Brewer, C. and Lait, J. (1980), *Can Social Work Survive?* Maurice Temple Smith, London.

Brown, M. A. G. (1964, 1971, 1977), 'A review of casework methods' in *Welfare in Action*, M. Fitzgerald (ed.), Open University/Routledge & Kegan Paul, London.

Butler, A. and Pritchard, C. (1984), *Social Work and Mental Illness*, Macmillan, London.

Fischer, J. (1973), 'Is casework effective?' *Social Work*, January, pp. 5-20.

Fisher, M., Newton, C. And Sainsbury, E. (1984), *Mental Health Social Work Observed*: National Institute Social Services Library No.5, George Allen & Unwin, London.

French, L. M. (1940), *Psychiatric Social Work*. The Commonwealth Fund, New York.

Hersen, M. and Barlow, M. (1976), *Single Case Experimental Design: Strategies for Behavioral Change*, Pergamon Press, Oxford.

Hudson B. L. (1982), *Social Work with Psychiatric Patients*, Macmillan, London.

Huxley, P. J. (1985), *Social Work Practice in Mental Health: Community Care Practice Handbook*, Gower, Aldershot.

Kraemer, S. (1987), 'Working with parents: casework of psychotherapy', *J. Child Psychol. Psychiat*, 28(2), pp. 207-13.

Olsen, M. R. (1984), *Social Work and Mental Health: A guide for the Approved Social Worker*, Tavistock, London.

Selby, L. G. (1965), 'Teaching From Case Material' (Talk given at a Study Day for Supervisors, University of Nottingham).

Sheldon, B. (1979), 'Not proven: the case of social work effectiveness', *Community Care*, 14 June.

1. Albert: public enemy number one?

Dale, P. (1986), *Dangerous Families*, Tavistock Publications, London.

Prins, H. (1986), *Dangerous Behaviour, The Law and Mental Disorders*, Tavistock Publications, London.

2. Ann: a problem in mothering

Crisp, A. H. (1980), *Anorexia Nervosa: Let Me Be*, Academic Press, London.

Lacey, J. H. (1983), 'Bulimia nervosa, binge eating and psychogenic vomiting: a controlled treatment study and long term outcome, *British Medical Journal*, 286, pp. 1609-13.

Perlman, H. H. (1971), 'The problem-solving model in social casework' in *Theories of Social Casework*, Robert W. Roberts and Robert H. Nee (eds), University of Chicago Press.

3. Tony Brown: the case of Prometheus Unchained

Birley, J. and Brown, G. (1970), 'Crises and life changes preceding the onset or relapse of acute schizophrenia: clinical aspects', *British Journal of Psychiatry*, 116, pp. 327-33.

Leff, J., Kuipers, L., Berkowitz, R. and Sturgeon, D. (1985), 'A controlled trial of social intervention in the families of schizophrenic patients: two year follow-up', *British Journal of Psychiatry*, 146, pp. 594-600.

Rutter, M., Cox, A., Egert, S. Holbrook, D. and Everitt, B. (1981), 'Psychiatric interviewing techniques IV. experimental study: four contrasting styles', *British Journal of Psychiatry*, 138, pp. 456-65.

Vaughn, C. E. and Leff, J. P.(1976), 'The influence of family and social factors on the

course of psychiatric illness: a comparison of schizophrenic and depressed neurotic patients', *British Journal of Psychiatry*, 129, pp. 125-37.
Wing, J. K. and Brown, G. (1970), *Institutionalism and Schizophrenia*, Cambridge University Press, London.

4. Colin: a quality of life

Goldberg, E. M. and Warburton, R. W. (1979), *Ends and Means in Social Work*, Allen & Unwin, London.
Martindale, B. (1987), 'Huntington's chorea: some psychodynamics seen in those at risk and in the responses of the helping professions', *British Journal of Psychiatry*, 150, pp. 319-23.
Mental Health Act Commission, (1985), *Consent to Treatment*, London.
Reading, P. (1985), *Relatively Speaking—A study of the Impact of Mental Disturbance on the Family as seen by Key Relatives*, MIND, Oxford.
Trethowen, W.H. (1979), *Psychiatry*, Baillière's Concise Medical Textbooks, London.

6. Eddie's story : a fragment

Green, Hanna (1964), *I Never Promised You a Rose Garden*, Pan Books, New York.
Rogers, C. (1967), *On Becoming a Person*, Constable, New York.
Rubin, S. (1972), 'Conversations with the author of *I Never Promised You a Rose Garden*', *The Psychoanalytic Review*, 59(2).
Winnicott, D. W. (1958), *Collected Papers: through paediatrics to psychoanalysis*, Tavistock Publications, London. (Other writers of the Object Relations school include Melanie Klein, W. R. D. Fairburn and Harry Guntrip.)

7. Fred: coping with long-term mental illness

Anderson, C. M. (1977), 'Family intervention with severely disturbed patients', *Archives of General Psychiatry*, 34, pp. 697-702.
Falloon, I. R. H., Boyd, J. L., McGill, C. W., Williamson, M., Razani, J., Moss, H. B., Gilderman, A. M., and Simpson, G. W. (1985), 'Family management in the prevention of morbidity of schizophrenia', *Archives of General Psychiatry*, 42, September, pp. 887-96.
Leff, J., Kuipers, L., Berkowitz, R., Eberlein-Vries, R. and Sturgeon, D. (1982), 'A controlled trial of social intervention in the families of schizophrenic patients', *British Journal of Psychiatry*, 141, pp. 121-34.
Leff, J., Kuipers, L., Berkowitz, R. and Sturgeon, D. (1985), 'A controlled trial of social intervention in the families of schizophrenic patients: two year follow-up', *British Journal of Psychiatry*, 146, pp. 594-600.
Stevens, B. C. (1972), 'Dependence of schizophrenic patients on elderly relatives', *Psychological Medicine*, 2, p. 17-24.
Tarrier, N. and Barrowclough, C. (1986), 'Providing information to relatives about schizophrenia', *British Journal of Psychiatry*, 149, pp. 458-63.

8. John: mania

Davies, M. (1981), *The Essential Social Worker: a guide to positive practice*, Heinneman/Community Care, London.
Weiss, R. S. (1974), 'The provision of social relationships', in Z. Rubin (ed.), *Doing unto Others*, Prentice-Hall, Englewood Cliffs, N.J.

9. Karen: the treatment of a case of phobic anxiety

Calof, D. L. (1985), 'Hypnosis in marital therapy: toward a transgenerational approach' in *Eriksonian Psychotherapy: Vol II—Clinical Applications*, by J. K. Zeig, Brunner Mazel Inc., New York.
de Shazer, S. (1985), *Keys to Solution in Brief Therapy*, W. W. Norton, New York.

Sim, M. (1981), *Guide to Psychiatry: Ed. 4*, Churchill Livingstone, Edinburgh.
Skynner, A. C. R. and Cleese, J. (1983), *Families and How to Survive Them*, Methuen, London.

10. Lydia: crisis work with a client with long-term problems

Sim, M. (1981), *Guide to Psychiatry: Ed. 4*, Churchill Livingstone, Edinburgh.
Waldron, G. (1984), 'Crisis intervention', *British Journal of Hospital Medicine*, April.

11. Mr L.: casework with a dementia sufferer

Gray, B. and Isaacs, B. (1979), *Care of the Elderly Mentally Infirm*, Tavistock Publications, London.
Gilleard, C. (1985), 'The impact of psychogeriatric day care on the patient's supporting relative', *Health Bulletin*, July, pp. 199-205.
Levin, L., Sinclair, A. C. and Gorbach, P. *Families, Services and Confusion in Old Age*, George Allen & Unwin, London (in press).
Pincus, A. and Minahan, A. (1973), *Social Work Practice: Model and method*, Peacock Publications Inc., New York.
Sullivan, H.S. (1954, 1970), *The Psychiatric Interview*, W. W. Norton and Company, New York.

12. Mrs D.: an integrated casework approach

Cochrane, R. (1983), *The Social Creation of Mental Illness*, Longman, London.
Currer, C. (1983), *Pathan Mothers in Bradford*, unpublished, University of Warwick.
Freud, S. (1925), 'Mourning and Melancholia' in *Collected Papers: Vol. IV*, Hogarth Press, London.
Glick, I., Weiss, R. and Parkes, C. M. (1974), *The First Year of Bereavement*, Wiley Interscience Publications, New York, pp. vii-viii.
Heimler, E. (1958), 'Odd Man Out', *New Statesman and Nation*, 5 April.
Hinton, J. (1973), *Dying*, Penguin Books, Middlesex.
Kubler-Ross, E. (1973), *On Death and Dying*, Tavistock Social Sciences Paperbacks, London.
Lindemann, E. (1944), 'Symptomatology and management of acute grief', *American Journal of Psychiatry*, 102, pp. 141-8.
London, M. (1986), 'Mental illness among immigrant minorities in the United Kingdom', *British Journal of Psychiatry*, 149, pp. 267-73.
Parkes, C. Murray (1972), *Bereavement*, Penguin, Middlesex.
Parkes, C. Murray (1978), *The Needs of Bereaved People*, The Family Welfare Association, London.
Perlman, H.H. (1970), 'The problem solving model in social casework' in *Theories of Social Casework*, R. Roberts and R. Nee (eds), University of Chicago Press, pp. 199.
Rack, P. (1981), *Race, Culture and Psychiatry*, Tavistock, London.
Rapaport, L. (1970), 'Crisis intervention as a mode of treatment' in *Theories of Social Casework*, R. Roberts and R. Nee (eds), University of Chicago Press, pp. 309.
Roberts, C. (1978), *The Language Barrier in Employment: Fact paper 4*, Commission for Racial Equality, London.

13. Mrs E.: on managing our own fears of madness

Goin, M. K. and Kline, F. (1976), 'Countertransference: a neglected subject in clinical supervision', *American Journal of Psychiatry*, 133(1), pp. 41-4.
Selby, L. G. (1955), 'Helping students in field practice identify and modify blocks to learning', *The Social Service Review*, Vol. XXIX, March.
Waldinger, R. J. (1987), 'Intensive psychodynamic therapy with borderline patients: an overview', *American Journal of Psychiatry*, 144(3), pp. 267-74.

16. Mrs R.: depression following a delayed grief reaction

Hudson, B. L. (1982), *Social Work with Psychiatric Patients*, Macmillan, London.

18. Sheila: a 'suicide' attempt

Butler, A. and Pritchard, C. (1983), *Social Work and Mental Illness*, Macmillan, London.
Goldberg, D. P., Benjamin, S. and Creed, F. (1987), *Psychiatry in Medical Practice*, Tavistock Publications, London.
Isaac B., Minty, B. and Morrison, R. (1986), 'Children in care—the association with mental disorder in the parents', *British Journal of Social Work*, 16, pp. 325-39.

19. Sue: a client with personality problems

American Psychiatric Association (1980), *Diagnostic and Statistical Manual of Mental Disorders: Edition 3 (DSM III)*, APA, Washington, D.C..
Brodsky, A. M. and Holroyd, J. (1981), 'Report of the task force on sex bias and sex-role stereotyping in psycho-therapeutic practice' in Howell, E. and Bayes, M. (eds), *Women and Mental Health*, Basic Books Inc., New York.
Brown, M. A. G. (1971), 'A review of casework methods', in E. Younghusband (ed.), *New Developments in Casework*, Allen & Unwin, London, pp. 11-37.

20. Peter: encopresis and child protection

Dingwall, R., Eekelaar, J. and Murray, T. (1983), *The Protection of Children*, Blackwell, Oxford.
Minuchin, S. (1974), *Families and Family Therapy*, Tavistock Publications, London.
Packman, J., Randall, J. and Jacques, N. (1986), *Who Needs Care?*, Blackwell, Oxford.

21. Maureen and Wendy: the behavioural approach

Eysenck, H. J. and Eysenck, S. B. G. (1974), *Manual of the Eysenck Personality Inventory*, University of London Press.
Hersen, M. and Barlow, D. (1976), *Single Case Experimental Designs*, Pergamon Press, Oxford.
Hersov, L. and Bentovim, A. (1977), 'Chapter 37: Inpatient units and day-hospitals, in M. Rutter and L. Hersov (ed.), *Child Psychiatry: Modern Approaches*, Blackwell Scientific Publications, Oxford.
Hudson, B. L. and Macdonald, G. (1986), *Behavioural Social Work: An Introduction*, Macmillan, London.
Quay, H. C. and Werry, J. S. (1986), *Psychopathological Disorders of Childhood: Edition 3*, John Wiley & Sons, New York.
Rutter, M., Tizard, J. and Whitmore, K. (1970), *Education, Health and Behaviour*, Longmans, London.
Sheldon, B. (1982), *Behaviour Modification: Theory, practice and philosophy*, Tavistock Publications, London.
Snaith, R. P., Constantopoulos, A. A., Jardine, M. Y. and McGuiffin, P. (1978), 'A clinical scale for the self-assessment of irritability, depression and anxiety (IDA)', *British Journal of Psychiatry*, 132, pp. 164-71.
Wolff, S. (1977), 'Chapter 20: Nondelinquent disturbances of conduct' in M. Rutter and L. Hersov (eds), *Child Psychiatry: Modern Approaches*, Blackwell Scientific Publications, Oxford.

22. Julie: a case of chronic pain

Hudgens, A. J. (1979), 'Family orientated treatment in chronic pain', *Journal of Marital and Family Therapy*, October, pp. 67-78.
Swanson, D. W. and Maruta, T. (1980), 'The family viewpoint of chronic pain', *Pain*, 8, pp. 163-6.

23. Tim: death in the family

Black, D. (1978), 'The bereaved child', *Journal of Child Psychology and Psychiatry*, 19, pp. 287-92.

Marris, P. (1959), *Widows and their Families*, Routledge & Kegan Paul, London.

Speece, M. W. and Brent, S. B. (1984), 'Children's understanding of death: a review of three components of a death concept', *Child Development*, 55, pp. 1671-85.

24. Yvonne: casework with an adolescent with hysteria

Austin, L. (1968), 'Dynamics and treatment of anxiety hysteria'. Reprinted from an earlier publication in F. J. Turner (ed.), *Differential Diagnosis and Treatment in Social Work*, The Free Press, New York.

Freud, S. and Breuer, J. (1895, 1974), *Studies on Hysteria: Vol. 3*, Penguin Books Ltd., Middlesex.

Jones, E. (1953, 1961), *The Life and Work of Sigmund Freud*, Pelican Books Ltd., Middlesex.

Reiner, B. S. and Kaufman, I. (1959), *Character Disorders in Parents of Delinquents*, Family Service Association of America, New York.

INDEX